YOUR BABY

YOUR BABY

Dr. Miriam Stoppard

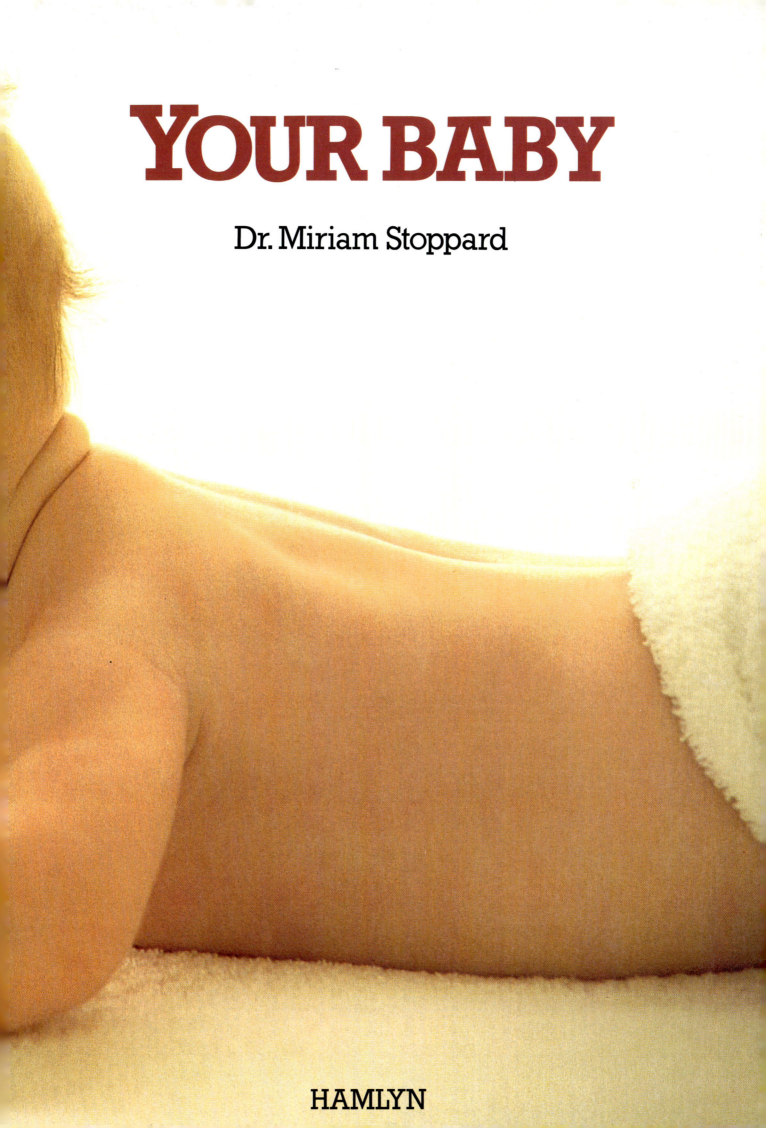

HAMLYN

dedication
For my Mother and Father

CONTENTS

LADY IN WAITING
Physical: The development of your pregnancy from fertilization to the ninth month 10
Medical: The care of your body, signs, symptoms and complaints 22
Psychological: Your state of mind during pregnancy 32
General: Planning for your baby 34

BIRTH DAY
Physical: The three stages of labour 42
Medical: What happens in hospital 50
Psychological: Your reactions to the birth 59
General: Preparing for home or hospital confinement 60

NEWLY BORN
Physical: Breast or bottle feeding your new baby 66
Medical: Postnatal discomforts and minor illnesses in the newborn 84
Psychological: Father and mother 88
General: Who helps look after the baby 91

LOOKING AND LEARNING
Physical: Following the development of your baby through crying, sleeping and feeding 96
Medical: Common baby illnesses and the different methods of contraception 109
Psychological: Encouraging and amusing your baby 117

General: Practical details from toys to safety procedures 120

ONE AT LAST
Physical: Weaning your child 126
Medical: Looking after a sick child 130
Psychological: The critical phases of learning 136
General: Everyday care and further safety procedures 139

FIRST STEPS
Physical: The developing child from learning to walk to bladder control 144
Medical: Some common illnesses and first aid 151
Psychological: Your child's behaviour from fears to temper tantrums 156
General: Useful toys and equipment 160

NEW HORIZONS
Physical: Daytime activities to night-time problems 166
Medical: Illnesses and immunization 170
Psychological: The development of language and speech plus some behaviour problems 173
General: Helping your child and your child helping you 177

SPECIAL ORGANIZATIONS 184

INDEX 185

First published in 1982 by
Octopus Books Limited

Published in paperback in 1987 by
Hamlyn Publishing
A division of the Hamlyn Publishing Group Limited
Bridge House
London Road
Twickenham
Middlesex
England

© 1982 Octopus Books Limited

ISBN 0 600 553 639

Printed in Hong Kong

INTRODUCTION

The trouble with babycare for modern women is that we don't get much chance to practise, due to the decline of large families and the curtailing of the extended family. My mother was one of thirteen children. By the time she was eight years old, she had charge of two smaller children, one of whom was still bottle-feeding. Girls were bound to learn about childcare because they were part and parcel of it.

Women denied this early field training turn elsewhere for advice – including to books. However, to try to set a blueprint for your unique relationship with your child would be quite wrong. All you need is the self-confidence to follow your maternal instincts, added to a little bit of background on what makes your baby tick and how to differentiate between something serious and something trivial. That's what this book sets out to give you.

It also hopes to achieve a little more. A recent visit to the birth clinic of a French obstetrician, Michel Odent, left me convinced that nature more often than not knows best. In Dr Odent's clinic, women are allowed to have their babies how they want, where they want and with whom they want. Dr Odent's episiotomy rate, Caesarean section rate and infant mortality rate are among the lowest in the world. Though not everybody can have her baby like that, by being quietly insistent about preferences we can have an influence. The same goes for bringing up your baby: do what comes naturally to you. There is one course of action I'd strongly recommend. Observe your child and take your lead from him. His most precious possession is his individuality. Your invaluable contribution is to safeguard it.

Miriam Stoppard
London

LADY IN WAITING

Fertilization – the first event

If you become pregnant it will be on or about the 14th day after your last menstrual period began. Fertilization, the very first event in pregnancy, therefore happens only about a week after you finish menstruating. Seven to 10 days after this, the fertilized egg (called the ovum) will become embedded in the lining of the womb and this is known as implantation. In a further week it will be firmly attached there by its primitive placenta. The placenta, or afterbirth, attaches the developing baby to its mother and is also the organ through which nutrients are carried from the mother to the baby and waste from baby to mother. It also produces pregnancy hormones that are responsible for maintaining the pregnancy and the health of the developing baby. At first quantities of placental hormones are small but as pregnancy progresses they become enormous and appear in the mother's urine. Placental hormones can be chemically detected in the urine of a pregnant woman and this forms the basis of pregnancy tests. Using ordinary laboratory tests, they can rarely be detected sooner than three weeks after implantation, i.e. 40 days after the first day of your last period although recently more sensitive methods have worked one week earlier.

Usually, doctors describe the developing baby, once its various parts are distinctly formed, as the foetus, i.e. at about twelve weeks. Before this time it is called the embryo.

It is also an accepted medical convention that pregnancy is counted from the first day of bleeding of your last period. Using this method of calculation you conceive on the 14th day, implantation takes place on the 21st day and by the time you have missed your first period you are '1 month pregnant'.

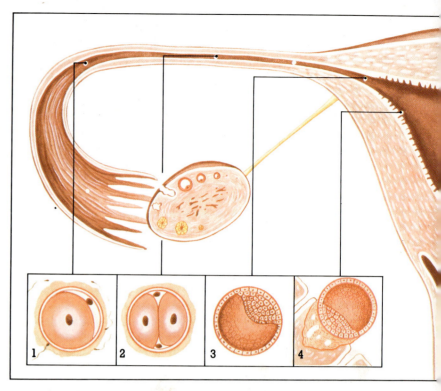

1   2   3   4

Your date of delivery

Calculating your EDD or expected date of delivery is a simple arithmetical exercise. Pregnancy lasts 266 days from conception, or 280 days – 9 calendar months and 1 week – from the first day of your last period. You can calculate your expected date of delivery by taking the date of the first day of your last period, adding on 12 months, that is one year later, subtracting 3 months and adding 1 week. So if your last period began on the 17 October, the expected date of delivery is 17 October next year, minus 3 months, which brings you to the 17 July. Now by adding 7 days, you arrive at a

(Below left) A chart to help you calculate the estimated date of your delivery. The upper line of figures represents the first day of your last period. Underneath this is the expected date when your baby will be born, which is 280 days later.

January	1	2	3	4	5	6	7	8	9	10	11	12	13	14	15	16	17	18	19	20	21	22	23	24	25	26	27	28	29	30	31	January
OCTOBER	8	9	10	11	12	13	14	15	16	17	18	19	20	21	22	23	24	25	26	27	28	29	30	31	1	2	3	4	5	6	7	**NOVEMBER**
February	1	2	3	4	5	6	7	8	9	10	11	12	13	14	15	16	17	18	19	20	21	22	23	24	25	26	27	28				February
NOVEMBER	8	9	10	11	12	13	14	15	16	17	18	19	20	21	22	23	24	25	26	27	28	29	30	1	2	3	4	5				**DECEMBER**
March	1	2	3	4	5	6	7	8	9	10	11	12	13	14	15	16	17	18	19	20	21	22	23	24	25	26	27	28	29	30	31	March
DECEMBER	6	7	8	9	10	11	12	13	14	15	16	17	18	19	20	21	22	23	24	25	26	27	28	29	30	31	1	2	3	4	5	**JANUARY**
April	1	2	3	4	5	6	7	8	9	10	11	12	13	14	15	16	17	18	19	20	21	22	23	24	25	26	27	28	29	30		April
JANUARY	6	7	8	9	10	11	12	13	14	15	16	17	18	19	20	21	22	23	24	25	26	27	28	29	30	31	1	2	3	4		**FEBRUARY**
May	1	2	3	4	5	6	7	8	9	10	11	12	13	14	15	16	17	18	19	20	21	22	23	24	25	26	27	28	29	30	31	May
FEBRUARY	5	6	7	8	9	10	11	12	13	14	15	16	17	18	19	20	21	22	23	24	25	26	27	28	1	2	3	4	5	6	7	**MARCH**
June	1	2	3	4	5	6	7	8	9	10	11	12	13	14	15	16	17	18	19	20	21	22	23	24	25	26	27	28	29	30		June
MARCH	8	9	10	11	12	13	14	15	16	17	18	19	20	21	22	23	24	25	26	27	28	29	30	31	1	2	3	4	5	6		**APRIL**
July	1	2	3	4	5	6	7	8	9	10	11	12	13	14	15	16	17	18	19	20	21	22	23	24	25	26	27	28	29	30	31	July
APRIL	7	8	9	10	11	12	13	14	15	16	17	18	19	20	21	22	23	24	25	26	27	28	29	30	1	2	3	4	5	6	7	**MAY**
August	1	2	3	4	5	6	7	8	9	10	11	12	13	14	15	16	17	18	19	20	21	22	23	24	25	26	27	28	29	30	31	August
MAY	8	9	10	11	12	13	14	15	16	17	18	19	20	21	22	23	24	25	26	27	28	29	30	31	1	2	3	4	5	6	7	**JUNE**
September	1	2	3	4	5	6	7	8	9	10	11	12	13	14	15	16	17	18	19	20	21	22	23	24	25	26	27	28	29	30		September
JUNE	8	9	10	11	12	13	14	15	16	17	18	19	20	21	22	23	24	25	26	27	28	29	30	1	2	3	4	5	6	7		**JULY**
October	1	2	3	4	5	6	7	8	9	10	11	12	13	14	15	16	17	18	19	20	21	22	23	24	25	26	27	28	29	30	31	October
JULY	8	9	10	11	12	13	14	15	16	17	18	19	20	21	22	23	24	25	26	27	28	29	30	31	1	2	3	4	5	6	7	**AUGUST**
November	1	2	3	4	5	6	7	8	9	10	11	12	13	14	15	16	17	18	19	20	21	22	23	24	25	26	27	28	29	30		November
AUGUST	8	9	10	11	12	13	14	15	16	17	18	19	20	21	22	23	24	25	26	27	28	29	30	31	1	2	3	4	5	6		**SEPTEMBER**
December	1	2	3	4	5	6	7	8	9	10	11	12	13	14	15	16	17	18	19	20	21	22	23	24	25	26	27	28	29	30	31	December
SEPTEMBER	7	8	9	10	11	12	13	14	15	16	17	18	19	20	21	22	23	24	25	26	27	28	29	30	1	2	3	4	5	6	7	**OCTOBER**

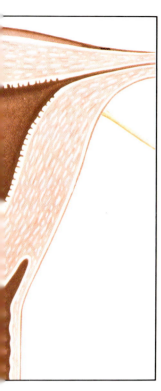

(Above) The egg (or ovum) is fertilized (inset 1) when it's about a third of the way along the Fallopian tube. The cell divides (inset 2) and continues to grow, forming a sphere of cells on the outside (inset 3). By the time it's implanted in the wall of the uterus 7-10 days later (inset 4) it has become a hollow ball of rapidly developing cells. The egg nearly always implants in the upper part of the wall of the womb, on either side.

delivery date 24 July next year.

At the bottom of page 10 is a chart from which you can easily estimate your expected date of delivery. It should be stressed that 280 days represents an average and your ability to calculate your EDD will depend on your remembering precisely when your period started, so do put this date in your diary every month. It also depends on your having regular 28 day cycles. many women have menstrual cycles which are either somewhat shorter, or somewhat longer, which may affect the length of pregnancy. A normal pregnancy may be anything between 39 and 41 weeks.

Signs of pregnancy
Missing a period

There are many signs of pregnancy which an observant woman may notice before she goes to her doctor or uses a pregnancy test for confirmation. The first and most classical sign is amenorrhoea or missing a period. Though pregnancy is the commonest cause of amenorrhoea it is by no means the only one. Stress, strain or worry may delay menstruation. Any severe disease such as anaemia, tuberculosis or a renal infection may disturb the menstrual cycle. A sudden shock, a surgical operation and recently even jet-lag have been known to make a period late. However, it is also not uncommon for there to be a very slight menstrual period even though a woman is already pregnant, at the time when one is due. If she counts this as her last menstrual period her baby will be born after eight months instead of nine and is one of the explanations of a so-called short pregnancy.

Nausea and vomiting

Nausea, or in some cases, vomiting, is an early sign and may be the only one for several weeks. It usually lasts no longer than three months, then gradually dies away. The commonest symptom is morning sickness which is a feeling of nausea on waking. Some women, however, find that it's worst in the evening and a few unfortunate ones find that it never quite leaves them all day. Early morning sickness is probably due to a low blood sugar and the best cure is to remain in bed and have your husband bring you a cup of tea and a piece of toast or a biscuit. Better still, is to have a glass of milk by your bed which you can drink on waking. Milk contains lactose and this sugar can be absorbed rapidly from the stomach into the blood stream and will raise the level of blood sugar quickly and relieve the nausea. If possible you should not get out of bed until the nausea passes. Other than hypoglycaemia (low blood sugar), no-one knows what causes the nausea and vomiting of pregnancy, however, it is almost certainly related to the high level of pregnancy hormones which can irritate the stomach directly but which also reduce the blood sugar.

Many women find that nausea is brought on by cooking smells, particularly from frying and that it is impossible to eat cooked or fried foods. Cigarette smoke and coffee may also make women feel sick. If this is the case they should try to confine their diet to fresh uncooked foods, salads, fruit and vegetables, to hard boiled eggs and cheese. Nausea is normal in pregnancy and should not cause concern unless it leads to frequent and profuse vomiting when you should consult your doctor. When medically necessary, there are several drugs which can do much to alleviate, if not cure it. It is very unusual for nausea and vomiting in pregnancy to continue beyond the 16th week but if it does, you should always seek medical help.

Change in taste

A distinctive change in taste is one of the early signs that makes a woman know she is pregnant, sometimes even before she has missed her first period. The sensation varies from woman to woman but is often described as metallic. Women may also find that they go off certain foods and drinks, the most common being fried foods, coffee and alcohol, as well as cigarettes. Others find that they have strong cravings for a particular food. If you satisfy your craving, try to make sure that the rest of your diet is varied to compensate. These changes are thought to be due to rising hormone levels and are often experienced in the second half of the menstrual cycle, too, for the same reason.

Passing urine more often

Many women notice that the frequency of passing urine increases, sometimes as early as one week after conception. The enlarged womb due to the implanted embryo presses against the bladder so that it tries to expel even small amounts of urine. Some women find themselves having to pass urine as often as every hour in the early stages but unless there is a burning sensation or pain (rather like cystitis) when you pass urine there is no need to consult your doctor about the increased frequency.

Breast changes

Nearly all women experience changes in the breast; the earliest ones are tingling and soreness of the nipple and shortly afterwards the breasts feel heavy and tender. This is an exaggeration of what happens in a mild form during the week prior to menstruation when the breast tissue may become enlarged due to fluid retention. By the sixth week of pregnancy the breasts may be measurably larger, as milk glands start to replace the fatty tissue. The small part of the breast that extends under the armpit, may be particularly swollen and tender. You may notice that the veins over the surface of the breast become more prominent and enlarged, and anything between 6 and 12 small creamy nodules appear in the nipple area which gradually enlarge as pregnancy progresses. The nipple also becomes bigger.

Confirmation of pregnancy
Laboratory tests

It is very difficult for a doctor to confirm pregnancy by internal examination any earlier than four weeks after you have missed your first period. In practice a doctor will not perform this examination for six to eight weeks after a missed period and most women want an answer before then. In this case a laboratory pregnancy test may be the answer. Your doctor will ask you to take along a specimen of your early morning urine which, because it is concentrated overnight, contains the largest amount of pregnancy hormones from the placenta during any 24 hours. If the urine has to go off to a laboratory, the result will not be available at the earliest for 48 hours. There are now pregnancy tests on the market which you can buy yourself to perform in the privacy of your own home and which will give you an answer within minutes.

Modern laboratory and home kit pregnancy tests all depend on the same process. Scientists have developed an antibody to the hormones which are produced by the developing placenta and which appear in the pregnant woman's urine. When the urine containing these hormones is mixed with the antibody, the hormones and the antibodies join together and this produces a change which can be seen quite easily. There is a small risk of a false positive or a false negative as there is with all laboratory tests. None is guaranteed 100 per cent. A positive result indicates pregnancy in nearly every case. If you get a negative result but the symptoms of pregnancy persist, then it is possible that you have performed the test too early in your pregnancy and so you should wait a week and then try again.

Internal examination

By six or eight weeks an internal medical examination along with all the other signs will fully confirm pregnancy. However, you may not have an internal examination until you begin labour, whilst some doctors like to confirm pregnancy at the first antenatal visit. It is left to the doctor's discretion unless there is something in particular to find out. Both the cervix (neck of the womb) and the lining of the vagina feel rather swollen and softened and when seen with the aid of an instrument called a speculum they have a bluish tinge. This is due to the increased blood flow in all the genital organs. The uterus has increased in size and can be felt by the examining doctor. An internal examination will not harm you or your baby. Very little except direct mechanical interference, like abortion or attempted abortion, and some drugs, can do anything to upset a normal pregnancy.

Miscarriage

Miscarriage is common. One in three of all first pregnancies miscarry and normally for very good natural reasons to make sure only the strongest babies survive and sometimes to give the uterus a trial run to bring it to full maturity. Many women are unaware that they have miscarried and almost all go on to have perfectly normal subsequent pregnancies with normal babies. Sexual intercourse can begin as soon as bleeding stops and you can try to conceive as soon as you like.

Helping yourself
Diet

Throughout pregnancy the relationship between your developing baby and you is parasitic as far as dietary needs are concerned. The baby's needs will always come first at no matter what cost to the mother. This means that you must pay particular attention to certain important foodstuffs which you must take in adequate quantities.

Protein

The first is protein. All kinds of meat, bacon, ham and poultry, fish, cheese and eggs are good sources. A fairly cheap way of getting protein every day is to have an egg for your breakfast.

Calcium

Milk is a rich source of calcium but you need not drink a pint of milk a day if you don't like it. You can have it in drinks, puddings, soups or cereals. Any dairy product, including cheese or butter each day will give you part of your calcium requirements.

Vitamins and minerals

During pregnancy you are in special need of these. You should make it a rule to eat some fresh fruit and vegetables every day together with green vegetables which are a source of roughage and help to counteract the constipation which quite often occurs during pregnancy (see page 28).

Liver, kidney and most kinds of offal are rich in vitamins and minerals, particularly iron, and you should try to eat these several times a week if they are to your taste. Oranges, grapefruit and tomatoes are good sources of vitamin C and will help to keep your skin healthy.

Try not to take too much starchy food like potatoes, bread, cakes and cereals. If you find that your bowels are a bit sluggish, do not resort automatically to proprietary purgatives. Instead try eating stewed prunes or figs each day or more fruit and green vegetables. You might try adding some fibre, in the form of wholemeal bread and pulses, or bran to your diet.

Watching your weight gain

It is absolutely essential that you keep your weight under control. It is quite unnecessary to eat for two because any weight gain over 20

(Right) It's a good idea to prepare yourself plenty of salads. They provide the necessary vitamins and, because there will be no cooking smells, they will be more acceptable if you are feeling nauseous.

pounds (9.1 kg) will remain after delivery and will unfortunately be in all the places from which it is most difficult to lose weight, such as the upper arms, the thighs, the waist, the hips and the tummy.

Your appetite will almost certainly increase in the second three months of pregnancy but do not indulge yourself by eating fattening foods. Try to stick to high protein foods. Keep a store of non-fattening foods in the larder and fridge for your weak moments, like several hard boiled eggs, low fat cottage cheese and natural low fat yogurt. The 20 pounds (9.1 kg) that you can gain are accounted for in the table (right).

Rest during pregnancy
Resting

Many women get more tired in pregnancy than at any other time of their lives. Indeed, unexplained fatigue, may be one of the first signs of pregnancy. It is very important to get sufficient rest. You should try to get 10 hours rest out of every 24: 8 hours sleep if at all possible at night and 2 hours some time during the day, preferably in the afternoon or just after lunch. Very often it's not possible to arrange this, especially if you are working but if you can't have a routine rest during the day, try to rest whenever you can. Always put your feet up when you are sitting down unoccupied and always lie down even if you're not asleep, whenever you can. If you are feeling extremely tired, don't fight it, give in. During the second three months of pregnancy, you may not feel tired at all but more energetic than you have ever felt before. But in the last 3 months, particularly the 6 weeks before you go into labour, you may feel extremely tired and need to rest 12 or 14 hours a day with your feet up. One small but important point is to try to avoid sitting with your knees bent and with one leg crossed over the other. This can make the circulation sluggish in the lower part of the legs which may lead to swelling and may aggravate varicose veins. Sit with your legs stretched out in front of you, as much as you can.

Sleeping

Sleep is just as important as rest. The secret of going to sleep at any time is relaxation, both physical and mental. Relaxation classes for pregnant mothers will help you to learn the art. While on the one hand many pregnant women find they are tired to the point of exhaustion, they may also paradoxically suffer from insomnia. A common pattern is to fall asleep easily but to wake quite refreshed two hours later and be unable to go back to sleep for the rest of the night. This leads to frustration and further exhaustion. If you are unfortunate enough to suffer from chronic insomnia, you should consult your doctor. Though drugs are given in pregnancy only when absolutely essential, there are sleeping pills available which if given under medical supervision will not harm your baby.

How the total weight gain is made up:

Weight of the baby	7 pounds (3.2 kg)
Weight of the placenta	1½ pounds (0.7 kg)
Weight of the amniotic fluid	2 pounds (0.9 kg)
Weight of the uterus	2 pounds (0.9 kg)
Increase in the weight of the breasts	1½ pounds (0.7 kg)
Extra fluids in blood and tissues	4 pounds (1.8 kg)
Increase in fat of mother	2 pounds (0.9 kg)
Total	20 pounds (9.1 kg)

Your schedule of weight gain should be as follows:

Up to 14 weeks –	No weight gain
14-20 weeks –	Gain 5 pounds (2.3 kg)
20-30 weeks –	Gain a further 8 pounds (3.5 kg)
30-36 weeks –	Gain 5 pounds (2.3 kg)
36-40 weeks –	Gain 2 pounds (1 kg)

Exercises for early pregnancy

As your abdomen enlarges, a severe strain is put on the muscles of the back and hips to maintain a good upright posture. These muscles need to be strengthened so that they can take the strain later in pregnancy. Moreover, muscles, ligaments, tendons and joints tend to slacken as confinement approaches in readiness to stretch and accommodate the baby as it is born. Strengthening muscles will help to keep the joints stable and to prevent over stretching. The exercises will also help to forestall backache. Above are some simple exercises for early pregnancy for the abdomen, the back and the hips. They can be started as soon as you know you are pregnant and should be stopped if they fatigue you or when your enlarged abdomen makes it too awkward for you to bend.

Activity

As long as your pregnancy is progressing normally, there is no reason why you should not follow normal exercise for as long as you feel comfortable doing so. If you feel tired you should stop whatever you are doing and rest. The chart on page 15 gives you some guidelines.

Dental care in pregnancy

Dentists no longer believe that calcium is lost from the mother's teeth during pregnancy but it is important that you make sure that your mouth, like the rest of your body, is in good condition and that you take advantage of free dental care. Some women notice that their gums tend to bleed, this is because in pregnancy there may

be an exaggerated response to plaque (bacteria on the tooth surface) which causes inflamed gums. This can be controlled by regular and careful daily brushing to get rid of the plaque. Your dentist will advise you on how to improve your tooth-cleaning techniques.

Special clothing

Until the fifth or sixth month, it is normally unnecessary to go to the expense of buying special pregnancy clothing. With the exception of form-fitting garments, most of us can adapt our ordinary clothes to accommodate a swelling abdomen in the early months. Smocks, which are always fashionable, will cover up a thickening waist and an enlarging stomach and unzipped skirts and trousers can be tethered with tape. Many current fashions can look just as good on a pregnant woman as one who is not. Often trousers and skirts have loose fitting waist lines with a drawstring which allow considerable expansion of the abdomen. There are also many stretch fabrics available. This saves money and means you can avoid buying garments which you only wear for a short time.

But as your pregnancy progresses, it does wonders for the morale to have one or two outfits in which you are comfortable and elegant, so it is worth splashing out on these. In the early months don't be afraid of wearing belts or tight jeans, as there is no truth in the old wives' tale that you will be squashing the baby. It wouldn't come to any harm whatsoever. But later when the enlarging uterus becomes easily felt, you should avoid wearing anything which restricts the abdomen. As long as you have firm abdominal muscles and you have done exercises in early pregnancy to

(Above) Exercises for early pregnancy.
(1) For strengthening your hips. Stand with legs astride, hands on hips. Twist body from waist through 90° to left and to right.
(2) For strengthening your back and hips. Stand with legs astride. Stretch up with right arm and down with left as far as it will go. Repeat with left arm raised.
(3) For strengthening your abdomen. Kneel with knees apart, arms high above head. Bring both arms down to the left, twisting at waist to touch feet behind. Repeat on right side.
(Above right) A chart of what you can and can't do. Keep up any regular sport, provided your pregnancy is normal, until you feel you cannot. But don't take up a new sport or get overtired.
(Below right) Yoga is a good preparation for labour and if you are practised in the art (like this teacher) you can carry on when pregnant.

	Things you can do	Things you can't do
SWIMMING	Swimming does no harm in pregnancy.	Don't swim for the first time. Don't swim in cold water. Don't dive from more than three ft (1 metre).
WALKING	Walk as much as you like.	Don't go hiking. Don't let yourself get overtired.
CYCLING	Cycling does no harm in pregnancy, up till the fourth month but take it easy.	Don't cycle after the fourth month because of your enlarging abdomen.
HORSE RIDING	–	Never ride in pregnancy.
SKIING	–	Never go skiing or water skiing.
DANCING	If not too energetic you may go dancing until labour begins.	Don't dance very actively or acrobatically.
LIFTING	Only lift light weights and always squat down to do it. (This includes picking up a child.)	Don't lift heavy weights or move heavy objects.
DRIVING	Driving is all right till your enlarged abdomen makes fast movements impossible, usually about the seventh month.	Never attempt a long journey on your own.
TRAVELLING	It does no harm to travel in pregnancy. Travel by train rather than car.	Don't undertake long, unbroken journeys, or travel any distance from home in the last six weeks.
FLYING	You may fly only before the seventh month, or with a medical up to eighth month.	Never fly in unpressurized aircraft, or across several time zones, e.g. London to New York which means a five hour time difference.
WORKING	Carry on working if you want to and the job is not physically taxing.	Don't continue a job that involves very energetic work or lifting.
SEX	Sex does no harm in pregnancy. May be more enjoyable than ever, right up to labour.	—

strengthen them, there is absolutely no need to wear any sort of supportive garment for your abdomen throughout pregnancy. You will find your feet become very tired as your weight increases and even swollen towards the end. So abandon the high heels and for once in your life go for sensible, low-heeled, well-fitting shoes.

Bras for pregnancy

As the breast tissue increases and the glands inside the breast enlarge ready to produce the milk for your baby, this extra weight is quite a strain on the ligaments which support the breast. If some of this strain is not removed, then the ligaments become stretched and you may find that your breasts will sag. Unfortunately they may sag for ever. It is not breast feeding which affects the shape of the breast, it is the state of being pregnant. The best thing that you can do to prevent this is to wear a good supportive bra with underwiring and you should change it for a larger size if your breasts get bigger. Only if your breasts become unduly heavy will it be necessary to wear a bra at night. There's no need to buy a special maternity or nursing bra until very near the end of pregnancy.

Supportive hose

If you have varicose veins, or if your mother has them, it's a good idea to give your legs some support by wearing elasticated tights. You should not wear stockings with elastic at the top because this will impede the return of blood from your legs to your heart and will only worsen varicose veins and encourage swollen ankles. Garters should also be avoided.

The development of the baby

For the developing baby, pregnancy is a spectacular growth spurt. At the end of the second week, when fertilization has just taken place, the embryo is a single cell and is only visible under a microscope. In 38 weeks it grows tens of millions of times. The embryo becomes just visible to the naked eye about the end of the fourth week.

End of the fifth week: the embryo is approximately 0.08 inches (two mm) long and is plainly visible to the naked eye with a distinguishable spinal column beginning to develop.

Sixth week: the head begins to form and very shortly afterwards the chest and the abdomen take shape. About the same time a primitive brain forms and by the end of the sixth week the primitive heart is beating, blood cells have been formed and are ready to circulate around the tiny body. Blood vessels in the umbilical cord are forming and will carry food from the mother through the placenta to the developing baby and similarly waste products from the baby to the mother who will eliminate them. There is no face but there are small depressions where the ears and the eyes will develop and the beginning of the mouth and jaw is just visible. The developing embryo is a little over half an inch (12.7 mm) in length.

Seventh week: the small buds of the arms and legs are growing and you can see tiny indentations which will develop into fingers and toes. Solid lungs are forming in the chest and the intestines are almost complete. But the most dramatic development is in the head. The inner parts of the ears are forming and the eyes are also developing, although the baby does not yet have eyelids. And while there is not a nose there are openings where the nostrils will be.

End of eighth week: all the internal organs are formed. The shoulders, the elbows and hips and

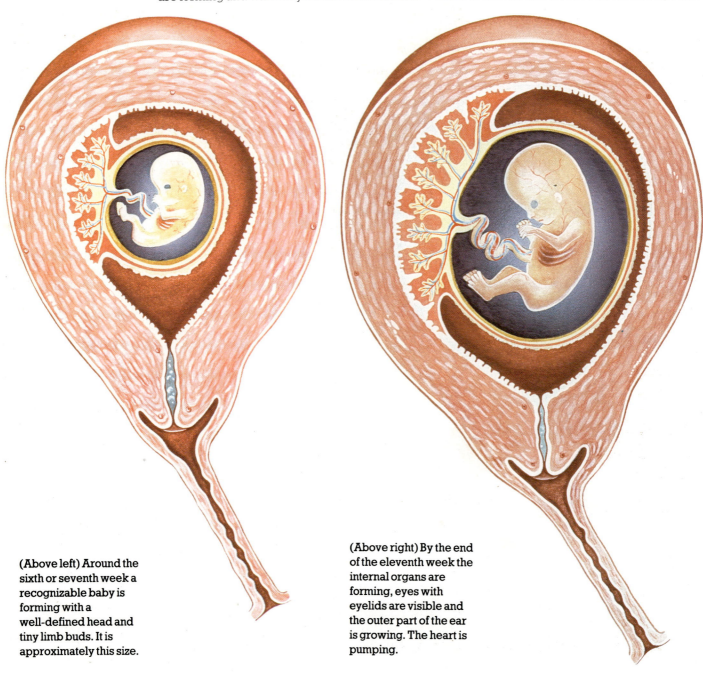

(Above left) Around the sixth or seventh week a recognizable baby is forming with a well-defined head and tiny limb buds. It is approximately this size.

(Above right) By the end of the eleventh week the internal organs are forming, eyes with eyelids are visible and the outer part of the ear is growing. The heart is pumping.

the knees are obvious and for the very first time, movements of the spine begin. The baby is 0.9 inches (2.2 cm) long.

Ninth week: the nose appears and the mouth begins to develop. The limbs, hands and feet are growing rapidly. The baby can move quite a lot now but the mother cannot feel it.

End of tenth week: the eyes are well formed and have eyelids and the external part of the ear is beginning to grow. The head is very large compared with the rest of the body and although the fingers and toes can be seen easily, they are joined by webs of skin.

At the 11th week all the internal organs of the body are functioning. The ovaries and testicles are formed and so are the external genital organs. The heart is fully formed and can pump blood to all parts of the body, the face is developing rapidly and the eyes are complete. The baby is 2.2. inches (5.5 cm) long, which is about as long as your little finger and its weight is ⅓ ounce (10 g). This is a very important milestone for the baby to have reached because once its organs are fully formed, they rarely come to any harm, although their rate of growth may be affected, so it is virtually impervious to drugs or infections.

At the 12th week: the face becomes properly formed, the eyelids are distinguishable and the external part of the ear becomes well developed. Muscles start to grow in the body and the limbs making more foetal movements possible. When the baby is 13 weeks old, the uterus or womb is approximately 4 inches (10.2 cm) wide and can be felt to be enlarged by a doctor doing an internal examination. The baby is completely formed and during the remainder of the pregnancy it will simply grow to a size when all its vital organs have matured so that it is capable of life independent of its mother.

End of 16th week: the limbs and the joints are fully formed and movement is quite vigorous, though rarely felt by a woman during her first pregnancy. About this time a fine downy type of hair grows over the skin of the foetus. This is called lanugo hair. The eyebrows and the eyelashes also start to grow.

By the 20th week: the baby is growing very rapidly in both weight and length and has the beginnings of hair on its head. As the muscles in its limbs develop, so movements become more obvious and can now usually be felt by the mother. The sac in which the baby is suspended is full of fluid, called amniotic fluid, and there is plenty of room, so that the baby can move and twist around quite easily. The baby is 10 inches (25.4 cm) long and weighs approximately three quarters of a pound (0.34 kg).

At the 24th week: it is just over 12 inches (30.5 cm) long and weighs a pound and a quarter

(Above) At 16 weeks, muscles and joints are formed and functioning – your baby can move! Hair is starting to appear, including eyebrows and eyelashes. From 20 weeks onwards your baby starts to grow and put on weight.

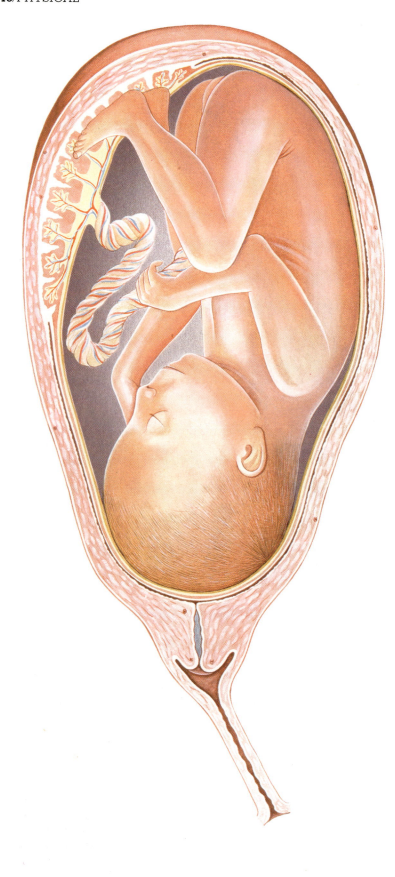

(Above) By 28 weeks your baby's lungs are capable of functioning and she is over a foot (30 cm) long. She will be twisting and turning inside the womb.

(0.57 kg) and though it has well-developed muscles it is still very skinny because no fat has been laid down.

At the 28th week: the baby is now legally viable which means that if it is born it must be registered as a pre-term infant. The lungs are reaching maturity and the baby would be able to breathe if it were born. The skin is covered with a greasy white substance called 'vernix'. It prevents the skin from becoming soggy from immersion in the amniotic fluid. The baby is now 14½ inches (36.8 cm) long and weighs two pounds (0.9 kg).

By the 32nd week: the baby is not just perfectly formed but is in proportion and if delivered it will open its eyes. Its chances of survival will be about 1 in 6. It is beginning to get a little rounder but it is still quite thin, has reached a length of 16 inches (40.6 cm) inches and a weight of three and a half pounds (1.6 kg). It lies with its head pointing downwards into its mother's pelvis most of the time.

At the 36th week: the baby stands a 90 per cent chance of survival if it is born. It is now getting fatter with more subcutaneous fat being laid down and the skin is covered by a liberal quantity of vernix. It is 18 inches (45.7 cm) long and about five and a half pounds (2.5 kg) in weight. From this time onwards the baby gains about 1 ounce (28.4 g) a day, so that by the 40th week it is approximately 20 inches (50.8 cm) long and seven and a half pounds (3.4 kg) in weight. Vernix becomes less in quantity after 38 weeks and at 40 weeks is usually only on the head and in the skin folds, e.g. neck, armpits and groins.

The changes in your body
The uterus

The growing baby makes huge demands on your body, which has to change to adapt to them. The uterus grows from about one and a half ounces (42.6 g) to nearly two pounds (0.91 kg) in weight so that it can accommodate, feed and finally contract with sufficient strength to push out the baby during labour. The muscles in the uterine wall not only thicken but also increase in number. At 12 weeks the uterus is just beginning to emerge from the pelvis and can be felt by a doctor or nurse examining your abdomen. It grows higher in the abdomen until at 36 weeks it touches the bottom of the breast bone.

The uterus contracts throughout a woman's fertile life. Sometimes the contractions can be painful and cause dysmenorrhoea, or painful periods. During pregnancy the uterus contracts about every 20 minutes, though a woman is rarely aware of it because the contractions are painless and may only be detected as a hardening of the wall of the uterus. These painless contractions are called Braxton Hicks contractions (see page 45) and they can be interpreted as trial runs for the real thing – labour.

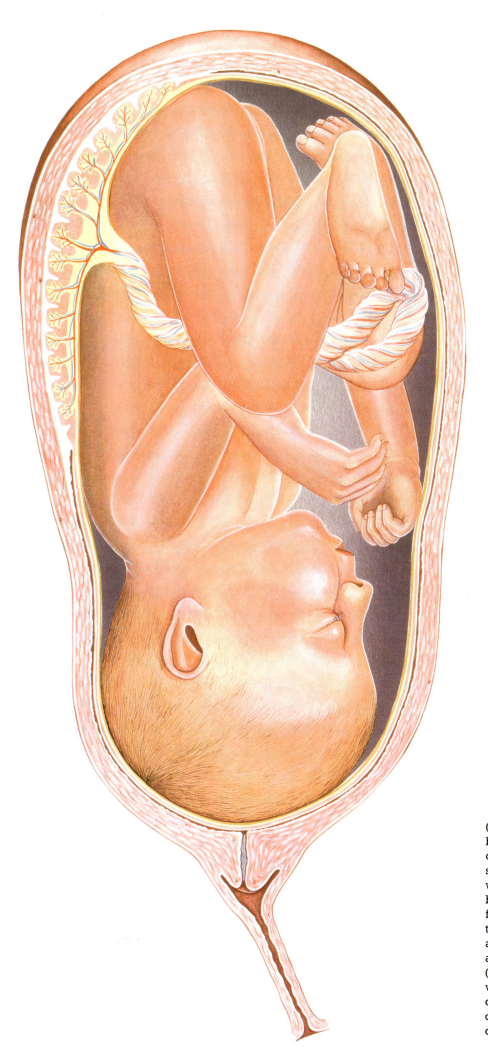

(Above) The older your baby gets, the better chance she stands of surviving alone. From 36 weeks onwards your baby gets rounder and fatter. In the four weeks to birth she will grow almost two inches (5 cm) and put on two pounds (0.9 kg). The greasy vernix which once covered her body now only remains in the skin creases.

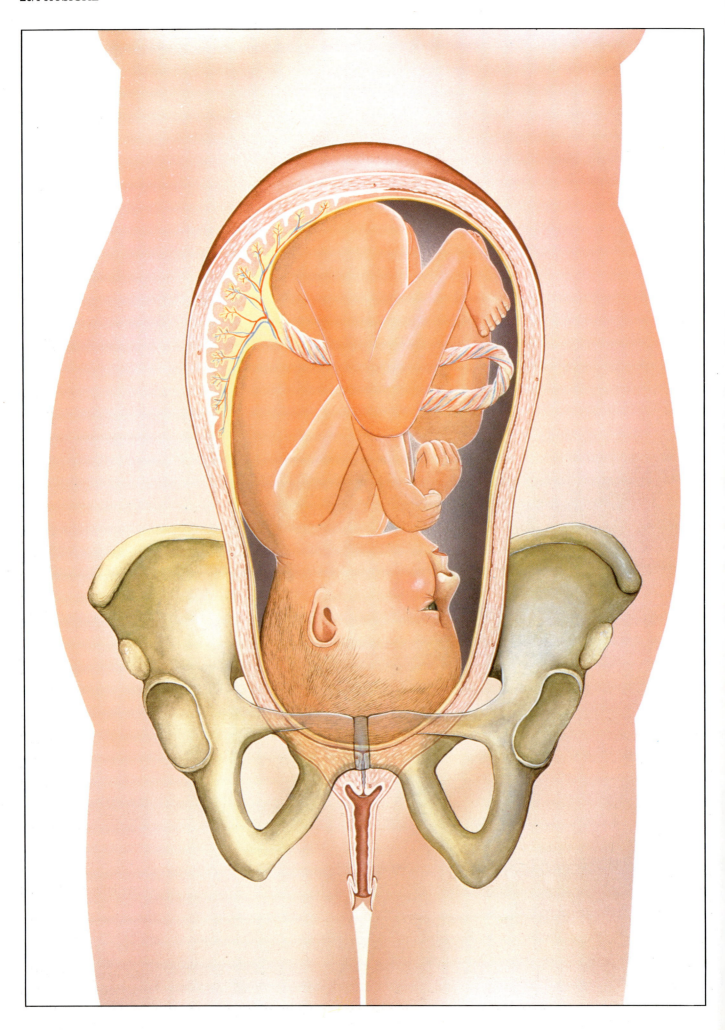

The vagina

As early as the sixth week, the blood supply to the vagina increases and the vaginal lining takes on a slightly bluish tinge. The secretions of the vagina and the cervix increase and may even cause some discharge, see page 28.

The blood

The body needs more blood than normal to meet the increased demands from the uterus and placenta. The average woman has 8 to 10 pints of blood. During pregnancy the amount of blood circulating round the body may increase anything up to 40 per cent. The demand is too rapid to give the body time to manufacture new blood and the increase in volume is largely achieved by increasing the fluid content of the blood, thereby diluting the number of blood cells. This is anaemia. Every pregnant woman is in danger of becoming anaemic and is usually given iron supplements and vitamin supplements to help prevent this.

The heart

Because of the increase in blood volume, the heart has to work harder than normal during pregnancy and by about the 28th week, its workload has increased by nearly 50 per cent. This is one of the reasons why women feel tired in the latter months of pregnancy. It is also a reason why you must control your weight gain. Extra weight puts an extra load on the heart and it has enough to do already. By the end of pregnancy your heart will be beating ten times more per minute than it did at the beginning. In one day this is 14,000 extra beats.

Breathing

For nearly every woman breathing becomes difficult towards the end of pregnancy. This is because the baby is pushing up against the diaphragm and so you cannot breathe in and out efficiently. Breathing is particularly difficult in the last four weeks especially when you sit down, so you should always try to choose a chair that will keep your back upright. You may experience a little pain on the right side of your chest where the ribs are being pushed out because of the pressure of the expanding uterus.

Skin pigmentation

In nearly all women there is an increase in skin pigmentation during pregnancy, which is due to the increased level of circulating hormones. It is most pronounced in brunettes, less pronounced in blondes and there is hardly any increased pigmentation in redheads who have little pigment in their skin to begin with. Darkening of the skin is most obvious in the nipple area in a line running down the centre of the abdomen, the linea nigra, and on the insides of the thighs. Occasionally patches appear on the face (chloasma). All but these may be permanent.

Skin stretch marks

Stretch marks occur when the elastic fibres in the lower layers of the skin are stretched to the point of rupture. They are usually a fairly bright pink in colour. Whilst the colour may fade after pregnancy, the stretch marks do remain as they are impossible to repair. They are associated not only with sudden stretching of the skin but also with the very high level of circulating hormones which may weaken the elastic fibres. No amount of massage or rubbing in oil will be of any avail in preventing or curing them.

The breasts

The breast is a collection of tiny glands which open out through ducts on to the nipple and are surrounded by a thick layer of fat. The breasts may become heavy, tender, and the nipples may tingle before normal periods. This process is exaggerated by and is continuous throughout pregnancy.

The glands grow rapidly in size and the blood supply to the breast increases. This shows up as a greater number of veins on the surface of the breast and these can be seen through the skin. They disappear when you stop breast-feeding.

(Left) Your baby usually, but not always, lies with her head pointing downwards into your pelvis. Until 'engagement', the head doesn't usually sink below the brim of the pelvis. The head 'engages' when it slips down into the pelvic cavity.

Milestones of development

You can chart the development of your baby through 'milestones'. These are developmental events which can be predicted with a fair degree of accuracy. You may like to chart your own pregnancy with your own milestones.

4 weeks	Amenorrhoea
6–8 weeks	Breast changes
	Nausea, morning sickness, lack of appetite, loss of interest in food, dislike of cigarette smoke, alcohol
	Increased frequency in passing urine
12 weeks	Uterus can be felt enlarging in the abdomen for the first time
14 weeks	Nausea and sickness disappear
	Increased pigmentation of the skin including the nipples and the linea nigra and darkening of moles and freckles
12th–14th week	Foetal heart can be heard with a special stethoscope
16th–18th week	Foetal movements first felt in a 2nd and subsequent pregnancy
18th–20th week	Movements first felt in a 1st pregnancy
24 weeks	Foetal heart can be heard with an ordinary stethoscope
36th week	The uterus has been enlarging in the abdomen and by this time has reached the level of the lower ribs
	Lightening, or the time when the baby's head drops down into the pelvis ready for labour to begin

Care of your body
Care of the breasts

You should pay particular care to breast hygiene and you should wash and dry them carefully every day. Once colostrum has been secreted, be careful that none of it becomes encrusted on the breast but wash it away gently. You might also practise expressing colostrum from the breast so that you are able to express milk once lactation has begun. First you should lubricate the skin of the breast and your hands with baby oil. Then with the palms against your breast, you should grasp it between fingers and thumb and firmly stroke downwards towards the nipple.

Next with your finger and thumb on the outer margin of the nipple area, gently squeeze the colostrum from the breast.

It is very important that your nipple is prominent so that your baby can suck easily. If you have an inverted nipple, do not worry because you can evert the nipple yourself by the time you have your baby. You do this by wearing breast shells. The shell is basically a disc of plastic with a hole in the middle. You wear it each day inside your bra with the shell over the breast so that the hole is in line with the nipple area. Every day a little pressure is exerted on the skin around the nipple and gradually it will evert and protrude forwards through the hole in the centre of the shell. The time you start wearing the shells will depend on advice from your doctor. Most women wear them during the last two months of pregnancy, usually for only a couple of hours in the beginning and then longer and longer each day until at the end of the month they are being worn for the whole of the day but not at night.

If your nipples are of normal shape, there is no need for any care other than daily washing with soap and water. There is no need to massage your nipples with oil or alcohol to harden them and never scrub or abrade the nipple area.

Drugs

The placenta is designed to carry nourishment and oxygen from the woman's body to the foetus and waste from the foetus to the woman. It follows that most of the substances in the woman's body can pass into the foetus and this applies to chemicals and viruses. If a medicine has a small enough molecule it will pass across the placenta into the baby's body. A medicine with a large molecule may not. Many commonly used drugs like aspirin, codeine and barbiturates have small molecules but they have been used for a long time without producing harmful effects on the foetus, so it is generally accepted that they do not harm it, if only taken occasionally in small doses.

Generally a drug taken by the woman will be in the baby's circulation within an hour. The development of the vital organs occurs during the first 12 weeks and it is during this time that they are susceptible to damage from external agents. The vast majority of congenital abnor-

malities occur during the first 12 weeks of pregnancy and so a pregnant woman should be rigorous about not taking drugs then. She should certainly never administer them to herself. She should only take them if prescribed by a doctor. Exceptions would be those drugs that a woman needs to take to maintain her health, such as insulin in a diabetic. A good rule of thumb should be to take no drugs whatsoever unless your doctor regards them as necessary.

Alcohol in moderation (i.e. a glass of white wine, lager or beer a day) does not seem to cause any harm to either the woman or her baby, though women may find that they are more susceptible to alcohol during pregnancy. This is because the enzyme which metabolizes alcohol is less available now. Excessive alcohol intake should be avoided both for the pregnant woman's sake and the baby's. The babies of alcoholic mothers very often suffer withdrawal symptoms when they are born, they may be underweight and may go seriously short of vitamins if the alcoholism is severe.

The case against smoking during pregnancy is incontrovertible. It has been shown that babies born from mothers who smoke more than 10 cigarettes a day are underweight, have difficulty in starting to breathe and are more prone to infections and to the respiratory disease which can affect newborn babies. This is an extremely serious condition in newborn infants as it may prevent normal breathing and cause death. There is also a higher incidence of stillbirths with smoking mothers. Even one cigarette a day may be harmful.

It is important that hormones are not taken during the early stages of pregnancy. At one time they were used as part of a pregnancy test but medical research has now shown that this may be harmful to a developing baby and the practice has been discontinued. However, hormones may be useful when given by an obstetrician for treatment of a threatened abortion, or for maintenance of pregnancy in women who have previously miscarried several times. It is particularly useful when a woman is deficient in progesterone.

Injections of local anaesthetic for dental treatment during pregnancy are quite safe unless you have a known allergy to them.

Among the drugs which are often given during pregnancy are iron supplements to prevent iron deficiency anaemia. These tablets are specially formulated for pregnant women and contain trace elements like copper, manganese, magnesium and cobalt. Folic acid is given in the U.K. from the first antenatal visit onwards and there are tablets which combine iron and folic acid. It is customary in some clinics to give calcium supplements, specially to women who suffer from muscular cramps.

X rays

We have known for some years that exposure to X rays in the early weeks of development may result in foetal deformities. It is an absolute rule

(Above) To express colostrum, hold your breast in both hands. Whilst the hand underneath supports the breast, stroke firmly downwards towards the nipple with the other.

Next bring your fingers and thumb down to the nipple area (the areola) and gently squeeze the nipple. Colostrum will then be expressed from the nipple.

that a woman in early pregnancy should never be exposed to X rays. In the latter stages the foetus is much less likely to be harmed but some authorities go as far as banning X rays of the teeth and chest even when the abdomen is protected by a lead screen.

Immunization

Immunization and vaccination should be avoided during the first four months if possible, certainly during the first three. Standard immunizations may be carried out after that time if absolutely necessary, with the exception of smallpox. Smallpox is now very rare. However, if it is needed, a first smallpox vaccination should not be carried out at any time during pregnancy unless the woman has been in contact with a case of smallpox. It follows that if you have not been vaccinated against smallpox, you should not travel abroad to an area where the illness occurs. It's a good idea to have all the immunization and vaccination you think you might need before trying to start a family.

German measles

German measles is a fairly mild infectious disease but the rubella virus can cross the placenta. If you contract the condition while you are pregnant, your baby will also become infected. After the 16th week, it is probably of little consequence but before that time the virus can cause serious abnormalities to your baby. The earlier in pregnancy you contract the disease, the worse the abnormalities are and include deafness, blindness and heart disease.

It is best if you have either had German measles or an inoculation against it when you were young. If you have not had it by the time you are thinking about having a family, you should have an inoculation against it before doing so and then wait three months. An inoculation will give you a mild attack of the disease but immunity from future attacks. All schoolgirls in the U.K. are now offered inoculation between the ages of ten and thirteen.

If you are pregnant, have never had German measles and come in contact with someone who has, make sure that you get in touch with your doctor immediately. He can give you an injection of gamma globulin which will protect you and your baby. If you contract German measles during the first three months of pregnancy, then your doctor will almost certainly suggest termination. As this cannot be undertaken lightly you will need to have a very full discussion with your husband and your doctor.

Antenatal care

Recent statistics have shown that Britain has one of the highest infant mortality (including stillbirths) rates in Europe. This is directly related to a lack of antenatal care. Women who seek antenatal care latest are those who are unmarried or those who have an unwanted pregnancy. The longer you go without antenatal care the greater are the chances of a mishap. You should go to your doctor immediately you suspect that you are pregnant and enrol at an antenatal clinic immediately after.

Antenatal care aims to maintain your good health. It lays emphasis on educating you about your own and your baby's health during pregnancy, on careful monitoring of all aspects of your health throughout pregnancy and ensures that you and your family are well prepared for your labour and for motherhood.

Less than 5 per cent of pregnant women attend their first antenatal visit during the first eight weeks of pregnancy and more than half of pregnant women attend only after the 16th week of pregnancy. Latest research shows that the chance of a woman having a live, healthy, normal baby, is directly related to the number of antenatal visits she makes.

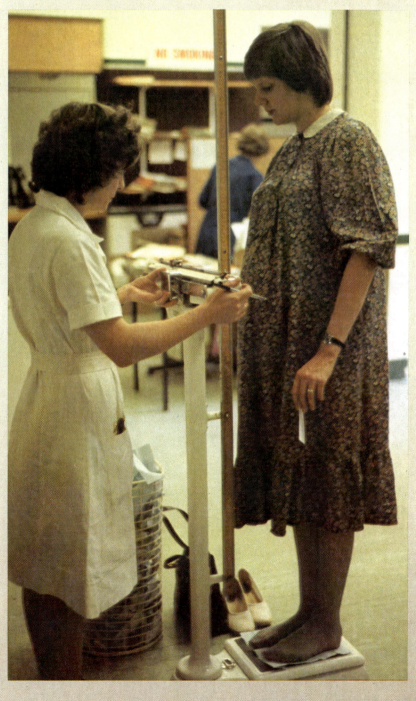

(Below) Regular antenatal visits are essential to you and your baby. They ensure your health, your baby's health and give doctors the chance to deal with minor problems before they become major ones. Weighing is a routine part of the visit.

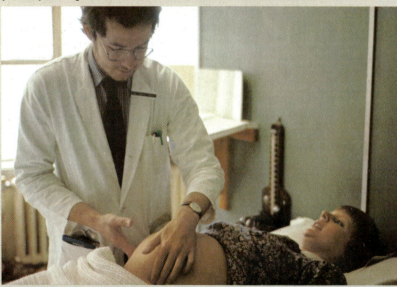

(Above) Blood pressure is taken at each antenatal clinic visit.

(Above) At a later stage the doctor can feel the baby through your abdomen.

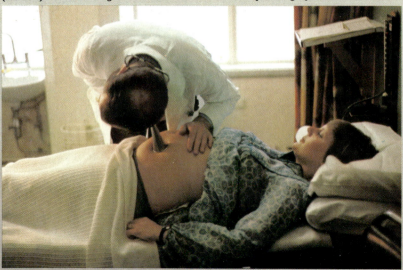

(Above) The baby's heart beat can be heard through a special stethoscope.

Antenatal visits

The first visit can be a pretty intimidating affair if you don't know what is going to happen. It should not be – it is very simple and straightforward and nothing unpleasant will happen to you.

First you will be interviewed by a doctor who will ask about your medical history, childhood illnesses, whether or not you have been in hospital and whether you have had any serious diseases. He will also ask you about any illnesses in your family. There will be a lot of questions about yourself besides your name, age and date and place of birth. He will want to know how long you have been married, whether you planned a family, whether you used contraceptives and if so which ones. Then he will ask you about your work, or the work you did before you became pregnant and your husband's job.

You will be asked at what age your periods began, how long your normal menstrual cycle lasts, how many days you bleed and what your period is like – heavy or light. The doctor will also want to know when you had your last menstrual period, what your weight was at the time you became pregnant and any of the symptoms you have had since you conceived.

You will be asked whether you want to have your baby at home or in hospital.

Then you will be examined, first for standard physical statistics and then to confirm your pregnancy. You will be measured for height (this gives some idea of the size of your pelvis) and you will be weighed regularly (the doctors and nurses will keep a careful check to see that you do not gain too much).

Your urine will be tested for protein and sugar, the latter to make sure that you do not have diabetes. Your blood pressure will be taken at each visit and recorded. Your breasts will be examined for signs that confirm pregnancy and the condition of your nipples will be noted, especially if you wish to breast feed. Your heart and lungs will be examined with a stethoscope to make sure that they are healthy and your abdomen will be examined very carefully to feel the uterus and later, the baby. Later a special foetal stethoscope will be applied to your abdomen so that the midwife can listen to the baby's heart. Your pulse will be taken and your fingers will be examined for swelling. One of the first signs of raised blood pressure and fluid retention (pre-eclampsia) is swelling of your fingers and tightening of your rings. Your legs will be examined for evidence of varicose veins and your ankles for swelling. It is not necessarily routine for you to have an internal examination at your first antenatal visit. Indeed most doctors are loath to examine a woman internally during pregnancy.

You will have a specimen of blood taken for a variety of tests. The first is to see whether or not you are anaemic and if so you will be given the appropriate iron and vitamin treatment. The second test is to group your blood, in case you should need a blood transfusion in an emergency. Your blood will also be typed for rhesus factor, either positive or negative. A rhesus negative woman will be tested to see whether or not she has antibodies (see page 31). If so, you may need special antenatal care and expert attention for you and the baby during and after labour. Everyone has a routine screening test for the presence of syphilis and rubella antibodies. At the end of your interview and/or your examination, you will almost certainly be given iron and vitamin tablets.

You will be asked to visit your antenatal clinic every 4 weeks until the 28th week. From the 28th to the 36th week you will visit every 2 weeks and from then onwards you will visit weekly, so the doctor can keep a careful eye on you as pregnancy advances. You will normally have more blood samples taken at the 36th week to confirm that all is well.

If any symptoms occur between visits, or if you have any questions that are causing you concern, take advantage of your antenatal visit to discuss them with your doctor. Quite often small things are worrying and the doctor will be able to reassure you with a simple explanation. Never keep your fears to yourself.

When you enrol at the antenatal clinic, you will also be asked if you would like to attend antenatal classes and will be given a list of where they are held and at what times. Some areas have special classes for husbands, whereas in others husbands are encouraged to attend with their wives.

Co-operation card

You will be given a co-operation card, where your details are recorded, at your first visit. Certain technical terms and abbreviations may be used and these are explained below.

Primigravida	This is your first pregnancy.
Multigravida	This is not your first pregnancy.
D.L.M.P.	Date of last menstrual period.
E.D.C.	Estimated date of confinement.
Oedema	Swelling of fingers, feet or ankles.
Micturition	Passing urine.
Urine/ Alb. Sugar	Your urine is tested for albumin (signalling high blood pressure) or sugar (may indicate diabetes).
B.P.	Blood pressure.
Height fundus	The height of the top of the womb.
P.P.	Presenting part of baby.
Ceph. or Vx	The head is presenting.
ROA/ROP	Back of baby's head (occipito) lies to your right and either front (anterior) or back (posterior).
LOA/LOP	Positions same but to your left.
RSA	Right sacrum anterior (bottom is presenting).
FMF	Fetal movement felt.
FH	Fetal heart.
Hb	Haemoglobin.

Twins

Twin or multiple pregnancies put a much greater strain on the mother's body. Twins occur in one in eighty European pregnancies. Twins usually run in families but the tendency to twinning often skips generations. Though transmitted by both men and women, the characteristic is usually carried on by a woman. There are two types of twin, identical and non-identical. Non-identical twins have arisen from two separate eggs and are no more similar than brothers and sisters. Identical twins arise from the same egg, which is split in two and look not just alike, but the same. They are about a third as common as non-identical twins, who usually have separate placentas. Quite often identical twins share the same placenta. On the face of it, it ought to be fairly easy to diagnose a twin pregnancy, but it isn't and five out of every one hundred twin pregnancies are only discovered when the second baby is born. But there are certain clues:
☐ If you suffer from excessive nausea and vomiting beyond the fourth month, it may be a sign.
☐ If, when the doctor examines your abdomen, the uterus is consistently larger than the date suggests.
☐ If foetal movement is excessive. You should ask your doctor about this. Movement will be first felt at about the same time in a twin pregnancy as in a usual pregnancy, see page 17.
☐ If the doctor hears two foetal hearts. If he has been alerted he can use a special electronic stethoscope which can pick up two heart beats immediately, as early as the fourth month of pregnancy.
☐ If the midwife or doctor feel more foetal parts than can belong to one baby, especially if they are able to feel two heads.

Twin pregnancies tend to be slightly shorter than normal ones. They usually last between 36 and 38 weeks. Miscarriage is no more common but anaemia and pre-eclampsia are.

The treatment of anaemia must be prompt and the warning signs of pre-eclampsia must be understood by the pregnant woman so that she can report them immediately they occur, see page 42.

(Below) There are two kinds of twins – those that develop from one ovum and share a placenta, identical (below left) – and those who develop from two ova and have separate placentas (below right). Non-identical twins need be no more alike than brother and sister. As you'd expect, twins are rarely the size and weight of a single baby, who has all the space of the uterus to fill and is the sole call on the mother's food supply.

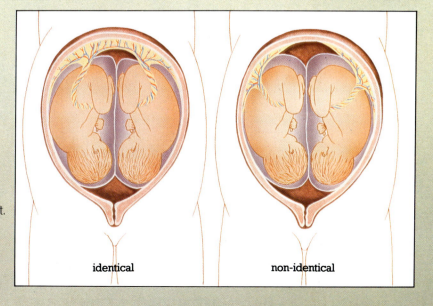

identical   non-identical

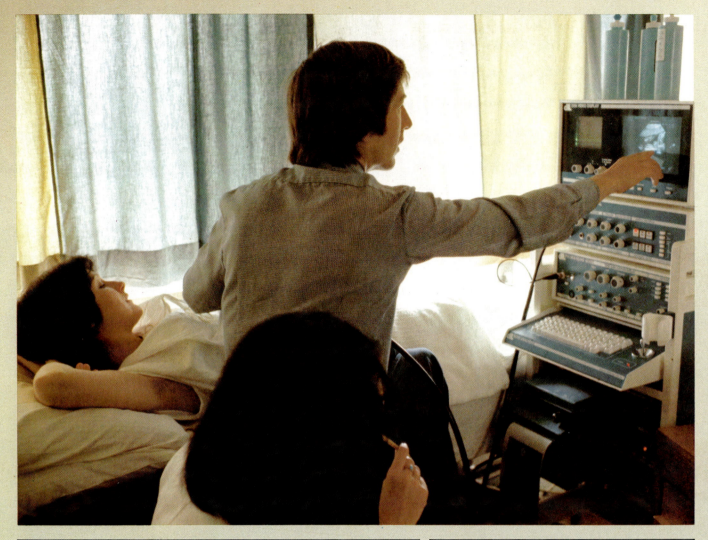

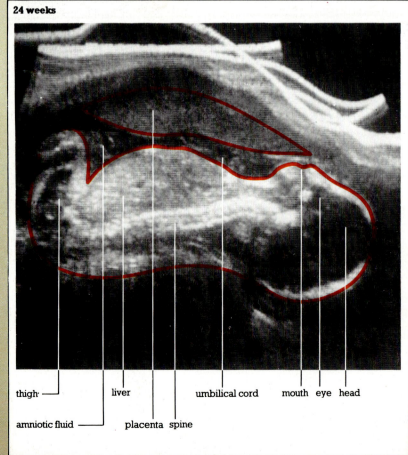

24 weeks

thigh

amniotic fluid

liver

placenta spine

umbilical cord

mouth eye head

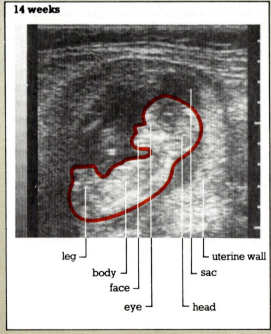

14 weeks

leg

body

face

eye

uterine wall

sac

head

(Top) You will be able to see a picture of your baby during the ultrasonic scan. (Above) This is a photograph of the screen image of a 14 week old foetus. On the scale at the side each division represents 1 cm. The foetus measures 7.6 cm from crown to rump. (Left) A 24 week old foetus. The lines at the top are the scanner lines.

Amniocentesis

There is a procedure whereby a sterile needle is passed through the abdominal wall and uterus under local anaesthetic in order to draw off a small sample of the fluid surrounding the baby for analysis. It is rarely performed before the sixteenth week and then only in very specific circumstances such as where there is a family history of spina bifida or mongolism or if the mother is old or if she has had German measles. It is never justified simply to find out the sex of your child. It is always performed in a special room under sterile conditions.

(Above) This is a very relaxing posture to rest in.

Ultrasonic scan

This is a diagnostic aid used by obstetricians to help them date the age of a developing baby or sometimes in the diagnosis of twins and triplets. Ultrasound waves are used in the same way as X-rays to give a picture of the baby, only they cause neither the mother nor the baby any harm. An ultrasonic scan will give an accurate picture of all the baby's parts. It can be performed safely at any stage of the pregnancy but it is commonly done twice. At 16 weeks it is used to measure the diameter of the foetal skull at its widest point from which the pregnancy can be dated with reasonable accuracy to within 6 to 7 days either side. At 34 weeks the abdominal circumference is taken, to size the liver, which will indicate how well the baby is growing. Problem mothers may be scanned more often.

(Above) Breathing exercises can help to relieve pain in labour.

Antenatal classes

These classes will explain the various aspects of mothercraft listed below. Make sure you fully understand them. The numbers in brackets refer to pages in this book where the relevant topics are covered.

1. The growth and development of the baby in the womb and how the womb itself will increase in size (pages 16 to 19).
2. Antenatal care including care of yourself, the importance of diet, exercise (including how to relax during labour if you wish for a natural childbirth), relaxation, sleep during pregnancy, care of the teeth, the bowels and the feet (pages 12 to 29).
3. Labour, including the signs which tell you it is beginning, what will happen during its three stages and which are the common things that may go wrong. You should examine and practise using the machine through which anaesthetic gases may be administered during labour and find out about the various forms of pain relief that are available during labour and the times when they will be useful (pages 51 to 53).
4. Breast feeding and bottle feeding, care of the breasts and special maternity bras (pages 15, 22 and 73).
5. Planning the baby's room and layette (pages 35 to 39).
6. Visit the maternity ward and labour ward (pages 61 and 51).
7. How to bath the baby (pages 80 to 81).

(Above) Husbands should participate too.

(Above) Many women take up this restful position without prompting.

Common minor complaints

Early morning sickness

Nausea and early morning sickness (see page 11) may cause you to lose weight in the early weeks of pregnancy, but the symptoms will probably go at about the 14th week. In the meantime, remember it is a normal phenomenon of early pregnancy – and try your best to keep yourself occupied. It has often been noted that the women with least to do are those who suffer most.

However, profuse and prolonged vomiting is a serious condition and should always be dealt with by a doctor.

Vaginal discharge

This may be profuse in pregnancy but still be normal. Generally speaking if the discharge does not smell offensive and does not cause irritation and soreness, then it is probably normal. But if in doubt, you should visit your doctor, because one of the commonest causes of an offensive vaginal discharge is thrush. Pregnant women are particularly susceptible to this infection which is easily treated.

Backache

Backache is one of the commonest complaints of expectant mothers. It is due partly to the slackening of the muscles and ligaments in the pelvis and spine under the influence of progesterone and partly to the enlarging abdomen which puts an unusual strain on the back. The best treatment is prevention and you will go a long way towards helping yourself by practising good posture when standing or sitting, by avoiding long periods of standing and lifting heavy weights and by taking adequate rest particularly in the middle of the day in the first few months of pregnancy.

There is nothing to be gained by wearing a supporting corset unless you have an underlying weakness of the spine. You may get some relief from massage or heat treatment.

Heartburn

Quite a number of pregnant women suffer from heartburn which is a burning sensation behind the lower part of the breast bone. The sensation is caused by the high level of circulating progesterone which relaxes the valve from the gullet into the stomach and allows regurgitation of the acid contents into the oesophagus.

It is not a symptom of an ulcer and can usually be cured by a drink of milk, an alkali tablet or alkali medicine. Alkalis will not harm your baby if taken occasionally. If the heartburn is persistent and troublesome, get in touch with your doctor.

Constipation

This is a common complaint due to high levels of progesterone which relax the muscle in the wall of the bowel and slow down the passage of food along the bowel. The food tends to stagnate in the intestine. More and more water is drawn from the stool which gradually becomes harder. You can help cure constipation by obeying the call to stool immediately. This usually occurs after eating and if you obey the call promptly you will retrain your bowel and encourage regular opening.

Help yourself by eating plenty of fresh fruit and vegetables to give your bowel bulk and roughage to work on. Adding bran or fibre to your diet in the form of drinks or on cereal will do nothing but good. Stewed prunes or figs will also help. You should not resort to purgatives regularly as this simply encourages a lazy bowel.

Shortness of breath

This is most common towards the end of pregnancy when the uterus is so large that it prevents the normal movement of the diaphragm and hinders respiration. Climbing a flight of stairs may be sufficient to make a pregnant woman breathless and you should stop and rest as soon as the shortness of breath comes on. If you have shortness of breath at night, you can help it by propping yourself up.

Fainting

Most pregnant women feel faint at some time. There are several reasons for this. During pregnancy the blood vessels to the skin are often dilated and can divert a large volume of blood from the brain. If the brain is deprived of blood even for the shortest time, there is a feeling of faintness. Also blood pressure can be

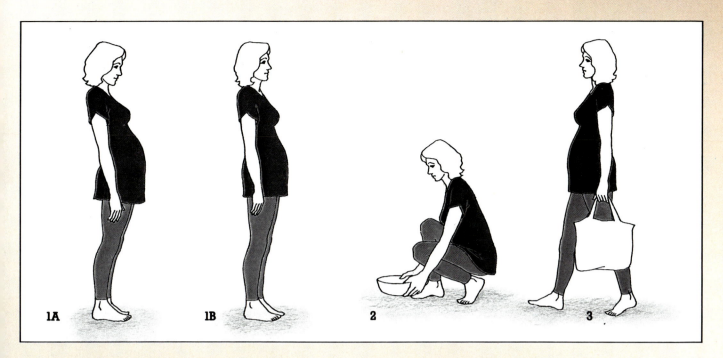

low particularly in the first few months. If you stand for any length of time, the blood may pool in the legs and fainting may occur if you suddenly stand from a sitting position and your blood pressure drops. Feeling faint and even fainting is not harmful to the baby.

Varicose veins

Few women get through pregnancy without suffering some form of varicose veins. Some have an inherited predisposition to them. But they may also be caused by relaxation of the muscles in the vein walls due to high levels of progesterone. The pressure of the developing uterus on the veins from the legs is another factor and excessive weight gain should be avoided.

You can help prevent varicose veins by avoiding standing and crossing the legs. It's a good idea to wear support tights but never wear stockings with a constricting band round the top, or garters. When you sit down, keep the feet on a stool and try exercising the foot by pulling it up, letting it down and making circular movements with the ankles.

Piles

Piles (haemorrhoids) are varicose veins around the anus and have the same causes as varicose veins in the legs. They may be aggravated by a chronic cough and by chronic constipation which causes straining when you use the toilet. If they are severe you should consult your doctor about treatment early in pregnancy. For less severe piles, the best treatment is to make sure you don't develop constipation.

Nose bleeds

Nose bleeds in pregnancy are usually minor and stop spontaneously after a few minutes. They can usually be controlled by simply pinching the nose between your finger and thumb. What-ever you do, do not put your head backwards because if you swallow blood it may make you vomit. Put your head forward over a sink or bowl.

Abdominal pain

Towards the end of pregnancy, most women experience some pain in the right side of the abdomen underneath the lower part of the ribs. This is due to the enlarging uterus pushing up against the rib cage and forcing the ribs outwards. It is perfectly normal, there is no need for any treatment and it will disappear after delivery. You may also experience soreness where your baby kicks persistently but this will be shortlived too.

A pregnant woman can suffer abdominal pain that has nothing to do with her pregnancy but it is always a frightening symptom at this time and if you ever experience severe or prolonged abdominal pain, you should inform your doctor immediately.

Swelling of ankles and hands

During pregnancy, blood volume may increase by as much as 50 per cent and this causes a large amount of fluid in the body. In the last three months it tends to accumulate in certain areas, particularly the extremities, so you may notice that your ankles swell and you are unable to take off your wedding ring towards the end of the day. You may also notice that your face becomes puffy, especially first thing in the morning. The treatment of these symptoms varies according to their severity but you must draw them to the attention of your doctor or midwife as soon as they occur. If your blood pressure and urine are normal, you will probably simply be advised to rest more. If your blood pressure is raised even slightly your doctor will almost certainly confine you to bed or you may even be taken into hospital for enforced rest. With this treatment the swelling (oedema) nearly always subsides.

(Above) To avoid backache, it is important to know how to stand correctly, how to lift and carry.
(1A) shows an incorrect posture with the abdomen sagging forwards and the neck muscles slumped. (1B) shows the right way: the back is straight and the head is held high.
(2) shows how to pick up something from the ground. You should bend your knees and squat before attempting to lift any object.
(3) shows how to carry something heavy. Try to keep your back straight. It is better to distribute a heavy load in two bags so that you are balanced.

Falling down

You are almost certain to suffer some kind of fall particularly in the latter part of pregnancy when your large abdomen makes you ungainly and upsets your balance. Even if you fall on to your stomach it is almost impossible to injure your baby because it is completely surrounded in a protective cushion of liquid. And if your abdomen strikes something sharp like a stone, it is again impossible for your baby to be damaged from the outside.

Visual disturbances

One of the effects of retaining fluid may be a slight change in the shape of the eyeball. This may result in minor visual disturbances such as spots before the eyes or flashes of light but they rarely signal any serious condition. Nonetheless you should report them to your doctor. You should also tell your doctor or midwife if you are wearing contact lenses so that they are not damaged when your eyes are examined and you should always remove your contact lenses before labour begins.

Warning signs

If any of these warning signs occur at any time during pregnancy you should get in touch with your doctor at the earliest possible moment.

1. Vaginal bleeding.

2. Severe, continuous abdominal pain.

3. Breaking of the waters.

4. Blurring of vision, difficulty in seeing, or any visual disturbance.

5. A continuous severe headache.

6. A temperature of over 101°·

7. Frequent and painful passing of water.

8. Swelling of the hands, face or ankles.

9. Absence of foetal movements for more than 24 hours.

10. Excessive vomiting.

Pre-existing problems
Heart disease

It is very rare for pregnancy to be terminated in a woman who is suffering heart disease unless it was severe enough to put a serious restriction on her ordinary life. On the contrary, most women who suffer mild to moderate heart disease go through pregnancy with ease and their heart condition may even improve.

Occasionally, heart disease is detected for the first time at the first antenatal visit, or the woman may have a known heart condition. In both cases, it means meticulous antenatal supervision, so that precautions can be taken to prevent any strain on the heart. Rest is mandatory – 12 hours in bed each night and at least 2 periods of rest lasting 2 hours during the day. The doctor will be on the lookout for anaemia and excessive weight gain and will probably take special precautions to guard against infection, especially influenza and the common cold. The patient must be informed that any swelling of the hands or feet, or the onset of shortness of breath, or a cough, or any minor infection should be reported to the doctor immediately.

The heart's workload peaks around the 30th week and at this stage many patients with heart disease are advised to go to bed and stay there for a fortnight. You may be advised to do this in hospital so you can be constantly supervised. Dental care is particularly important, as infected gums and decaying teeth are dangerous to a patient with heart disease and if any dental extractions are done they must be covered by the administration of an antibiotic.

Labour is usually allowed to run its own course in a patient with heart disease. Usually it is very easy and quick. Nonetheless, women with cardiac disease are admitted to hospital at about 38 weeks so that they can have a complete and supervised rest before labour begins.

Diabetes mellitus

If diabetes mellitus is well controlled with insulin and other drugs, the patient will have no difficulty in becoming pregnant but will be given special care throughout pregnancy. If you are diabetic and you do become pregnant, it is specially important that you go and see your doctor immediately. Latent diabetes may become overt as the result of pregnancy. This is one of the reasons why every woman's urine is tested very carefully for the presence of sugar at each antenatal visit. Because diabetes is so easily treatable, most women who have the condition explained to them can manage it extremely well themselves and there is no reason why they cannot do just as well during pregnancy.

The control of diabetes during pregnancy is crucial, or both mother and baby are exposed to dangers like prematurity. Adjustments in insulin and drug requirements may be necessary so diabetic women must be seen by their doctors frequently. Weight gain and diet must also be watched.

Doctors will take an extra special interest in the diabetic mother from the 32nd week onwards and at the 36th week they will probably do hormone estimations to make sure that the baby is healthy and that the diabetes is properly controlled. There is a tendency for diabetics to have large babies and if this is the case it may be delivered by Caesarian section (see page 56). Otherwise labour in a diabetic woman is usually straightforward. From 36 weeks onwards, the pregnancy will be artificially induced (see page 42) if there is any sign that the baby is ready to be delivered. During labour, a diabetic mother will be given glucose solution into a vein to control the diabetic condition while her baby is being born and the baby will be watched carefully by paediatric doctors and nurses for the first few days of its life to ensure that everything is O.K.

Rhesus incompatibility

A woman who has a rhesus negative blood group is given special care especially if she is carrying a rhesus positive baby. During pregnancy, blood cells from the baby may escape across the placenta into the mother's own circulation. The mother's body interprets the rhesus positive cells as foreign and tries to destroy them by forming antibodies to them – rhesus antibodies. They are harmful to the baby if their level is high.

A rhesus negative woman who is having a baby for the first time will probably have no antibodies at all because they can only be formed once she has been exposed to rhesus positive blood cells and this may or may not occur during the first pregnancy. Most doctors agree that there is no danger whatsoever during the first and there may be very little danger during subsequent pregnancies because antibodies may never be formed in large quantities. But they take the precaution of finding out what the level of antibodies is by testing the mother's blood during pregnancy, because above a certain level it is known that they may damage the developing baby. A previous termination or miscarriage may also affect the number of antibodies produced. This level is reached in less than 10 per cent of women who are rhesus negative. So because you have a rhesus negative blood group there is no need for immediate alarm. In fact, the outlook is good. Rhesus incompatibility is uncommon nowadays because after labour a rhesus negative mother will have a blood test to see if any of the baby's cells have entered her circulation. If the test is positive she will be given an injection of anti rhesus globulin, which destroys the baby's cells remaining in her blood, so that antibodies are not produced.

Even if you do have antibodies which can cross the placenta and attack your own baby's blood cells, we know so much about rhesus sensitivity that hospital obstetrical units are quite capable of dealing with the situation and will give you a lovely healthy baby at the end of your pregnancy. It does mean, however, that your antenatal care will be meticulous, that you will have to attend the clinic more often than the other mothers and that you may have regular blood tests. You may also have one or more amniocentesis tests, see page 27 and if the baby is found to be affected, an inter-uterine transfusion may be carried out.

In a few cases the newborn baby needs a blood transfusion to replace its own cells which have become damaged during pregnancy and occasionally all the baby's blood must be changed, especially if it is jaundiced at birth. Paradoxically your baby will be given a transfusion of rhesus negative cells even though it is rhesus positive itself. This is to prevent the new blood cells being destroyed by any of the mother's rhesus negative antibodies that remain within the baby's system. A rhesus positive baby cannot produce antibodies to rhesus negative cells and the transfused cells will die over a period of time to be replaced by the baby's own healthy rhesus positive blood cells.

Once the antibody and the yellow pigment (bilirubin), which is responsible for the jaundice, have been washed out of the baby's system it will come to no further harm and be a normal healthy child. To give the child the best chance of this happening, a doctor will take a specimen of blood from the umbilical cord as soon as it is delivered to test for the presence of anaemia and jaundice.

When a transfusion is performed, the baby's own blood is withdrawn at about a third of an ounce (10 ml) at a time and the same quantity of blood is transfused back into the baby. By doing so about 80 per cent of the baby's own blood can be removed and replaced with the new rhesus negative blood. In about 72 hours an infant will have got rid of all the antibodies that have been passed on from his mother and after the third day there is generally no need for any further transfusions to be carried out.

Boy or girl?

It is said that you can be 70 per cent successful in sexing your baby if you really want to know its sex by simply counting the foetal heart rate; a heart rate persistently below 140 beats per minute is said to be male and one persistently above 140 beats per minute female.

A Swiss company is hoping to market a test for sexing your baby which involves nothing more than your spitting on to filter paper. It is claimed to be 90 per cent certain by the fourth month and will cost around £12. It takes some of the fun out of being pregnant in my opinion. Furthermore as the test could be used as a possible basis for claiming an abortion because the baby isn't the sex you want, I'm morally against it. We should not have the choice. The sexes are biologically balanced and to meddle with this natural selection is tantamount to human pollution. We may bring about ecological changes we would greatly regret.

(Below) In the first pregnancy (1) there is little danger when a rhesus negative mother is carrying a rhesus positive baby. However, at birth (2) the baby's blood enters the mother's circulation and she reacts by forming antibodies (3) to kill the unwanted blood cells. If the build-up of antibodies is not prevented by an injection immediately after birth, then in a subsequent pregnancy (4), many more antibodies will be formed which will reach the new baby's circulation and will destroy his blood. In this case the baby may need an inter-uterine transfusion.

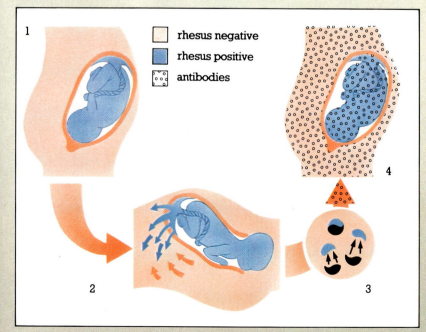

1

☐ rhesus negative

■ rhesus positive

▨ antibodies

2   3   4

Fears in pregnancy

When they find they are pregnant, most women feel happy and content. However, it is also quite normal, later on, for them to experience anxieties about the birth.

The best way to allay any fears that you have about your pregnancy is to find out as much as you can about it. There is nothing more fearful than the unknown and you would be wise to ignore the alarmist advice, old wives' tales and horror stories about pregnancy, which every woman hears at some time while she is carrying her child. Instead seek sensible and balanced advice from books, nurses, midwives and doctors and anyone who is medically qualified to give you accurate information. Your pregnancy and labour will be easier and happier if you fully understand what is happening and why, and how you can cope with it.

It is perfectly natural to fear that your baby will not be normal. There is nothing that you can do about this other than try to put the thought out of your head, for the chances are that you will have a perfectly normal baby. What you must not do is to link incidents you experience with the possibility of having an abnormal baby. Abnormalities are not caused by frights, shocks, falls or any incident in the outside world so ignore chance associations. Your fears will almost certainly increase as confinement approaches but you should try to distract yourself with the pleasant side of your waiting, such as planning and preparation for the coming baby.

Involving your husband

It will do a great deal to keep you emotionally calm and confident if you involve your husband from the very beginning. He should be encouraged to take up an active parental role from the moment your conception is confirmed and, if you encourage him to take the trouble to learn all about your pregnancy, he will almost certainly become interested, involved and supportive. He will also be more inclined to be a loving, involved father once the baby arrives.

It is now quite an accepted fact, indeed, it is expected, that the husband should be an active participant throughout a woman's pregnancy.

Most women attend antenatal classes to learn about and to be introduced to the process of psychoprophylaxis – making pregnancy easier by dispelling the fears about it. Nowadays most classes include a father's evening, when husbands can go along to find out more about pregnancy and labour.

It is commonplace for a father to be present during his wife's labour and delivery. If he wants to be there, it is his responsibility to be as well informed about what is going on as his wife is. Even if he doesn't attend the birth he should be as fully informed as possible so that he can give his wife the help she needs. It is his job to know as much about fathercraft as she will learn about mothercraft, and to find out about relaxation techniques. You both need it.

If your husband is to be with you during labour, warn the hospital well in advance. It is a

(Below) As part of the general familiarization with the hospital lay-out and procedures, you are taken round the wards during one of the antenatal classes. Husbands are, of course, welcome to come, too.

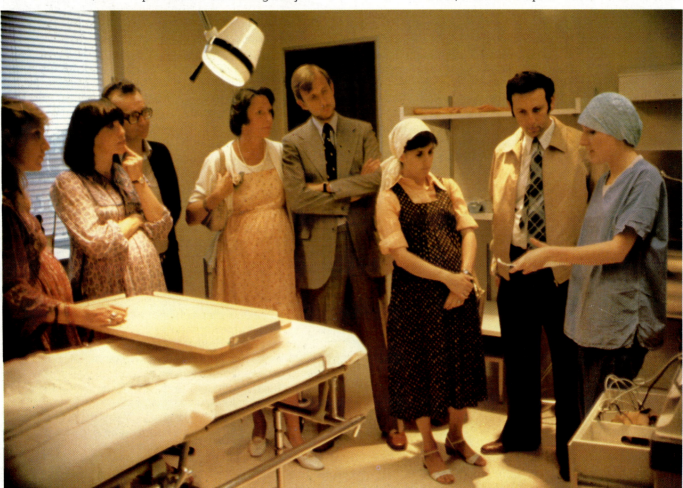

good idea for him to work out a schedule of what he will do when you go into labour so that he is prompt and efficient in informing the hospital of your condition and in taking you there.

Make sure that your husband is aware of your inevitable swings of mood: the fact that you may well be confident and outgoing one moment, then depressed, introspective, even tearful the next. The reason being that you are hardly in control of your emotions, which are being affected by the high level of female hormones that circulate in the blood during pregnancy. Warn your husband to be prepared for your tiredness and fatigue and later on in pregnancy, your nesting instinct to prepare everything for the new arrival.

Moodiness

Every woman is subject to fits of depression and moodiness, irritability and tearfulness at this time. They are common in pregnancy and quite normal. During one of these attacks the instinct is to remain alone. But your mood will lift more quickly if you seek the company of happy, friendly, supportive people, who will do much to make you forget your depression. Friends with children are particularly useful as they understand the problems and can discuss the ups and downs of becoming a parent calmly and coolly with you.

Working

There is no reason at all why you should not continue working for a good part of your pregnancy. The length of time you will be able to work depends on the sort of job you do and whether you are physically able to cope with it. If it is sedentary you should be able to continue until a few weeks before labour begins. But if it involves strenuous physical work, then you should certainly give it up no later than the 32nd week. Whatever your job is, you will have to make adjustments to your routine and to the extent to which you push yourself. You will no longer be able to move as fast or as dextrously as you could. You will be unable to work as long or stay up as late as you did before you were pregnant. Certain areas of your domestic life can be neglected and allowed to slide and you would be well advised not to worry about them. It is much more important to rest than to have a spotlessly clean house. It is better to have an early night than stay out late at a party. Forego your shopping in the lunch hour, put your feet up and take the weight off your legs. Don't hesitate to ignore housework or hard physical effort if you feel like it. It's the one time in your life when nothing is as important as the way you feel. Your family should realise you can't dash about like you used to as well. Your husband especially must appreciate that you cannot keep going at a fast pace. So must your boss. In pregnancy you can neglect almost anything but yourself.

Try not to worry about things that don't matter. The important thing is the baby that is growing inside of you. Once you understand this priority, most other things will fall into place and you should not face many crises and indecisions where you find it impossible to choose between two loyalties.

Self-discipline

You will find your pregnancy easier and more enjoyable if you discipline yourself to accept the changes in your life and adapt yourself to them. You must also try to exert some control over your emotions and not to indulge yourself in tantrums, fiery rages, or pessimism. Plan your days carefully so that you get enough rest and be strict with your diet so that you don't gain an excessive amount of weight.

Think positively. Make a detailed plan for yourself of what you will do when your labour starts. How you will go through each step in 'phoning your husband; 'phoning for an ambulance; informing your doctor; changing into your clothes for hospital; picking up your case, which has already been packed and contains all that you will need for yourself and the baby in hospital; putting on the kettle and making a cup of tea while waiting for the ambulance; getting into the ambulance, arriving at the hospital, changing into your nightdress, climbing into bed and awaiting the onset of labour. If you 'practise' this in your head until you have confidence in your ability to cope with everything, you will await confinement with few fears and little distress.

(Above) Work by all means if it keeps you happy and doesn't tire you. But don't stay on late in pregnancy at a physically taxing job. Try to keep as sedentary as you can. If it's financially possible give up as soon as you become fatigued and certainly if your hands or ankles begin to swell.

Services and benefits

Under the National Health Service you can claim a wide variety of services and benefits which are available to all pregnant women and you would be well advised to take advantage of them all. They fall into the following categories:
☐ Medical Help
☐ Auxiliary Help
☐ Nutritional help
☐ Financial Help

Medical help

Your own family doctor is the mainstay of your medical advice. He is the first person you should inform when you think you are pregnant because he will arrange for your antenatal care, and admission to hospital. He will also arrange a close liaison with local authority services such as the midwife, the health visitor, your enrolment at the local authority clinic. You cannot and should not bypass your own doctor because he is the only person who knows about your family and past medical history and your domestic environment, all of which may significantly affect the sort of care you need.

The midwife works very closely with your own doctor. Even if you have your baby in hospital it will be your midwife who takes care of you when you are discharged and for the first few days. If you are going to have your baby at home, she and your doctor will share the responsibility for your confinement.

Your health visitor, besides being a trained nurse, has had special training in looking after young babies and will visit you regularly after your baby is born and will help and advise you on his welfare.

If you are going to have your baby in hospital, you can do so at a General Practitioner Maternity Unit, an obstetric hospital run by GPs in that area. If you are interested in having your baby delivered in one of these units, you should ask your doctor for further details. Otherwise you may have your baby in a hospital maternity unit under the care of a consultant obstetrician. In either case, you can opt for the length of stay in hospital that suits you. If you would like to take your baby home quickly, you need only stay in hospital for 48 hours (see page 59). You may like to stay for a few days longer, say five days, or a week and then your discharge can be appropriately arranged. There is no given time that you must stay in hospital if your pregnancy is normal. If you wish you can insist on only staying 48 hours but this should be arranged before you go into hospital.

Auxiliary help

In some circumstances, you may qualify for the services of a home help. The midwife will be able to advise you about this, see page 91. She or the health visitor will also be able to put you in touch with a social worker if you have longer term problems over finances or difficulties in coping with a young child.

Nutritional help

You should enquire at your local child welfare or maternity clinic about the free milk and welfare foods which are available to some pregnant women and their children. You may qualify for one pint of free milk a day or two free packs of dried baby milk and free children's vitamin drops and mother's vitamin tablets if either of the following apply to you:
1. You are an expectant mother, all your children are under school age and your family is in receipt of supplementary benefits, or is in special need because of low income.
2. You have a handicapped child aged between 5 and 16 who is not attending an educational establishment.

If you do qualify for free milk you should ask at your local post office or your social security office for the claim forms. You will qualify for welfare foods if your income does not exceed a certain level and you are pregnant, and you should enquire as above for the claim forms. You are also entitled to free dental care and exemption from prescription charges. You should ask your doctor when you attend the hospital booking clinic and you will be given a signed form which you then complete and send to your local executive council whose address you will find on your medical card. A form will be returned to you which you should use to claim these exemptions and your milk token book.

You may also be entitled to free spectacles and dentures and you should consult your optician and your dentist about this so that you may make the claims on an appropriate form and send them to your local social security office.

Financial help

The two main financial benefits are the maternity grant and the maternity allowance.

The maternity grant is a lump sum. The contribution conditions for it are to be abolished from July, 1982. From that date, all mothers who can show they have been resident in Great Britain will qualify.

Maternity allowance is only for women who have been working and paying the full rate of insurance contributions. You may still qualify even if you gave up work some time ago. It is a weekly payment covering a certain period before and after the baby is born and it is available to both married and single women.

Conditions of payment
Maternity allowance
☐ before the 11th week prior to your expected date of confinement you must have worked for at least 25 weeks and paid Class I (employee's) contributions.
☐ can be paid at £20.65 a week, but is less if you have not paid 50 Class I contributions in the tax year relevant to your claim (your Social Security office will tell you which year is relevant).
☐ if claimed later than the 11th week before the expected delivery date you may lose it.

(Above) Organizing the nursery is one of the best parts of a pregnancy.

☐ claims can only be made for payment in arrears if you can show good reason for doing so (any claim in arrears will only apply to the preceding 12 months). Claim late and you could lose money.

☐ may be increased to allow for dependents.

Maternity grant

☐ may be claimed at any time from 14 weeks before the week in which your baby is expected to 3 months after the birth of your baby.

☐ if you claim later, your grant may be refused unless you have a good reason for being late.

☐ if you claim more than 12 months after the birth the grant cannot be paid.

☐ is paid if either you or your husband satisfy the contribution conditions for it or if you satisfy the contribution conditions for maternity allowance.

☐ is paid for a stillbirth if pregnancy lasted at least 28 weeks.

☐ can be paid for each baby born at a confinement provided each survive more than 12 hours.

How they are paid

Your maternity allowance is payable by means of a book which can be cashed weekly at your local Post Office. Tokens remain valid for up to three months. The maternity grant is paid by Giro Order and again may be left for three months.

Working mothers

If you are a working mother, it is now law that your job must be kept open for you for 11 weeks prior to your pregnancy, and 29 weeks after your confinement providing you have been with your employer at least 2 years. You should discuss these conditions with your employer so that your rights are satisfied and that it is made clear that you wish to return to work.

Planning your baby's room
Colours

One of the happiest activities you can indulge in is to plan your baby's room and her layette. If you are lucky enough to have the space, design a nursery. But whether it is a separate room or just a special corner, redecorate it specially, make new curtains and furnish it as brightly and as cheerfully as you can. We know that babies like bright primary colours, particularly blue and yellow, so set aside the traditional pastel colours of baby pink and baby blue and go for colours that are sunnier and more natural.

Mobiles

From an early age babies are fascinated by things that move. If you can, get a few toys that will move in a current of air and catch the light as they move, or make a soothing, tinkling sound. There are a variety of mobiles available and you will find that a fairly cheap mobile suspended over the cot in a position where your baby can watch it easily will keep her fascinated for ages.

The floor

For the sake of hygiene, most baby books recommend that the floor covering is linoleum or tiles that can be easily washed and disinfected. I personally think this gives the nursery a rather cheerless feel and would recommend a cosy fitted carpet.

Storage

It is useful to have a chest of drawers and some shelf space so that the baby's linen, creams, toys and clothes can be kept together, conveniently close to the cot.

Curtains

Babies respond dramatically to daylight and darkness. They tend to wake when it is light and go to sleep when it is dark. You can capitalize on this by lining your curtains with fabric which completely blocks the light. The lining will also help to keep out draughts.

Guards

Don't forget to take the precaution of barring windows, installing fireguards and putting a gate across the door, long before your baby becomes mobile. It is also a good idea to protect the power sockets. Further details about the various safety precautions you will eventually need to take are on page 141.

Lighting

A dimmer switch to control the main light source will be helpful.

Heating

If your baby is born in the winter you will have to take particular care to see that she is kept warm and out of draughts, preferably in a part of the house where the temperature is equable for the rest of the family and fairly constant. In very cold weather it's probably better not to take a very young baby out of doors.

Conversely in warm sunny weather your new baby will need less clothing. Avoid the tendency that every new mother has to cover her baby with too many layers. In really warm weather it's a good idea to give your new baby a few hours outdoors in the sunshine, well-shaded, protected and out of draughts.

It's unwise to keep a new baby in an unheated kitchen. Rather keep your baby in any room in the house which has heating. However, the kitchen is quite adequate if it's all you have but make sure the baby is warm and not in a draught.

Layette

Every mother instinctively wants to spend a lot on her baby's layette but babies grow very quickly and your expenses will be high later on. It is best to buy only the essentials described here in the first few weeks.

(Above) The basic essentials of the layette can be purchased before the birth. You can add the extras afterwards when you have the practical experience to know what's missing.

Nappies

There are several options open to you in choosing your baby's nappy. You can use:

1. Disposable nappies (2 kinds)
2. Terry towelling nappies (2 kinds sometimes in conjunction with muslin nappies and nappy liners)
3. Nappy service

The nappy service is expensive and is out of the question for many mothers. Disposable nappies are very attractive as they involve no special cleansing, disinfecting and washing but they too are on the expensive side. There are two kinds, one type is just a pad which needs to be worn with plastic pants into which it will fit, the other type incorporates the plastic pants as an integrated outer layer. They are made so that the layer nearest the baby's skin allows moisture to pass through completely and be absorbed by the rest of the nappy, thus keeping an almost dry surface next to the skin. This minimizes the chances of the baby getting a nappy rash, see page 85. They come in different sizes and some are extra absorbent for night-time use. Whilst they are an expensive alternative, they are very convenient to use on certain occasions, such as when you are travelling or on holiday. It is also very helpful to use disposable nappies when the baby first comes home, while you are settling in to a new routine.

Start off with several packets and make sure that you have at least one spare packet in store.

The terry-towelling nappies are traditionally squares of soft, absorbent towelling but they are also available in specially shaped designs, either triangular or T-shaped which fit the baby's bottom, thus avoiding bulk and making fitting and pinning easier. Since they are of double thickness towelling they do take much longer to dry. You will need two dozen.

Muslin nappies are squares of soft, lightweight material which are useful for very young babies.

Nappy liners help to keep the towelling nappy from getting very soiled. They can usually be flushed away once used. They come in packets of 100 or 200.

One-way nappies are also used as a lining to terry-towelling nappies. They are made of a material specially designed to stay fairly dry, whilst allowing the moisture to be absorbed by the towelling nappy.

Four vests

Four stretch 'babygrow' garments

Nightdresses are not essential, as the baby does not need different clothing for night and day. Make sure that you choose a size which will not cramp your baby's feet.

Six pairs of waterproof plastic pants

As already mentioned, some types of all-in-one disposable nappies incorporate pants, whilst the other type requires pants specially designed to take the disposable pad. With terry towelling nappies you have a choice. There are pull-on ones or popper pants with an adjustable waistband or tie pants. For very young babies

(Below) While it's nice for you and the baby if the nursery is pretty, your main concerns should be comfort and practicability. This clever 'baby-changing area' is a very good idea. It speeds up the whole nappy changing operation if all the necessary equipment is to hand.

the type that tie at the sides and do not have elasticated legs can be preferable. Otherwise make sure the elastic gives easily, so that it doesn't cut into your baby's skin.

A coat for going outdoors
Or if your baby is born in the winter, consider getting an 'all-in-one' hooded jump suit which will keep out the draughts.

A shawl

A woollen helmet with ear flaps and a pair of mittens

Equipment

Equipping your baby's room depends very much on the amount of money you have available but essentials will include:

A cot If it is painted, make sure that the paint contains no lead. To my mind the most hygienic ones are chrome-plated cots, though they are rather expensive. A cradle or crib is not essential but does provide a young baby (i.e. for the first four months) with a smaller and therefore snugger bed. Also, rocking it is very soothing to both mother and baby and if decorated prettily it will be a very attractive addition to your nursery. A carry cot (see below) can be used instead of a cradle or crib.

Four cot sheets Babies find the slightly fluffy flannelette variety the most comforting. The baby only uses a bottom sheet.

Waterproof plastic sheet Essential for a cot.

Two cot blankets The cellular type made of wool are probably the warmest (see page 36 for temperature of nursery).

A plastic baby bath on a steady stand. Some stands will also fit the carry cot and therefore have a dual use.

Two bath towels Try to have ones which are soft and fluffy and are used only by the baby. If you can afford them, the kind which are in the shape of a square with a hood in one corner enable you to wrap your baby completely.

Feeding and sterilizing equipment (for bottle-fed babies). You can purchase four bottles and the sterilizing unit in one pack.

Non-biological washing powder or soapflakes For washing the baby's nappies and clothes as

(Right) Your confinement case should be packed during the last two-three months, ready for you to take to hospital. It will contain clothes for you and the new baby. (Below) Few people can resist the temptation to buy all the equipment so attractively on display in baby shops. However, it's better to start with the bare minimum, get used to that, then build as you need more.

Baby expenses

No baby is cheap and you would be sensible to start thinking about what you are going to need for your baby quite early on in pregnancy so that you can budget your expenses and spread your expenditure out. It's up to you of course how much you spend, how expensive your equipment is and how expensive you make your baby's layette. I would suggest that you should count on spending about £250 before the baby arrives, broken down as follows:

☐ Nursery – decoration, curtains, floorcovering, furniture £100
☐ Baby equipment – carry cot and transporter or pram and cot, bath, sterilizing equipment, linen, baby bag etc. £100
☐ Layette – nappies, clothes, shawl, etc. £50

By sticking to the bare essentials this sum might be reduced by £50-60.

Baby preparations

You may also decide to have a baby 'medicine' chest. Items you might keep in here include:
☐ antiseptic baby cream – Cetrimide is the kind used in many hospitals.
☐ infant vitamin drops, from your baby clinic.
☐ nappy rash cream.
☐ saline solution for cleansing eyes or nostrils.
☐ thermometer.
☐ paracetamol elixir – a mild analgesic.

Your confinement case

Some time in the last three months of pregnancy, prepare an emergency case to take to hospital. It should always be ready packed so that you can pick it up at a moment's notice. Some hospitals issue their own 'clothes list' and this may vary slightly from the one given. You should include the following items:

For you
☐ 2-3 nightdresses, preferably in cool fabric, e.g. cotton and front opening
☐ A bedjacket
☐ A dressing gown and slippers
☐ Several pairs of pants
☐ A packet of sanitary towels
☐ A sanitary belt
☐ 2-3 maternity or feeding bras and bra pads
☐ Basic make-up and hair accessories
☐ An outfit of loose fitting clothes for you to wear when you leave hospital*

*Some hospitals prefer you to leave this outfit at home to be brought in on the day you leave. If this is so, have the clothes ready in a particular place, so that they can be easily found.

For the baby
☐ 2 nappies of any kind with safe-lock pins (in case there's a delay on the way home and you need to change your baby)
☐ A pair of plastic pants
☐ 1 vest
☐ 1 'babygrow'
☐ 1 hat
☐ 1 shawl
☐ 1 jacket (if baby born in winter)

these will not irritate baby's skin.

A toilet box This will hold all you will need for your baby's toilet, including baby soap, baby cream, baby lotion, cotton wool, baby hairbrush and at least two dozen large curved nappy pins and a box of cotton wool buds.

A bucket Keep this standing by, filled with nappy cleanser to drop your dirty nappies in.

A bin The sort with a plastic bucket inside in which you can place your soiled oddments.

A carry cot with wheels. This will convert to a pram or can be used on its own as a cot.

A chair Preferably low, in which you can sit comfortably to feed and tend to your baby.

There are certain other items that I personally found indispensable. One was a padded plastic mat on which I changed the baby. The second was a plastic baby holdall with lots of pockets to keep all your baby's bits and pieces together, which you can carry around with you. The third was an endless supply of tissues.

The pram

A pram is not an essential as a carry cot with transporter will serve exactly the same functions. There are certain features you should look for whichever alternative you choose:

☐ It should be the right weight and height for you, so try pushing it before buying it to make sure it feels comfortable and not too heavy.
☐ It is important that you can see ahead of you when the hood is up. So check this.
☐ Good brakes are essential for safety, so only buy a pram or transporter that accords with British Safety Standards.
☐ Make sure the mattress is firm.
☐ Your pram needs a canopy which will act as a sunshade in summer and a pram net to keep off insects and cats when the baby is outdoors. Make sure that you can buy both items to fit the pram you choose.

BIRTH DAY

What kind of labour?

Long before you go into the labour ward, make certain that you have opted for the kind of labour you want. Make sure that the hospital staff know how long you want to stay in hospital because they have to make their plans too.

You may have decided during your antenatal classes that you wish to have natural childbirth. This means having your baby under normal, conditions without the help of any drugs, without any analgesics to relieve the pain, and without any inhaled anaesthetics to take the edge off the strongest contractions. This kind of labour is available to everyone so make certain that you have stated your preference clearly well in advance. It is also advisable to find out about what pain relief is available, how it works and why you might need it.

Induction

The necessity to induce your labour will have been discussed fully with you at the antenatal clinic before your admission to hospital and will not be undertaken without your agreement unless it is for an important medical reason. The reason why induction is desirable for you will have also been discussed with you and would include such factors as:

1. Medical reasons

High blood pressure.

Pre-eclampsia (the warning signs of which are high blood pressure, swelling of the ankles, hands and face and the appearance of protein in the urine).

Post maturity of your baby (probably signified by your failure to gain any more weight and usually means pregnancy has gone over 41 weeks.

Placental insufficiency (the baby is outgrowing the food supply provided by the placenta).

Diabetes.

Rhesus incompatibility. (See page 31.)

2. Social reasons

Social reasons are usually understood to mean that the labour is being induced for the convenience of the patient or the doctor and are therefore frowned upon. The general disapproval stems from two separate schools of thought; the first is that labour and delivery is an entirely natural process and should not be interfered with, especially for reasons as apparently frivolous as the convenience of the doctor or patient. The second stems from the fact that in the past induced labour was not as safe as spontaneous labour. This last argument is now irrelevant since induction in our hospitals today is as safe as spontaneous labour as long as the woman is fit and healthy and near term.

Given that an induced labour is as safe as a spontaneous labour, it is bound to be used more frequently so that patients can benefit from being looked after by doctors who are alert and fresh and who have at their disposal all the ancillary services they may require should an emergency arise. The services in the anaesthetics department, in the blood bank and in the paediatric unit are reduced during the night.

There are various ways of inducing labour. One of the most favoured is artificial rupture of the membrane followed by an injection of oxytocic drugs. This will happen very early in the

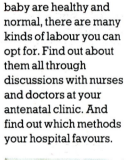

(Below) If you and your baby are healthy and normal, there are many kinds of labour you can opt for. Find out about them all through discussions with nurses and doctors at your antenatal clinic. And find out which methods your hospital favours.

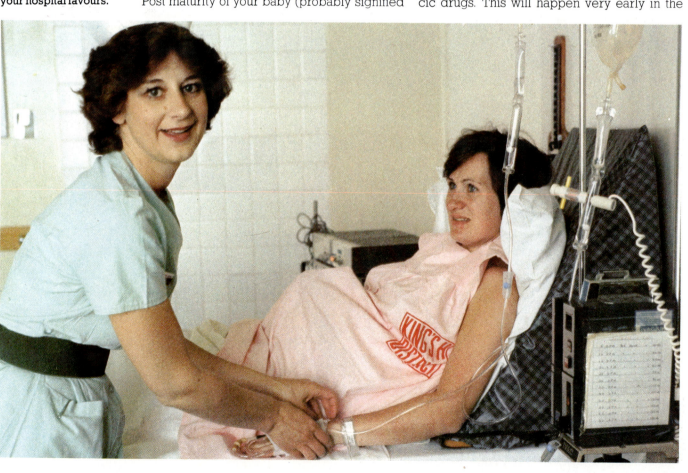

morning. You will be taken to the labour ward, where a doctor will examine you internally. He can usually feel the forewaters protruding through the cervical opening. By guiding a special pair of forceps up the vagina to the cervical canal the membranes can be gently perforated without you feeling any pain or discomfort. The amniotic fluid begins to drain away and pressure inside the uterus falls. It is thought that this alteration in pressure initiates labour which usually becomes well established within a few hours of rupture of the membranes and proceeds normally.

Oxytocic drugs are a group of chemical compounds which directly stimulate the uterus to contract rhythmically. The first drug to be used was pitocin and was given into a vein by means of a drip. Later, a form was devised which could be given by intramuscular injection. In some units, pitocin is given as tablets which are tucked up between the tongue and the cheek and slowly sucked. The drug is absorbed through the lining of the mouth into the bloodstream and its effect is to make the uterus start and maintain contractions. Women who have sucked these pitocin tablets will know from experience that by sucking hard they can increase the frequency of the contractions and slow them down by not sucking at all. More than one pitocin tablet may be given.

Alternatively, a synthetic drug, syntocinon, may be used to induce labour and it is given through an intravenous drip.

Recently, prostaglandin pessaries have been introduced to start off labour.

A dose of castor oil was once a commonly used method of inducing labour but it has been abandoned in modern obstetrics largely because it doesn't work well. A large dose of castor oil by mouth does little more than cause severe abdominal cramps which is one thing a woman in labour can well do without.

If you are interested in or even against an induced labour, make certain your feelings are known to the medical staff. If it is possible that your labour will be induced, find out as much as you can about it. It means that your labour is virtually under the control of the medical staff and it is performed most often so that doctors and staff can be present when your baby is born. Equal numbers of babies are born during every hour of the day, which means that, if left to their own devices, fifty per cent of all births would be during the night. Although most of the medical staff are equally spread over the 24 hours, some of the support staff may not be.

Leboyer's method

A French obstetrician, Leboyer, advocates a special environment in the labour ward when the baby is born. He suggests dim lights with no noise or loud sounds. Very often the maternal heart beat is played on a gramophone record. When the baby is born he is handled with great gentleness and care. The mother is actively encouraged to hold him immediately after delivery, obeying her own natural instincts to cradle the baby against her skin, croon to him, to sing, to chat, to caress, to smooth his skin. There is no rush to separate mother and child. Everything is done slowly, calmly, quietly.

There is much to be said for Leboyer's methods especially as you are given the baby as soon as he is born. On the other hand it is not always safe for a baby to be delivered in dim light, especially if things go wrong or the baby needs paediatric attention. In many maternity wards you will find the doctors and nurses quite prepared to accommodate a happy medium and will already be advocating early contact between mother and baby, beginning with breast-feeding immediately after birth.

The lie

During the early weeks of pregnancy the baby lies in any position and it twists around the uterus quite freely. By the end of the 32nd week with your first and the 34th week with your second and subsequent pregnancies, your baby will have settled into one particular position, called its lie. The lie may be
☐ longitudinal
☐ oblique
☐ transverse

Longitudinal lie

The baby's spine is parallel to the mother's with one end of the baby – either the head or the bottom – lying over the mother's pelvic brim. It begins to take up this position as the 28th week approaches. This lie occurs in about 98 per cent of pregnancies.

Oblique lie

Of the remaining 2 per cent of pregnancies, 1.5 per cent have an oblique lie, where the baby's spine is at a slight angle to the mother's. The lower part of the baby therefore lies just above the mother's groin. An oblique lie is commonest in women with several children whose abdominal wall muscles have become rather slack and lost their tone. Just before the onset of labour most babies with an oblique lie spontaneously move into the longitudinal position.

Transverse lie

The remaining 0.5 per cent of pregnancies have a transverse lie where the baby's spinal column is at right angles to the mother's. Again this occurs most often in women who have had a large number of pregnancies. Very rarely a transverse lie may be due to large cysts or fibroids which take up space within the uterus and prevent the baby from lying longitudinally. In nearly every case of transverse lie, the obstetrician can correct the position to a longitudinal lie by rotating the baby into position from the outside before or just after the onset of labour (see page 44).

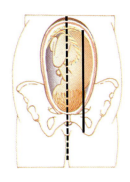

(Above) The longitudinal lie – the most common and convenient.

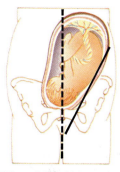

(Above) The oblique lie – more likely in women with several children.

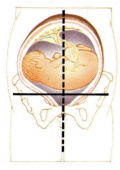

(Above) The transverse lie – a much less common position.

The presentation

This describes the part of the baby which is lying at the entrance to the birth canal: or, if engagement has occurred, in the pelvis. As nearly all babies assume a longitudinal lie just before labour begins, it is either the head (cephalic) or the bottom (breech) of the baby which is presenting.

Up to the 28th week, nearly all babies have a breech presentation with their heads lying under the mother's rib cage. During the 32nd week with the first and the 34th week in second or subsequent pregnancies, the baby spontaneously swings around, so that its head comes to lie over the pelvic brim and it becomes a cephalic presentation. Therefore, from the 37th to the 40th week, the normal time for deliveries, 96 per cent of babies are born head first.

In a cephalic presentation, the head and neck are pressed forwards so that the chin is resting on the chest. This is called a well-flexed head. This means that it is the top and back of the head which descend the birth canal first and which are delivered first. In 1 in 100 babies however, the neck and head are not flexed and the head may be bent so far backward that the face is looking directly down into the pelvis and is described as a face presentation. Neither presentation gives much difficulty in delivery. Due to the squeezing action as the head comes down the birth canal, swelling occurs in that part of the baby's head or face which presents. In a vertex (back of the head first) presentation, a swelling, called the caput, may form and in a face presentation the lips, nose and cheeks may be swollen and bruised. This swelling disappears within a short time and has no harmful effect on the baby at all.

In addition to a well-flexed head a baby lies with both legs bent at the hips and the knees and the feet turned inwards and crossed in front of the genital organs. The arms are also crossed so that the left hand rests on the right shoulder and the right hand rests on the left shoulder. Most babies who are in this well-flexed position lie with their backs to the front of their mother's abdomen. This is known as the anterior position. The back may be just to the right or just to the left of centre and the baby's position is described as right anterior or left anterior. When the baby's back is lying next to the mother's spine, the position is termed posterior and again because it can lie to the right or left side of its mother's spine, the position is described as right or left posterior.

One of the reasons why you will attend the antenatal clinic at two weekly intervals from the 30th week is so that the doctors and nurses can check on your baby's position and ensure that it is lying correctly. If your baby is still in a breech position by the 32nd week with your first, and the 34th week with your second and subsequent babies, your doctor may try to turn it into a cephalic presentation. This is a very simple, quick and painless manoeuvre. Both my babies were turned by the doctor though a few hours after leaving the clinic I felt them swing round to the breech position in which they seemed to be more comfortable. Despite this, both babies swung round to the cephalic presentation just before the onset of labour. In turning the baby round your doctor will use both hands on your stomach to gently push the baby's body up on one side and the head down on the other.

If your baby persists in presenting breech first, this is no cause for concern as breech deliveries are rarely accompanied by complications (see page 54).

Labour

Nobody knows exactly why labour starts. Most evidence suggests it is the baby who is in control. It is possible that the baby acts through the placenta to release a hormone which triggers off the onset of labour. The same hormone controls labour subsequently.

The time at which this happens varies. The length of a pregnancy can vary greatly between one woman and another and from pregnancy to

(Below) Most baby's 'present', that is are born, head first. Inside the uterus the neck is bent forwards with the chin on the chest. The baby can face backwards (1) or forwards (2), both positions are normal. So is the breech position (3). It's rarer but normal nonetheless.

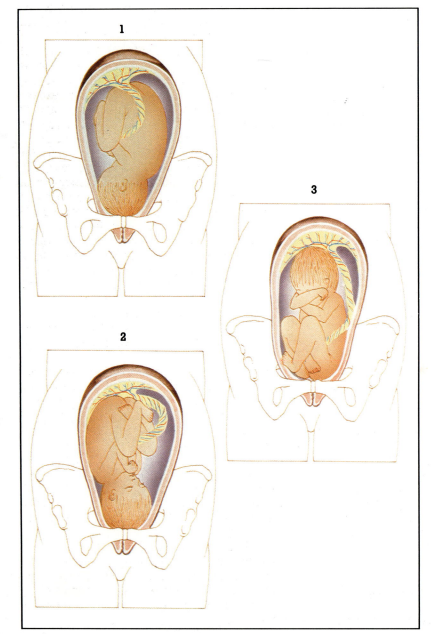

pregnancy in the same woman. It also depends on the father, as a woman may experience pregnancies of different lengths with different partners. Also, each baby seems to reach maturity at its own particular time. Forty weeks is only an average. Maturity may be reached at any time from the 36th week onwards up to the 42nd week, see page 54.

Similarly, there is no length of labour which can be described as normal because labour is different in every woman and every pregnancy. As a general rule however, women having their first child will experience a slightly longer labour. In most women, a first labour lasts about 12 hours but can range from 2 to 24 hours. About 3 in every 100 women will be delivered within 3 hours and about 10 will take as long as 24.

Labour in women having their second and subsequent babies lasts on average 6 hours but the range extends from 1 to 24 hours, labour being less than 3 hours in 10 out of every 100 women and more than 24 hours in one out of 100.

Fear about the health of the baby, about her own welfare and about pain or discomfort undoubtedly influences the length of a woman's labour. This fear is nearly always based on ignorance, so it is essential that antenatal care includes education and instruction about the mechanism of labour and what a woman can expect once labour has started. Education also includes reassurance that the complications of labour can nearly always be successfully treated resulting in no permanent harm to mother or baby.

Many women over the age of 40 having their first child have an extremely easy labour. However, as a rule of thumb, women over the age of 30 who are entering the last period of their fertile lives, or who are termed 'elderly primigravida', are usually given special attention during labour, so that any problems can be detected at an early stage.

It is not true that most babies are born at night. An equal number of babies arrive during each hour in the twenty-four. In contrast, the birth rate could almost be described as seasonal, with two peaks in March and April and in September. The first peak follows nine months after the summer holidays, and the September peak nine months after Christmas.

Signs of labour

If you have any fear that you will not recognize the onset of labour, be reassured by the knowledge that nearly every woman recognizes the symptoms easily. It may begin with any or all of the following three signs. You should go to hospital after you have had any of the three following indications:
1. You may pass a small quantity of blood-stained mucus called the 'show'.
2. The membranes or forewaters may break releasing fluid.
3. You may begin to have powerful regular uterine contractions.

The show is probably the commonest sign that labour has begun. The mucus is the plug which has been lying inside the cervix (neck of the womb) providing protection to the cavity of the uterus so that infection cannot get in. As labour begins, the cervix opens and the mucus plug slips out. It is easy to recognize because it is a half to one inch (12.7 mm – 25.4 mm) wide and formed of sticky, clear, semi-solid mucus. You may also get a low backache at the same time. The show is perfectly normal and does not mean the baby has lost blood.

As the cervix gradually gets wider and the baby's head presses down into the pelvis, the fluid which lies in front of the head is trapped. The ballooning of the amniotic sac (the membranes in which the baby develops) by this fluid is called the 'bag of waters' or the forewaters. As the pressure increases, the forewaters may break. Contrary to the old wives' tale, an early rupture does not mean a long, difficult labour.

As already explained in chapter one (page 18) the uterus contracts weakly and painlessly throughout pregnancy to keep its muscle toned up and to prepare it for the length and force of the contractions which it has to make during labour to expel the baby. These Braxton-Hicks contractions occur about every 15, 20 or 30 minutes and usually last for no longer than 25 seconds. If you put your hand on your abdomen during pregnancy you can feel it harden during a Braxton-Hicks contraction but you will experience no pain. As you near term, the contractions become more obvious and may cause you discomfort but never pain. When labour starts, however, the contractions become regular, strong and forceful, with a definite pattern.

All uterine contractions start off slowly and the sensation of pressure in the uterus rises gradually. The power of the contraction increases until it reaches its height which it maintains for a time and then disappears rapidly. The differences between Braxton-Hicks contractions and those which occur during labour are:
1. The pressure of Braxton-Hicks contractions is weaker.
2. They are only about half as long.
3. They are below the level at which pain is felt.
4. They disappear at about the same rate as they arise.

Despite this, in the four weeks before the onset of labour, Braxton-Hicks contractions may be powerful enough to stretch the cervical canal to its full extent and you may feel twisting and dragging pains over the lower part of the abdomen. Quite often in these last few weeks, the contractions and lower abdominal discomfort may be accompanied by backache, which comes at regular intervals of every 20 or 30 minutes and lasts 30 or 40 seconds. This signals that the Braxton-Hicks contractions are becoming stronger.

If labour is about to begin the contractions quickly become more powerful, the backache is obvious and discomfort begins to encircle the lower part of the abdomen. It may continue for 2 or 3 hours with contractions coming every 15 minutes or so.

The three stages of labour

Labour is the mechanism designed to push the baby from the womb and it can be divided into three clear stages

First stage is from the onset to when the cervix is fully opened (dilated). The cervix is fully dilated when it is stretched to only a thin rim which allows the baby's head to pass through.

Second stage is from full dilatation of the cervix to the complete delivery of the baby.

Third stage is from delivery of the baby to complete delivery of the placenta (after-birth).

First stage

The stretching of the cervical canal and taking up (effacement) of the cervix can only be achieved because the uterine muscle possesses several unique properties.

The uterus is the largest and one of the most powerful muscles in the body. It is divided into two parts, the upper and lower segments.

During labour, the muscles of the upper segment contract and exert pressure on the lower segment which in turn transmits the pull of the contractions to the cervix. The cervix, as a result, stretches and eventually the entire cervical canal is eliminated.

When the cervix has been effaced or taken up, further contractions are designed to open out or dilate the cervix. The rate at which this happens is dependent on the frequency and strength of uterine contractions. The average diameter of a baby's head is 3¾ inches (9.5 cm) and the cervix has to dilate to this size.

By the time contractions are occurring every five minutes, the cervix will be about 1.2 inches (3 cm) dilated and the longest part of labour is already over. When contractions are occurring every three minutes, the cervix will be approximately 2⅓ inches (6 cm) in diameter. At full dilatation, the uterine contractions will be coming every two to two and a half minutes.

The degrees of dilatation of the cervix have been standardized so that it can be described accurately and progress charted. Initially, dilatation is given in 0.4 inches (1 cm) increments up to 1.6 inches (4 cm). When the diameter of the cervix is 2–2½ inches (5 to 6 cm) it is described as being 'half dilated' and on internal examination, the rim of the cervix can be felt all the way around the head of the baby. At 2.8 inches (7 cm) the cervix is said to be 'three quarters dilated' and the examining hand can detect the cervix only at the front and the sides. When the last part of the cervix at the front has disappeared, the cervix is said to be fully dilated. The first stage of labour is complete and proceeds smoothly into the second stage.

Second stage

With full dilatation of the cervix, the baby's head passes into the upper part of the vagina. Uterine contractions aided by the voluntary and involuntary bearing down movements of the mother are designed to push the baby slowly down the birth canal and through the vaginal opening.

As the second stage of labour begins, the uterine contractions become different. With each contraction you experience a strong desire to push down. Initially, you will feel this urge only when the contraction is at its height but as the second stage progresses, the urge becomes more and more irresistible.

Bearing down is a reflex. Women who know nothing about the mechanism of labour automatically take a deep breath, hold it, bend their

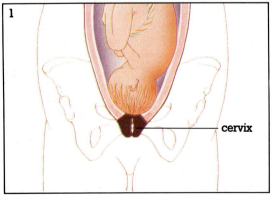
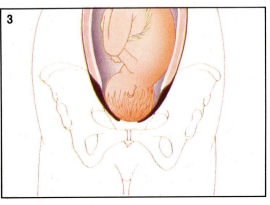
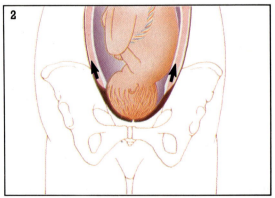
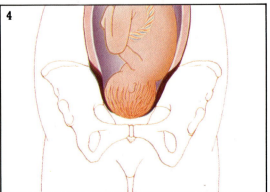

cervix

(Left) Before the cervix (1) can dilate and open up it has to thin out and spread around the baby's head (a process called effacement). This happens when the uterine muscle contracts, pulls on it and doesn't let it slide back. When the cervix is taken up (fully effaced) (2) it then starts to dilate (3) with each successive uterine contraction, until it's 'fully dilated' (4). Then you can start to push!

knees up, hold on to them and strain downwards as though trying to empty the bowels. All these sensations and movements will have been described to you during your antenatal classes and as soon as you find yourself uncontrollably doing them, you will know instinctively that this is now the second stage of labour and you are pushing your baby out.

Between contractions you will be told to relax and breathe steadily in and out. The uterine contractions by this time will be coming every one or two minutes and lasting approximately one minute. When the baby's head has descended to the pelvic floor, your desire to bear down will become even greater. The back of the baby's head now rotates round to the front and starts to stretch the pelvic floor and the vaginal entrance. This is called crowning and you will experience a feeling very similar to fullness in the rectum which will almost force you to strain downwards continuously.

As your baby's head emerges from the vagina, you may feel as though it is tearing. This should never be allowed to happen as the midwife will be gently controlling your baby's head, gradually easing the lips of your vagina over its brow. The sensation is due to the normal stretching of the muscles surrounding the vagina. If at this point it looks as though the muscles are not stretching but are going to tear, then you may have an episiotomy, see page 53. As your baby's head is delivered the chin is stretched away from his chest. The first part of its head to be born is the brow, followed by the nose, the face and finally the mouth and chin.

When the head is fully delivered, the baby's back is uppermost with the face pointing towards the bed. Almost immediately the baby rotates its shoulders so that it is facing its mother's right or left thigh and the midwife will wipe its eyes, nose and mouth with clean gauze and remove fluid from the mouth, nose and upper air passages with an aspirating tube. There follows a breathing space when uterine contractions stop for a few minutes and on restarting, the first contraction is usually sufficient to deliver one shoulder, the next contraction delivers the other and the rest of your baby will slide out.

The midwife may help this last part of delivery by putting her thumbs and fingers under the armpits of your baby and following the natural direction of the birth will lift your baby upwards towards your abdomen. If you are feeling bright and strong, ask if you can sit up and you will see your baby born. The second stage generally does not last longer than an hour for a first baby and may be as little as 15 or 20 minutes for subsequent babies. In some maternity units the final stage of delivery is helped by the use of low cavity forceps.

Your baby will probably be a bluish/purplish colour when she is born and her body, face and head will be covered with vernix. She will be wet and slippery and will almost certainly be streaked with blood. Her face will be screwed up and her head may be a peculiar shape due to the moulding which occurs when it passes through the birth canal.

Your baby may give her first cry when her head is delivered and will almost certainly be crying lustily a few seconds after birth. If the baby is breathing normally there is no reason at all why you should not hold her immediately. Ask the nursing staff if you can lay the baby on your abdomen and the two of you can be covered with a warm towel. Gently stroke your baby, talk to her, chat, croon, kiss her, in fact do whatever you like with her. Your gentle stroking movements, the sound of your heart beating and your soft voice will make her coming into the world a pleasant one.

Ask if you can hold your baby in this way for 20 or 30 minutes. Even in this short time a very

(Below) The head is said to 'crown' when it appears through the vaginal opening (5). The head is born by a straightening of the baby's neck. The baby's face is towards the mother's buttocks (6).

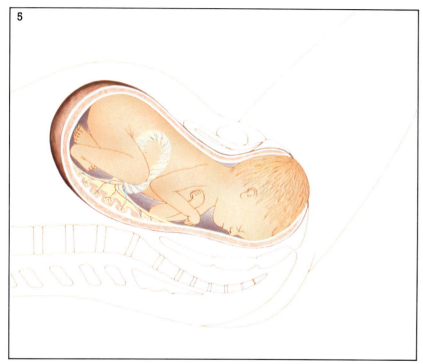

5

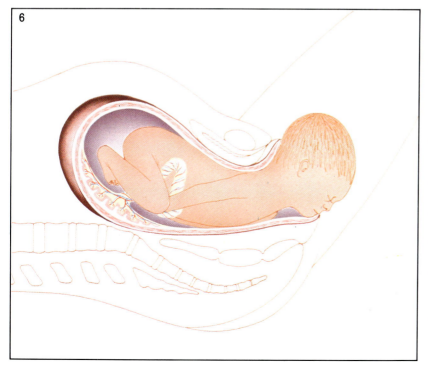

6

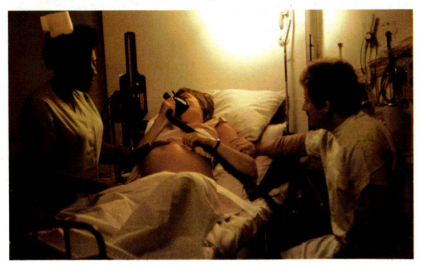

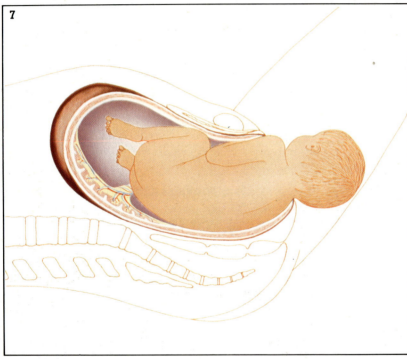

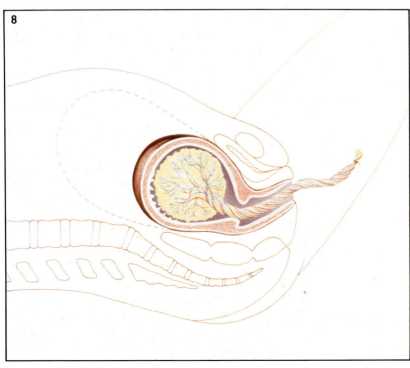

strong bond can be cemented between mother and child and it is crucial to her later development (see page 66). If you feel strongly about it, you can insist on holding your baby, unless there is some medical reason why you should not. It is best to explain to the medical staff before you go into labour that you want to hold your baby immediately after the birth.

If there is fluid in your baby's mouth or nose or air passages, the medical staff may want to make sure that it is cleared and breathing is normal. As soon as they have done this, ask if you can hold your baby. If she requires no medical or nursing attention, insist that you hold her. With the establishment of normal breathing your baby's skin will have turned from blue to a bright pink, first round the mouth, then the face, hands and arms and then the rest of the body. This indicates that her lungs have become fully expanded and are functioning properly. Don't worry if her hands and feet remain bluish for a few days, this is normal.

At this point the umbilical cord is divided between a pair of clamps placed five or six inches (12-15cm) from the baby's navel. She is now capable of living an entirely independent life. As your baby nestles close to you, you will no doubt feel tremendous relief and thankfulness that she has passed her first test by coming safely into the world. It is also natural that you should feel pride and satisfaction that you helped her achieve it.

Third stage

After delivery uterine contractions cease and the uterus rests. Left to work on their own, uterine contractions will restart about 15 minutes later. Initially they are weak but they quickly become strong enough to separate the placenta from the uterine lining and push it into the vagina. The mother can usually expel the placenta with one bearing down movement.

Nowadays it is usual to give an intramuscular injection of a hormone such as ergometrine or syntometrine usually into the mother's thigh as the baby's head is born or when the first shoulder has been delivered. The hormone stimulates the uterus to contract within about four minutes which speeds up the delivery of the placenta and minimizes bleeding. As can be seen in the illustration (bottom left) the size of the uterus reduces rapidly at this stage, although it takes about six weeks to contract to its non-pregnant size.

Once the placenta is in the upper part of the vagina, the midwife will help its delivery by a manoeuvre that is called 'controlled cord traction'. She will gently push your uterus upwards and backwards at the same time pulling gently on the cord. You will experience your final desire to bear down and with very little effort the placenta and its membranes will be delivered. The third stage of labour has been completed. The placenta is checked to make sure nothing has been left behind and your temperature and blood pressure are taken.

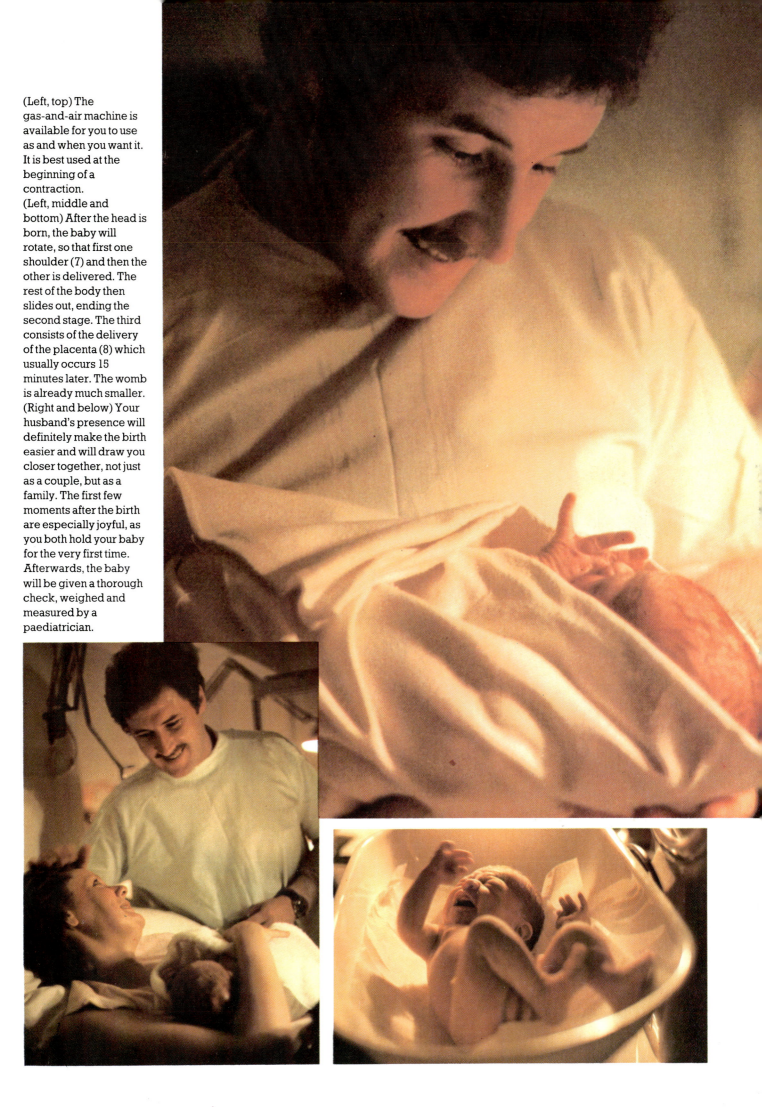

(Left, top) The gas-and-air machine is available for you to use as and when you want it. It is best used at the beginning of a contraction.

(Left, middle and bottom) After the head is born, the baby will rotate, so that first one shoulder (7) and then the other is delivered. The rest of the body then slides out, ending the second stage. The third consists of the delivery of the placenta (8) which usually occurs 15 minutes later. The womb is already much smaller.

(Right and below) Your husband's presence will definitely make the birth easier and will draw you closer together, not just as a couple, but as a family. The first few moments after the birth are especially joyful, as you both hold your baby for the very first time. Afterwards, the baby will be given a thorough check, weighed and measured by a paediatrician.

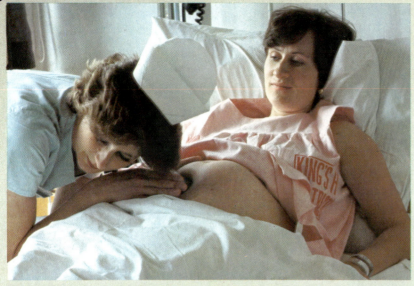

(Above) As soon as you arrive in hospital your baby's heart will be checked.

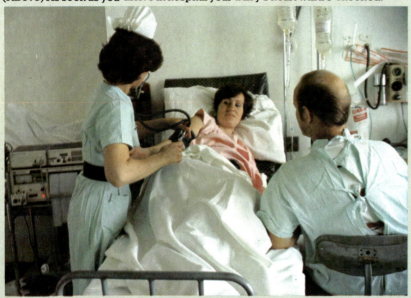

(Above) You will be examined regularly once labour is established.

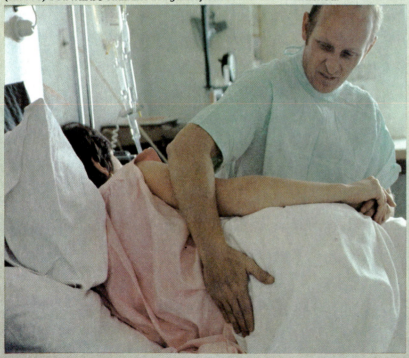

(Above) In the delivery room your husband can help relieve your backache.

Going to the hospital

You should be sensible about notifying your midwife that your labour has started. Remember that she is on call 24 hours a day. If you wake in the middle of the night with pains, wait and see if they are regular and continuous. If they are coming every half hour you can safely let your midwife sleep on until dawn. On the other hand if your labour starts early in the evening it would be only fair to notify your midwife so that she is not surprised by a call at 2 a.m. It is a good idea, if you don't have your own telephone, to have a supply of coins ready for the telephone during the last few weeks of pregnancy.

You should go to hospital as soon as you are sure that labour is fully under way, that is when the contractions are strong, painful and every 10 minutes. While you are still waiting, have a cup of tea or a snack, rest if that's what you want to do, or just potter about. But don't do anything strenuous, for instance avoid running up a long, steep flight of stairs. There is no need to rush and you should not be afraid that you will not get there in time. If you are doubtful that your labour has really started, telephone the hospital and talk to the midwife on duty who will be able to advise you.

Make sure you have attended to all of these things before you leave home:

1. Tell whoever is looking after the home and your husband that you are leaving for hospital.

2. Telephone the maternity ward to tell them that you are on your way.

3. If you are not being driven there by your husband or a friend, telephone the ambulance station and ask for an ambulance to take you to the hospital. Tell them you are a maternity case and give the name of the hospital.

4. Pick up your maternity case (see page 39) and put it and your coat by the door.

5. Put on the kettle, make a cup of tea and wait for the ambulance.

If you have children and no-one can come to look after them in your own home, you should arrange for them to go and stay with the family or friends a week before your delivery is due. However, make sure that you explain to your children exactly why they are going away, so that they do not feel left out or resentful. When you go into labour one of the worries you should be relieved of is having to get children dressed and packed and off to their temporary home.

As you will have telephoned the hospital, your midwife will be expecting you. Once at the hospital you will undress. Very shortly afterwards you will be examined by the midwife or the house doctor on duty. They will talk to you at some length, referring to your antenatal notes and noting the signs of labour that you have already observed. They will take your blood pressure, pulse and temperature and will examine you to see if there is any vaginal bleeding or loss of fluid. They will decide whether an internal examination is necessary to ascertain the baby's presentation (see page 44). You will be asked to provide a specimen of urine the first time you go to the lavatory.

As an empty lower bowel makes delivery cleaner and easier, you may be given an enema, then, if your membranes are ruptured, you will probably be asked to take a shower or a bath.

There are certain things about the progress of the labour which the doctor needs to know as soon as you are settled in hospital.

1. The abdomen is examined to assess your condition, your baby's condition and the stage to which labour has progressed.

2. The strength, frequency and length of uterine contractions are noted and recorded.

3. The position of the baby is defined and the presenting part ascertained.

4. The foetal heart is examined through a foetal stethoscope.

5. By internal examination the degree of dilatation of the cervix, its thickness, its texture and its consistency is examined.

6. During the internal examination, care is taken to make sure that the umbilical cord, a hand or a foot is not intervening between the presenting part and the cervix.

For some unknown reason the stomach does not empty from the time that labour begins, so you should not eat and you will not be given food once you are in hospital. But, if necessary, you will have drinks to give you energy in the form of milk and sugar.

In the early part of labour you do not have to stay in bed, indeed you will be encouraged to walk about the ward and relax. Later on, as labour is a very tiring process, you will be encouraged to rest and sleep as much as possible. When labour is fully established you will be encouraged to stay in bed in the position in which you can rest most comfortably. For many women this is lying on their side. From this time onwards your blood pressure, pulse, temperature and respiration will be recorded hourly or even half-hourly during the first stage of labour. Your baby's heart will be listened to every half hour or every 15 minutes after the membranes have ruptured. Once the first stage of labour is complete, you will be encouraged to take up one of the two positions which are most common in this country for delivery of the baby.

In the left lateral position you will lie on your left side with the buttocks at the edge of the bed and your legs slightly bent. The midwife or the doctor will stand behind your buttocks and there will be an assistant at the opposite side to raise your right leg.

In the dorsal position you will lie on your back, your knees bent and your legs widely splayed apart. The midwife and the doctor will stand on the right side of the bed.

The sitting position is less common. You should ask your doctor about it, then if the hospital agrees and you are fit enough, you could try it. You will need to have followed a full course of antenatal instruction in natural childbirth.

Pain relief

There are several ways of relieving pain in labour. These are listed first then described.

☐ Suggestion, which includes education about pregnancy and relaxation exercises which allow and encourage you to relax during the different stages of labour and psycho-prophylaxis.
☐ Drugs which alleviate anxiety (tranquillizers) or pain (analgesics).
☐ Local or regional anaesthesia using injections of local anaesthetics, very similar to those used at the dentist.
☐ General anaesthetics when complete consciousness is lost.

Suggestion

The main principle behind the theory of suggestion is that childbirth can and should be a pleasant and happy experience and that knowledge will create self-confidence, which will allay fear and tension and therefore pain. It would be quite wrong to go into labour believing that it will be entirely pain-free but you should have faith in your ability to cope, have a complete understanding of what is happening and know that by performing certain exercises like breathing and relaxing you can be distracted from a good deal of the pain.

Try to avoid being caught in the controversial cross-fire between believers in natural childbirth and prophylaxis and those who believe that drugs should be administered during labour to relieve pain. If you want to, you can enjoy the best of both worlds.

Drugs

Drugs which are used in labour usually fall into one of the following classes:

Sedatives and tranquillizers
The difference between a sedative and a tranquillizer is that a sedative relieves anxiety and makes you feel calm and drowsy; a tranquillizer relieves your anxiety without causing drowsiness. Sedatives and tranquillizers are usually used in the early part of the first stage of labour, especially if you go into labour in the evening when it may be considered best for you to sleep for the first part of your labour. Sedatives and tranquillizers are usually given in small doses and at this level they do not affect the baby.

Hypnotics
A hypnotic will make you sleep. Again these drugs are usually given during the early part of the first stage of labour, especially if the patient is very disturbed and anxious and if the midwife and doctor consider that established labour will not occur in the next few hours.

Analgesics
Analgesics relieve pain. Some also make you sleepy. Analgesics are given in pregnancy either by injection or by inhalation.

The analgesic drugs given by injection are of the pethidine or morphine type and are used after labour has become fully established to dull the pain of strong uterine contractions. An intramuscular injection of pethidine usually begins to act within 15 to 20 minutes and is extremely

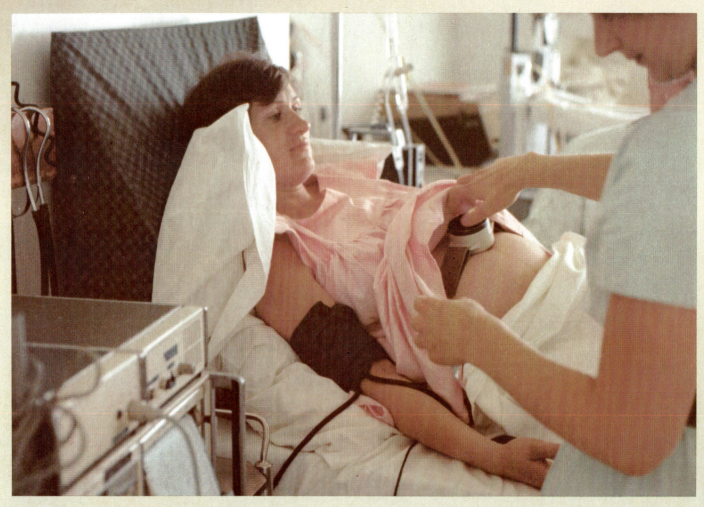

(Above) In a modern hospital unit there can be quite a lot of monitoring equipment which may appear impersonal. It's all to good purpose, especially if your labour has been induced. It will monitor such things as your blood pressure and the baby's heart beat.

efficient in relieving pain during pregnancy. Each injection will last about four hours and one of the most useful properties of pethidine is that it does not prolong labour. Despite its effect in making the mother drowsy and slightly hampering the baby's breathing, it is still probably the most commonly used analgesic.

The inhalation analgesics are administered through a mask which you or the midwife fits over your nose and mouth and you breath in. This is the so-called gas-and-air machine. The three analgesics most commonly used are nitrous oxide, trilene and penthrane. If this form of analgesia is available on your maternity unit you will have been shown the apparatus and how and when to use it during labour. You yourself are largely in control of the amount of analgesia you want with this apparatus. You can hold it, place it over your mouth and inhale the anaesthetic when the pain is at its worst and remove it when you no longer need it. Suffocation is impossible. You can also influence the depth of analgesia you obtain, because the more deeply and frequently you breathe the gas mixture, the greater the effect. You will feel the effect after about 20 seconds and it will reach its maximum about half a minute later.

As you will have been shown in your antenatal classes, the most efficient way to use the apparatus is to begin inhaling the gas just before or just as the uterine contraction begins. Incidentally, no one inhalational analgesic has been shown to be superior to the others.

Local anaesthetics

The simplest form of local painkiller is an injection of a local anaesthetic into the skin and muscles of the perineum in preparation for the episiotomy (see page 53).

A nerve block can be performed by the deeper injection of local anaesthetic and is usually done immediately before a forceps delivery. The block is done by injecting the nerves in the side wall of the pelvis. It is painless and causes numbness of the vagina, perineum and the vulva.

The **paracervical** block is widely used in America and Scandinavia but has never been popular in the UK. It is the most effective form of local analgesia in the first stage of labour and it involves the injection of local anaesthetic into a collection of nerve fibres which supply the uterus and the cervix. The injection means that pain in the uterus cannot be felt and the first stage of labour can be accomplished with very little discomfort.

Epidural anaesthesia

The aim of epidural anaesthesia is to introduce a local anaesthetic into the epidural space so that the fine sensory fibres carrying pain sensations to the brain are anaesthetized and the nerves which control movement are left relatively unaffected. This means that there will be a complete loss of sensation from the level of the injection downwards and labour will therefore be painless while movement of the legs is maintained though they may feel a little heavy.

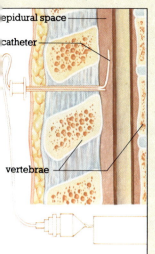

epidural space

catheter

vertebrae

(Above) This is an enlarged diagram of how the epidural injection is carried out. You will have a local anaesthetic first and so will not feel pain from the operation. An epidural anaesthetic is injected into the lower part of your spine. After the first injection the catheter is left in place, so that it can be used for top-up doses if necessary.

In most obstetric units the anaesthetist will insert a fine catheter into the lower part of the back (the lumbar region of the spine) or further down into the sacral part of the spine. This minor operation is performed under local anaesthetic and can hardly be felt at all. The catheter is left in place so that when one injection of anaesthetic wears off (in 3-4 hours) a topping-up injection can be given through it to maintain analgesia.

Again, you yourself are in control of how much analgesia you have and how quickly you have it. You can call for the anaesthetist to have the catheter inserted whenever you wish. It is usually advised that the catheter is placed well before the first stage of labour is complete so you should alert the nursing staff immediately your contractions become very painful. An anaesthetist will be called, you will be asked to turn on to your left side with your head bent forward and your knees pulled up into your chest. A little local anaesthetic is injected into the skin so that you cannot feel the entry of the needle and the catheter is introduced into the epidural space. Your legs and the lower part of your body will go numb and you will no longer feel the pain of contractions. Each dose of anaesthetic lasts between three and four hours and when the pain returns, you can have it topped up by the anaesthetist if you wish.

Epidural anaesthesia works in 95 per cent of patients but there is a remaining 5 per cent in whom the pain killing effect for some reason is less than satisfactory.

Most authorities agree that epidural anaesthesia is one of the most efficient methods of obtaining pain relief during labour. Furthermore, it has no ill effects on the baby.

It is quite common for women who have had an epidural anaesthesia to experience a fall in blood pressure causing dizziness or faintness and this is usually relieved by turning on to your left side. A few women may also experience slight headache after the anaesthetic.

General anaesthetic

Nowadays, a general anaesthetic is normally only used when a Caesarian section is performed, see page 56. Pre-operative medication is given intravenously and you will lose consciousness straightaway. Do not be perturbed by the speed with which things happen. In obstetrics, as a general rule, once the decision to proceed to surgery has been taken, things will go rather fast.

Monitoring equipment

You may notice a lot of equipment and display panels in the labour ward which are used, when necessary, for monitoring the wellbeing of the baby and mother. It is rarely necessary to use them. The exception being in an induced birth when the heart function of the mother and baby is tracked from the time labour is in full swing. The use of the equipment is mainly a precaution as an early warning system, the aim being prevention rather than cure. Most of the time it gives medical and nursing staff information which assures them that all is well. The equipment used in most units is so modern and streamlined that it hardly ever restricts the mother in any major way.

Episiotomy

During an episiotomy a cut is made in the skin or muscles at the entrance to the vagina called the perineum. This is to help the baby's head to pass through the entrance to the vagina. Those in favour of episiotomy maintain that with the average size of a baby's head at 9.5 centimetres (three and three quarter inches) in diameter it is bound to cause some tearing of the skin and tearing or over-stretching of the perineal muscles. Tears and overstretching are very difficult to repair and may later affect a woman's sex life. They may also lead to the collapsing of the wall of the vagina.

Those obstetricians who do not believe in routine episiotomy argue that a woman's vaginal tissues can stretch and accommodate the widest diameter of the baby's head as it is being delivered and due to their elastic properties will recoil to their previous size, shape and tone, particularly if encouraged to do so by performing special post natal exercises.

With neither of my children was an episiotomy performed and the rule of thumb used by my obstetrician struck me as being very sensible and logical. It was a genetic one. My mother had not needed one, so I probably wouldn't either. One thing you may be certain of, your medical attendants will not allow you to be torn. If your tissues stretch easily they will probably not intervene. If a tear seems possible they will perform an episiotomy.

When the obstetrician or midwife thinks that an episiotomy is going to be necessary, a local anaesthetic is injected into the skin and muscles of the perineum so that they become numb. Once insensitive to pain, a cut is made by the doctor usually at an angle to the right or left of the anus and this allows the baby's head to pass through perineal tissues which are too rigid or too tight to allow it through without tearing. An episiotomy must be performed when forceps are being used and when, in the opinion of the medical attendants, the perineum muscles are so rigid that they will hold up the completion of the second stage of labour. Very often the numbing effect of the original local anaesthetic injection is still acting when the third stage of labour is complete and the episiotomy has to be repaired. If not, a further injection is given so that the repair is painless. The various layers of the vagina, perineum muscles and perineal skin are stitched separately and a soluble cat gut is usually used so that the stitches do not need to be surgically removed. Sometimes the skin stitches are made of silk or thread and these are removed on the sixth day after delivery. Every doctor takes very great care in repairing an episiotomy.

Breech delivery

As a general rule a breech delivery is no more difficult or longer than any other kind of labour and difficulties after delivery are no more common than with a normal (cephalic) presentation. However, you will have to go into hospital for the delivery.

There is absolutely no problem in delivering a breech presentation if the baby is small and the mother has a normal pelvis. Mechanical problems may occur if the baby is large, if the mother's pelvis is small or if the baby's head is bent backwards. Because the head is delivered last, any factor which slows down a breech delivery may lead to lack of oxygen to the baby. Factors which hurry the delivery may cause injury to the baby because the birth canal has not been stretched first by the widest part of the baby, that is its head and shoulders.

In the cephalic delivery, the head is leading the way and passes through the birth canal very slowly and gradually. As it does so it will 'mould'. Moulding is the term used to describe how the soft bones of the baby's skull slide just a fraction of an inch (1 mm) over one another but this can reduce the diameter of the baby's head by more than half an inch (one centimetre). This makes its passage through the cervix and the pelvic cavity much easier. It occurs over several hours and is therefore gradual. But in a breech presentation, the head may not be given the time to mould as satisfactorily as it can when it is slowly easing its way through the birth canal. Whereas in a cephalic presentation the head takes several hours to travel from the brim of the pelvis to the vaginal entrance, in a breech delivery it must travel the same distance in approximately seven minutes. This is because the umbilical cord is squeezed between the bones of the head and the pelvic bones. This cuts down the baby's supply of oxygen and if delivery is too slow, the baby will suffer from lack of oxygen.

In most cases there are no problems at all. In a very few cases there is the simple mechanical problem of the baby's head being slightly too large for its mother's pelvis. This problem is accentuated if its head is not well flexed (with the chin resting on its chest).

In a breech delivery, every mother and her baby is judged individually. Before labour, various measurements and investigations are done to minimize the chances of a mechanical problem arising during delivery. If the obstetrician feels that there are any risks at all he may opt for a Caesarian section, see page 56.

The first stage of labour with a breech delivery is usually straightforward. You will be told not to push and to let your baby move down through the strength of the uterine contractions alone. When the baby's bottom appears at the perineum an episiotomy (see page 53) is always performed. Without any bearing down movements the baby's buttocks, legs and abdomen will be delivered and then the doctor will gently pull down a short loop of umbilical cord so that it will not be over-stretched as the baby's head comes through the pelvis. The arms and shoulders are then delivered. In nearly all cases of breech delivery, the head is delivered with the aid of forceps so that it passes through the pelvis slowly and gently so that damage and injury are avoided. Some form of anaesthetic will be given before the forceps manoeuvre so that this final stage of delivery will be painless.

The third stage of labour is not affected and proceeds in the usual way.

Pre-term delivery

The words 'premature' and 'prematurity' are no longer officially used. They covered a variety of conditions which are now referred to more specifically. The following terms are likely to be used:

Low birth weight: any baby weighing five and a half pounds (2.5 kg) or less at birth.

Pre-term: a baby born before the 37th week or, more exactly, 259 days after conception. 'Term' is the period from the 37th to the 41st week (259 to 287 days) after conception.

Post-term: a baby born after 41 weeks. This and the previous descriptions are applied whatever the weight of the baby. However, a pre-term baby is quite likely to have a low birth weight and such babies are still unofficially called 'premature'.

Appropriate for gestational age (A.G.A.): a baby whose weight falls within the expected range for the particular period of gestation.

Small for gestational age (S.G.A.)/Small for dates (S.F.D.) (the most commonly used)/**Light for dates (L.F.D.):** all these are applied to a baby whose weight is below the expected range.

The cause of a short gestation period is often unknown but certain conditions of the uterus and ovaries are associated with it, for example fibroids and ovarian cysts. 'Small for dates' babies may be associated with smoking, preeclampsia, twins, illness in pregnancy (e.g. rubella), maternal disease (such as diabetes), overwork, malnutrition or anaemia.

Pre-term labour usually begins without any advance warning and very often in a woman who is carrying her first baby in a pregnancy which has been otherwise entirely normal. The first sign will be the same as a normal onset of labour, i.e. either the breaking of the waters, or contractions or vaginal bleeding.

The general consensus of medical opinion is that once the pre-term labour has started nothing should be done to slow it down, except in the case of pregnancies which are less than 34 weeks. In this case, the mother will be admitted to hospital and special drugs will be given by intravenous drip in an attempt to stop labour. If it is successfully stopped, the mother will be confined to bed until term.

More often than not, pre-term labour is shorter and easier than a labour which occurs at full term. As the pre-term baby's skull bones are soft, an episiotomy is nearly always routinely performed and specially designed forceps are very often used to protect the baby's head from injury.

Variations of normal labour

Most labours run smoothly, but very occasionally their progress may vary from the usual routine in the following ways:

☐ The labour may be prolonged (see below).
☐ The mother may be distressed (see page 56).
☐ The baby may be distressed (see page 56).
☐ It may be necessary to use forceps to complete the second stage of labour (see page 57).
☐ It may be necessary to perform a Caesarian section to deliver the baby (see page 56).
☐ There may be bleeding after delivery of the baby (see page 56).

Prolonged labour

A labour can be longer than it should be because of delay in completion of the first, second or third stages. Slowing of progress in the first two stages is always due to one of three causes.
1. Abnormal uterine contractions which are usually either too weak or too short.
2. Abnormal or difficult position of the baby, the commonest being an incompletely flexed head.
3. Abnormality of the pelvic bones, the vagina or the muscles of the pelvic floor and perineum.

Abnormal contractions

If the uterine contractions are weak and short during the first and second stage the uterus is said to be in a state of inertia. Sometimes it is because the uterus never seems to rev up to forceful, frequent contractions. Sometimes it is because the contractions, once established, become weak and irregular, so that the cervix dilates very slowly and the first stage of labour becomes long. If the forewaters have not ruptured, this condition is sometimes treated by rupturing the membranes artificially and the uterus frequently responds with strong regular contractions and the labour progresses satisfactorily. It may also be treated by giving small doses of syntocinon through an intravenous drip.

The cervix will dilate slowly if the uterine contractions are strong but only last a short time. This most often happens when the baby is lying in a posterior position and the mother always experiences backache. Fear is the commonest cause of this kind of uterine activity and so antenatal instruction is designed to give reassurance through knowledge and understanding.

It is generally agreed that the second stage of labour has stopped when the head no longer descends. In a first pregnancy the baby should be delivered an hour after the second stage begins and in subsequent pregnancies within half an hour. Most midwives and doctors however, are so accustomed to judging the progress of pregnancy that they know a long time before this if it is not going as it should. The cause can be weak uterine contractions. It may also be due to overuse of sedatives or tranquillizing drugs. However, if the baby is in a good position, the delay can easily be overcome by using suction extraction (see page 58) or by forceps delivery (see page 57).

Difficult position of the baby

Delay in the first or second stages caused by the baby is nearly always due to the position or the size of the baby's head. The size of the baby's head rarely affects the course of labour. Even a large baby, say 10 pounds (4.5 kg) in weight, with its head well flexed (its chin resting on its chest) will present the smallest diameter of the head to pass through the pelvic brim and labour will progress quite smoothly. Most causes of delay due to the baby are because its head is not properly flexed.

When the head is not fully flexed, the diameter of the head which is presented to the pelvic brim may be too large to pass through with ease. The baby's head is completely normal in terms of its size and its shape but because of its position, the part of it which has to pass through the pelvis first is artificially increased.

Incomplete flexion of the head is most commonly seen when the baby is lying in the posterior position. Because the baby's spine is lying against the mother's spine, its body cannot be fully flexed simply for mechanical reasons.

This situation is most often found with first babies and means that the baby's head may not engage in the pelvis at the 36th week as expected, or even when labour starts. Labour may be slightly prolonged but in most cases the head will rotate itself within the pelvis and delivery will be perfectly normal.

Again during the second stage, a faulty position of the head is the commonest cause of a prolonged labour. It may be that the baby is in a posterior position and fails to rotate through the necessary 180 degrees. If it remains in this position it can be gently rotated into the correct position and then forceps delivery can be carried out. Sometimes the second stage takes longer because the head rotates through only 90 degrees and ends up facing sideways instead of backwards. Again, the head can be gently rotated and once in the correct position, forceps delivery can be performed.

If the baby's head is stretched backwards, then its face is too large a diameter to pass through the pelvis and labour cannot proceed until the head is flexed. If flexion can be achieved, then the labour can be completed by a forceps delivery but if not, by a Caesarian section (see below) so that no harm comes to you or your baby.

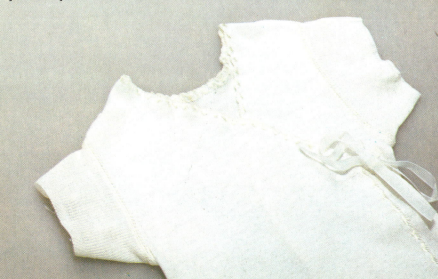

Abnormal pelvic bones

This is now a rare cause of prolonged labour. In the past it was most commonly due to rickets which made the pelvis asymmetrical and prevented the baby's head from passing through it. At your first antenatal visit your doctor will probably try to fit his or her closed fist (the approximate size of a newborn baby's head) between your pelvic bones by placing it on the outside of your body. As a rough guide this is not a bad first test and if a doctor's suspicion of disproportion (too large a baby's head for the mother's pelvis) is confirmed, further investigations, e.g. ultrascan (see page 27) will be arranged at the appropriate time. If disproportion prevents delivery once labour has begun a Caesarean section is performed, as it would not be possible for the head to be delivered normally.

Delay to third stage

If the placenta has not been completely delivered within 30 minutes of delivery of the baby, then the third stage of labour is delayed. Usually with the injection of oxytocic drugs the third stage of labour takes less than five minutes. But if there is no bleeding the midwife will be quite happy to wait a further few minutes to see if the placenta will be delivered spontaneously. In about three per cent of women, this does not happen and then a general anaesthetic is usually given when the placenta can be very gently removed from the uterus. The reason for doing this is that while the placenta remains in the uterus there is always the possibility of bleeding. Every mother is closely monitored to make certain that this does not happen.

Should it occur then you will be given another injection of an oxytocic drug which will cause the uterus to contract into a small ball and prevent any further bleeding.

Maternal distress

Maternal distress is really a medical term, used by doctors and midwives, for anything, emotional or physical, which interrupts the smooth progress of labour and may potentially harm the mother or baby. If a woman has regularly attended antenatal classes, maternal distress is very rare. Psychological distress usually only occurs in women who have not been properly instructed and the treatment is to find out what is causing her anxiety and then to allay her fears.

Doctors and midwives are most concerned when there is the possibility that physical maternal distress will occur. This could happen if the mother were suffering from some underlying medical condition, such as diabetes, high blood pressure, heart disease or kidney disease. In these cases particular attention is paid to the mother's comfort to help prevent distress.

Real physical distress is a thing of the past which occurred when a labour had lasted more than 48 hours and a mother was exhausted, dehydrated and possibly feverish. Nowadays this is never allowed to happen.

Foetal distress

Foetal distress, that is when the baby shows signs of discomfort, means that it is short of oxygen. This may happen suddenly (acute) or it may have been present for some time (chronic).

The commonest cause of acute foetal distress is frequent uterine contractions. When the uterus is contracting down hard, the blood supply to the placenta and therefore to the baby is greatly reduced. If contractions are coming every three minutes and lasting for one minute, this means that sufficient blood has to reach the baby in between to last it during the contraction. The placenta and the uterus usually have reserves to call upon so that the baby does not go short of oxygen but occasionally, the reserves are not sufficient. The same thing can happen if the umbilical cord is twisted very tightly round the baby's neck, or if there has been bleeding behind the placenta which prevents oxygen passing into the baby's blood from the mother.

There are three main signs of foetal distress.

1. The amniotic fluid becomes stained with meconium.
Meconium is a thick green substance which stays in the baby's intestine until after delivery but if the baby is short of oxygen, the rectum empties and the meconium passes into the amniotic fluid. It becomes visible as it passes down the vagina.

2. The foetal heart rate drops. The baby's heart has a normal rate of between 120 and 160 beats a minute. During a contraction the heart rate slows and as soon as the contraction is over, it rises again within seconds. Beyond these changes which occur with uterine contractions, a persistent heart rate of more than 160 beats per second or less than 120 beats per second means that the baby is short of oxygen.

3. Violent foetal movements. When the baby is starved of oxygen it not surprisingly makes violent twisting and turning movements.

Doctors and midwives are always on the lookout for foetal distress and signs that the baby is under severe stress prompt medical attendants to make the delivery as fast as possible. If the cervix is not fully dilated, this will be done by Caesarian section. If it occurs during the second stage, it will be done using forceps.

Caesarian section

Caesarian section is now a safe operation and in most hospitals accounts for about 6 in every 100 deliveries. This seems a rather high figure and the reason for it is that anaesthetic and surgical methods have improved so much in the last 25 years that obstetricians would rather opt for an early Caesarian section than let you have a difficult prolonged labour.

One of the great advantages of Caesarian section is that the oxygen supply to the baby is never in jeopardy. Present day anaesthetic techniques insure that the baby is always well supplied with oxygen throughout the surgical procedure. A team of paediatricians is always standing by to look after the baby immediately it is taken from the abdomen by the surgeon.

There are some classical reasons why an obstetrician may have opted to deliver you by Caesarian section before labour begins and he will discuss them with you. They would include high blood pressure, pre-eclampsia, proven pelvic disproportion, fibroids, ovarian cysts and an abnormally situated placenta. The placenta normally lies in the upper part of the fundus of the uterus, but occasionally it implants lower down and may even cover the entrance to the cervical canal. This condition is called placenta praevia and indicates a Caesarian section.

As far as subsequent pregnancies are concerned, you need not think that because you have had a Caesarian section once you will always need a Caesarian section. Women who have had a Caesarian section for their first baby have gone through subsequent pregnancies quite normally and delivered their babies vaginally. There is no truth in the old wives' tale which says the number of your pregnancies is limited even if you have to have Caesarian sections each time. There are recorded cases of women having as many as ten Caesarian sections though most obstetricans would advise that three is a reasonable limit.

Your obstetrician will almost certainly advise that you should wait a year after a Caesarian section before becoming pregnant again and he will also tell you that once you have had a Caesarian section, subsequent deliveries, albeit by the vaginal route, should be performed in hospital. It is unlikely that you will be allowed to go beyond term with a subsequent pregnancy. If you don't go into labour spontaneously by your expected delivery date, your labour will almost certainly be induced but allowed to proceed as a vaginal delivery unless some event, as mentioned previously, occurs which indicates a Caesarian section.

Forceps delivery

Forceps were probably first used at the end of the 16th century by a family named Chamberlen, who kept them a secret for nearly 150 years. No-one was allowed to see them and the room had to be emptied before they were produced. Even then the patient was heavily draped in sheets before they were uncovered.

Modern obstetric forceps are designed so that the blades fit delicately and accurately around the baby's head and when properly applied they cannot possibly damage or harm him. In fact forceps provide a steel cage which protects the head from any pressure as it moves through the birth canal.

Your midwife and doctor will not consider the use of forceps unless the following conditions have been fulfilled:

☐ The cervix is fully dilated.
☐ The head is engaged in the pelvis.
☐ There is no obstruction to delivery.
☐ The membranes are ruptured.
☐ The uterus is contracting either spontaneously or under the action of an oxytocic drug.
☐ The bladder is empty (it may have to be emptied by passing a catheter).
☐ An anaesthetic, either local or general has been administered.
☐ There is no disproportion.

Disproportion needs a little explaining. It means that there is a discrepancy, either apparent or real, between the largest part of the baby, that is its head, and the size of the mother's pelvis. The disproportion can be apparent if, for instance, the head is not fully flexed, and therefore presents a larger diameter than normal to the pelvic brim, or real when the mother's pelvis is too small or distorted in shape due to previous

(Below) (1) Forceps delivery. The blades are carefully inserted one by one, so that they fit round the baby's head, avoiding his ears. (2) Suction (vacuum) extraction. A small metal cap is fitted to the baby's scalp and this is then attached to apparatus which will create a vacuum to keep the cap in place.

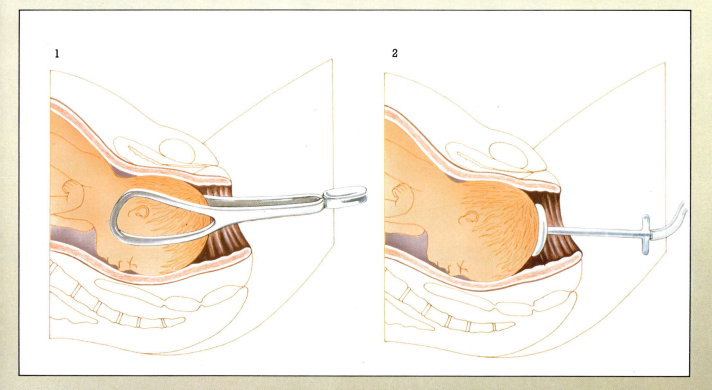

1

2

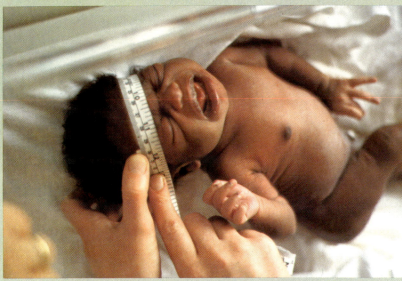

(Above) Immediately after birth your baby is examined. His head is measured.

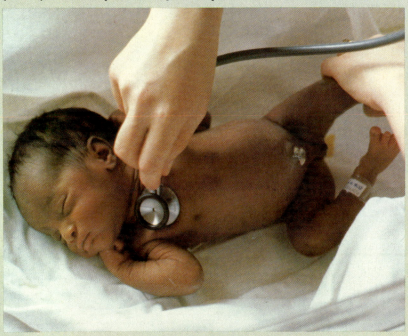

(Above) His heart beat is checked through a stethoscope.

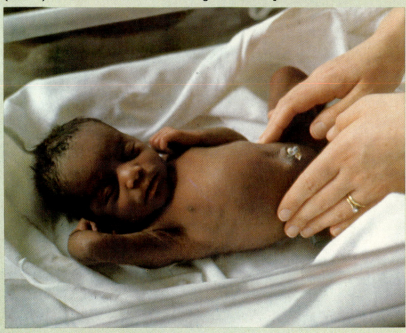

(Above) His limbs and organs are examined.

disease or injury, to allow the baby's head to pass through.

At the first antenatal visit the doctor examines a woman's pelvis to assess its size and late engagement of the head could indicate possible disproportion which would then have been investigated before labour began. If disproportion was found to be real, then a Caesarian section would be needed and appropriate arrangements would have been made. Unless a woman's pelvis had been distorted in some way, real disproportion is very rare, because a small woman tends to have a suitably small baby regardless of the size of her husband.

Forceps delivery is always performed under local or general anaesthetic. The obstetrician will locate the exact position of the baby's head and if necessary will gently rotate it manually. The forceps are applied individually. The first is placed by guiding the blade gently along the inside of the baby's head with the inner side of the hand between the forceps and the baby's face so that the blades do not even touch its skin until they are in a good position. A second blade is inserted in the same way between the baby's head and the wall of the vagina on the other side.

The obstetrician ensures that the blades are in the correct position and the handles fit together exactly. Gentle pulling for about 30 or 40 seconds at a time combined with your pushes and with periods of relaxation in between usually ensures that the baby's head descends on to the perineum when an episiotomy is performed and the baby is safely delivered.

Suction (vacuum) extraction

Suction extraction is used to speed up the second stage of labour. When the first stage of labour is complete a small metal cup is attached to the baby's scalp by creating a vacuum in it with a special vacuum apparatus. By pulling gently on the cup the baby's head is eased down the birth canal. This method of delivery is widely used in Scandinavia and has only one minor complication: the baby's scalp may become swollen where the cup is applied and the swelling may take several days to subside. But its advantage is that the cervix does not have to be as fully dilated as for forceps delivery.

Checks on your new baby

Almost immediately after your baby is born a paediatrician will give him an exhaustive examination, not just every part of the body, including the fontanelle, eyes, nose, ears, mouth, tongue, arms, legs, hands, feet, trunk and anus but also will perform some basic laboratory tests on his blood and urine to make sure he is not anaemic and that all his bodily functions are normal. His measurements will be taken, including the circumference of his skull.

If there are any unusual findings you will be told about them. If you're concerned because nothing is said this means everything is as it should be but ask if you need reassurance.

Dispelling fears

During pregnancy you should read as many sensible and practical books as you can find. You should ask your doctor and your nurses to clarify areas which are not clear, or which puzzle or frighten you so that you gain confidence both in yourself and in the medical staff.

In the last few weeks it can help a great deal to talk to other mothers in the same position. Antenatal classes are not just a way of preparing yourself for labour, they are also a way of meeting people. The National Childbirth Trust organizes social events as well as antenatal classes and will provide you with advice and help. Problems diminish when shared with a friend, while they may seem insurmountable if you try to cope with them yourself.

When you go into labour you should be free to concentrate on the job in hand. You should not have to worry about what is going on at home, so do make sure that you have made careful and detailed preparations so that home life can go on without you.

An understanding and supportive husband can give you special confidence.

Your husband and labour

Having your husband with you during labour will almost certainly help you. To experience your child's birth is one of the greatest moments that either parent can have and it is a pity if you do not share it. But if your husband has strong feelings about not attending your labour, do not force the point. It will only become a bone of contention between you.

Before your husband can be present in the delivery room, there are two things you must insure. First, establish with the hospital that he will not just be tolerated but welcomed. If he is there under sufferance, he will feel in the way. It is quite wrong if the medical staff give this impression but sometimes the bustle, efficiency and the speed with which things have to be done in a delivery room do not leave much time for the niceties of making a husband feel at home.

For his part, your husband must understand his role and conform to the rules of the delivery room. Part of his role is to be well prepared for what is going to happen. It is a great shock for someone to be present at the birth of a baby if they have no idea what is going to take place, so, if possible, your husband should have seen a film of labour and delivery. He should also have had detailed instruction about the normal mechanisms and physiology of labour and should have been taught how to help you to relax and breathe properly during the different stages. He should also be prepared to wait outside should any complications occur. The wishes of doctors and nursing staff vary and must be respected.

One of the advantages of having your husband there is that he will be participating in the birth and will not just be an observer. Moreover, he is much more likely to become an interested, active father, who is emotionally involved with the baby sooner, than someone who simply waits outside for the news that he has a son or daughter. Just as important, when you get home and find that your baby plays havoc with your routine, your husband will be more sympathetic if he has been involved with you and the child right through the birth.

Emotional reactions

Just after delivery your emotional state will be rather fragile. You will get upset easily and you may even become miserable and depressed, so try not to become too involved in other mothers' problems. If you cannot cope with the upset caused by a specific event such as a stillborn baby or an abnormal baby and the sympathy of the nursing staff does not help, then the best solution for you is to return home.

In the strange and clinical surroundings of a hospital ward, small things can get out of proportion, a nurse may seem unfriendly and the doctor may appear to handle your baby rather roughly. Your needs may not be immediately attended to. This is not because the staff do not care about you and your baby, it is simply because they are nearly always overworked. If something really upsets you however, do not bear a grudge, say so as frankly and as kindly as you can.

One of the hospital routines that causes most emotional upset is feeding (see page 62). It can be a very difficult time for a mother and a nurse who has seen many mothers start breast feeding successfully may seem rather unsympathetic. As you only have a short time in hospital and it is a nurse's responsibility to make sure that feeding routines are established, they may seem rather rushed to get the whole thing going. You may feel that you are not given peace and quiet to work things out for you and your baby. It may seem that the time allotted to breast feeding is unduly short and that the baby cannot take sufficient milk in the time you are given. Nurses of course are keen to complete one duty and go on to the next. If this upsets you, talk it over with sister, explain that your baby seems to be a slow feeder and ask her if you can take feeding time at a more leisurely pace. If approached in a reasonable and rational way, you will find that the nursing staff are only too eager to help.

Having a pleasant stay on the maternity ward is like everything else in life, a matter of give and take. The nurses and doctors have essential routines they must complete and they have to be done speedily and efficiently. In an emergency it is the saving of a life that they are concerned about and at such times human comforts go by the board. You should have an understanding attitude towards this. On the other hand, you and your baby have your rights. Ultimately you have the say in what happens to your baby and as long as you are doing things properly and have the confidence to carry them out well, then it is your right to explain calmly to the nursing and medical staff what you wish to do. In almost all instances, agreement can be reached. If you find that this is impossible ask if you can go home as soon as possible.

Home or hospital confinement

Only if you are having your second or third baby do you stand any chance of persuading your doctors and nurses to allow you to have your baby at home. If you are having your first, fourth or subsequent baby, then it must be delivered in hospital.

You will avoid disappointment if you appreciate that all the following conditions must be fulfilled at the time you enrol at your antenatal clinic for your doctor to feel happy about allowing you to have your baby at home. They are explained below.

☐ You must be fit and healthy.

☐ You are more than five feet (1.5 m) in height.

☐ This is your second or third pregnancy.

☐ Your previous pregnancies, labours and *postpartum* (i.e. after the birth) periods have been normal.

☐ You are over 17 years of age.

☐ You are under 35 years of age.

☐ There are no rhesus antibodies present in your blood.

☐ Your home conditions are suitable for confinement.

☐ There is sufficient help at home for you to get uninterrupted sleep and rest during the day, after your baby is born.

If you have your baby at home you can have almost all the expert care and facilities that are enjoyed by women during hospital confinement. In other words you will have your own doctor and midwife, your doctor can consult freely with an obstetrician, there will be a mobile obstetric emergency unit at your disposal and your doctor and midwife will have maternity packs and sterile supplies just the same as in hospital. You can also have the service of a home help.

Home conditions must be good before a doctor and midwife will agree to deliver the baby there. At least, there must be a suitable private bedroom. The doctor and midwife may want to see the room before delivery and they may ask you to change around the furniture or bring special items that they need into the room.

☐ You will also need:

Two large basins, one for you and one for your midwife.

A bedpan.

A jug that will hold at least two pints of water.

A large plastic sheet to cover the mattress.

A bucket into which can be placed soiled sheets and dressings.

A nailbrush and soap for the doctor and midwife to scrub up.

At least one hot water bottle.
Two warm blankets.
☐ For yourself:
Two nightdresses.
Dressing gown.
Pair of slippers.
Your own toilet articles.
Your own bath towel.
A smaller towel.
A flannel.
Two nursing brassieres.
Sanitary belt.
Maternal sanitary towels.
☐ For the baby (see pages 37, 38 and 39 for detailed advice):
A large soft towel in which he can be wrapped immediately after birth.
A cot.
Sheet and blankets.
Your baby's clothes.
A baby bath.
A baby bath towel.
Baby soap.
Baby lotion or cream.
Safety pins.
Nappies.
Waterproof apron for when you bath him.
A low feeding chair.

There are however, certain well-defined circumstances that make a hospital confinement desirable.
1. If it is your first baby, because it is not yet known whether you will have naturally easy labours or difficult ones.
2. If you are having a first baby when you are over the age of 35 because difficulties in labour are more frequently encountered by such women. It should be added that the majority of women over 35 seem to have very easy labours, despite the fact that statistically the likelihood of encountering complications increases with age.
3. If you have had previous labours that were difficult or complicated.
4. If you are expecting twins or the doctor suspects a multiple birth.
5. If you are of small stature and the doctor suspects disproportion, (see page 57).

The arguments about home versus hospital deliveries will always be controversial. Some of the bonuses of home confinement are:
☐ You are with your husband and family.
☐ You are in familiar surroundings and therefore feel less fearful.
☐ Your family feel that they are sharing in the coming of the new baby and will be more likely to welcome it right from the outset.
☐ You may have a friend or relative to help. Mothers are particularly invaluable at this time. They have been through it before and they can be very reassuring.
☐ You will not worry about your absence from the family.
☐ Your baby is always near you.
☐ You can do whatever you like with your baby whenever you want to.
☐ Your baby becomes a member of the family immediately and you can establish a domestic routine in a few days.

On the other hand some undoubted advantages of hospital confinement are:
☐ There are skilled personnel ready for any emergency or complication.
☐ The nurses will teach you how to deal with the everyday care of your baby.
☐ There is a paediatrician in-house who will examine your baby.
☐ You will have a chance to meet and talk to other mothers in the hospital ward and share fears, experiences and triumphs.
☐ You will be able to compare your baby with other newborn babies on the ward.
☐ You can share some of your troubles with the other mothers, for example, discomfort from stitches, difficulty in establishing breast feeding and soreness of the nipples.

However, I am sure we would all agree that if hospitals could be more like home, more mothers would be happier to be delivered there.

If you are going to have your baby at home you will have discussed with your midwife when you should call her.

The midwife

A midwife is a State Registered Nurse who has completed special training in obstetrics, antenatal care, labour, infant care and post-natal care. She therefore knows most of what there is to be known about pregnancy, labour, babies, new mothers and infant rearing. She will help in all stages of your having a baby and many midwives are so expert, experienced and dedicated that they have the full trust of doctors and specialists to take total responsibility for all aspects of you and your baby. Midwives are fountains of knowledge. Use their expertise. Get them on your side. Try to develop a special relationship with one whom you can use as a confidante and for advice and help. Few are the dragons they were once made out to be: they love mothers, motherhood and babies and put their welfare first. They can be especially reassuring in the first few weeks after delivery when you may be having difficulty establishing breastfeeding and you're anxious. On the other hand don't let yourself be browbeaten.

On the ward

You will enjoy your hospital stay most if you find out as much as you can about the maternity ward routine before you are admitted. If some routines seem odd to you, ask about them. You will have a happier stay if you understand why things need to be done in a particular way. You will almost certainly be sharing the ward with several others but remember that they are not sick people, they are mothers like you who are getting to know and enjoy their new babies. The social life on a maternity ward tends to be rather lively with mothers exchanging experiences and learning from one another. You will probably have a great deal of fun and new friendships

(Left) Many hospitals nowadays have flexible visiting hours, so that grandparents and sisters can get to know the new baby.

may be started. There is a lot to be said for the companionship and friendliness that exists in nearly every maternity ward.

Routines may seem to be established more with the nurses and doctors in mind than with you and your baby. Inescapable ward noises, such as those which come from the sluice room, food which you do not particularly enjoy and the interruption of your sleep may prove frustrating. Nearly every woman is tired and in need of sleep after delivery and lack of sleep can lead to irritability, depression and tearfulness. Also it is quite hard to sleep in strange surroundings and if you find this a problem discuss it with the ward sister and ask if she thinks sleeping pills are advisable. Lights are usually out at about nine p.m. and even if you are woken for the baby's first feed at six a.m. you can get a good nine hours' sleep. If you are a relaxed sort of person, try and cat nap whenever you can during the day when ward routine and your baby's feeding times allow.

It is accepted medical practice that a woman should be out of bed and walking (even a few steps) as soon as possible after delivery. Once you have had a chance to rest and perhaps have a nap, the nurses will encourage you to walk to the lavatory, pass urine and have a bath. You will find that there is an accent on cleanliness and hygiene during the time that you are on the ward. If the presence of episiotomy stitches causes you discomfort in the bath or when you are sitting down, ask for a rubber cushion.

A typical day's routine on a maternity ward would be as follows:

---

6 a.m. Feed, wind and change your baby.
7 a.m. Breakfast.
8 a.m. Bath, shower and change for the day.
9 a.m. A waggon comes round the wards with newspapers, sweets, fruit and toilet requisites for you to buy.
10 a.m. Bath the baby, feed, wind and change.
11 a.m. Your own free time.
12 midday. Lunch.
Rest until 2 p.m.
2 p.m. Feed, wind and change the baby.
Snooze till tea.
3.30 p.m. Tea.
4-6 p.m. Visitors.
6 p.m. Top and tail the baby, feed, wind and change.
7-8 p.m. More visitors.
8-9 p.m. Relax.
9 p.m. Lights out.
10 p.m. Feed, wind and change the baby.
11 p.m. Go to sleep.
2 a.m. Possibly you will be woken to give the 2 a.m. feed.

Before you go into hospital, make sure you know about visiting hours. Most hospitals have relaxed the rigid, short visiting hours of the past. Some hospitals may allow free visiting, though the rules regarding children visiting are not so uniformly flexible. Because of the dangers of infection, some sisters prefer children to remain outside the maternity ward, while others may welcome them.

Rooming-in

Some hospitals allow what is called 'rooming-in', so enquire about it. This means that the baby spends most of the 24 hours in a cot by your bed. He may even spend the whole night with you and with help from the nurses, which you should not hesitate to ask for, you will be able to look after nearly all of his daily needs right from the start. You can insist on having your baby with you if you feel strongly about it. A flexible attitude towards mother and baby contact is usually reflected in flexible visiting hours, encouraging father to be present at delivery and demand feeding routines.

Rooming-in is a real bonus for you and your baby. You are with him from his first hours of life. You are in a position to observe and react to his every need, his patterns of behaviour, to his likes and dislikes. He in his turn gets used to your voice, your smell, touch and your face. In this way, the relationship between mother and baby can be cemented from the first few hours. Indeed, these first few days are so valuable to you and your child in forming the basis of your future relationship and in forming his ability to have successful relationships with other people, that it is worth considering staying in hospital a little longer in order to fully establish a bond.

Feeding routine

You must also clarify your hospital's attitude towards feeding. Some stick rigidly to a 4 hourly routine, that is 6 a.m., 10 a.m., 2 p.m., 6 p.m., 10 p.m., 2 a.m., 6 a.m., and feeding is not allowed at any other time. This can be hard on some newborn babies who are naturally slow feeders. If feeding times are hurried, they do not have a chance to take in sufficient food to tide them over the next four hours. They become hungry, they wake and they may cry. This can be disturbing to a mother whose natural instinct is to go to her baby, pick him up, nurse him and feed him. If this is the ward routine however, you must be prepared to accept it while you are in hospital and establish your own routines when you get home.

Other hospitals follow a routine of demand feeding. In the end, this is not so different from feeding a baby every four hours. A normal baby is likely to want to suckle more or less every four hours. The difference in the two routines is that the former follows the feeding times laid down by the nursing staff, whereas the latter follows the natural inclination of the baby.

With both my children, I have been on a ward where the 2-6-10 routine was enforced. I acceded while I was there, tried not to let it upset me and attempted to make up for it by nursing my baby all the time I was with him. Once I got home, I established my own demand feeding routine. I do not think we suffered in the long run.

(Top right) During the first few days after delivery you will be getting to know your baby. Make sure you're allowed to have your baby whenever you want. Nurse her as often as you like. Most hospitals will let you have the baby by your side through the night but you may welcome the unbroken sleep.
(Middle right) Don't take too much notice of your baby's weight, or how much feed she takes. If she's happy and contented she's probably doing very well.
(Bottom right) As part of the daily routine in hospital, you and your husband, if he's there at the time, will be shown how to 'top and tail' your baby (or babies!).

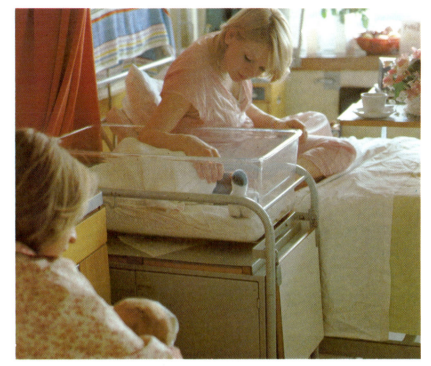

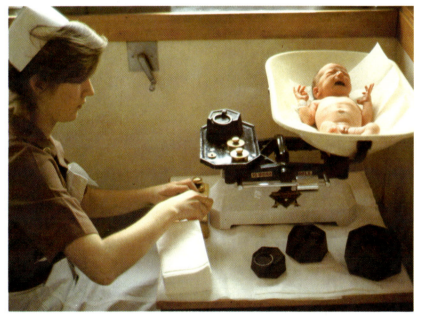

Other useful items to take

Besides the things you will have packed in your emergency case for yourself and the baby (see page 39), there are one or two other items which you may find useful when you are in hospital.

Books Though you can see from the hospital routine that your day is punctuated by a succession of ward activities, there will be moments when you can be quiet and on your own. So it is an idea to take a selection of light reading, which can be picked up or put down to fit in with events.

Writing paper & envelopes You will probably want to write thank-you letters for all the flowers, gifts and good wishes you may receive. This is best done while you are still in hospital and you are likely to be able to find an odd ten minutes when you are entirely free.

Cosmetics Your husband and your visitors will be cheered if you are looking neatly dressed with your hair well done and your make-up on, so take any of your usual items of make-up, shampoo, conditioner and curling tongs or heated rollers (if you use them) which are easy to pack. You will almost certainly find that the ward has a hair dryer which can be passed around.

Radio/Television You will probably find that for once in your life you do have time to glance at the newspapers in the morning but you may also like to keep up to date by having a portable radio on your locker and if it has an ear piece so that you can listen without disturbing the rest of the ward, all to the good. The ward will probably supply radios and a television set but if you want the flexibility of watching your own choice of programmes and are lucky enough to have a portable television set, do take it with you.

Small change It is very useful to have a bag full of coins for the telephone as you may want to ring friends and relatives during the day.

Clothes While you may shed 18 pounds (8.2 kg) while you are in hospital, it is unlikely that you will go back to your pre-pregnancy shape, so do not make the mistake of having a dress to go home in that antedates your pregnancy. It is very demoralizing not to be able to do up the zip. Similarly, if you have suffered from swollen ankles towards the end of your pregnancy, it may take six weeks to subside, so do not try to squeeze your feet into tight fitting shoes or boots. However, some hospitals prefer you not to bring in these clothes until you actually need them.

It will also do much for your morale if you can have something pretty and new to wear while you are going about the ward. You will almost certainly be feeling tired and it is easy to slip into the habit of slouching around in down-at-heel slippers and an old dressing gown. A new bed jacket which you can wear when your visitors arrive will pep up jaded spirits.

Perfume Giving birth to a baby is quite an achievement so pamper yourself. Save that bottle of new perfume to be opened after delivery and take with you all those unused gifts of bath salts, bath essence, sweetly scented soap and talcum powder.

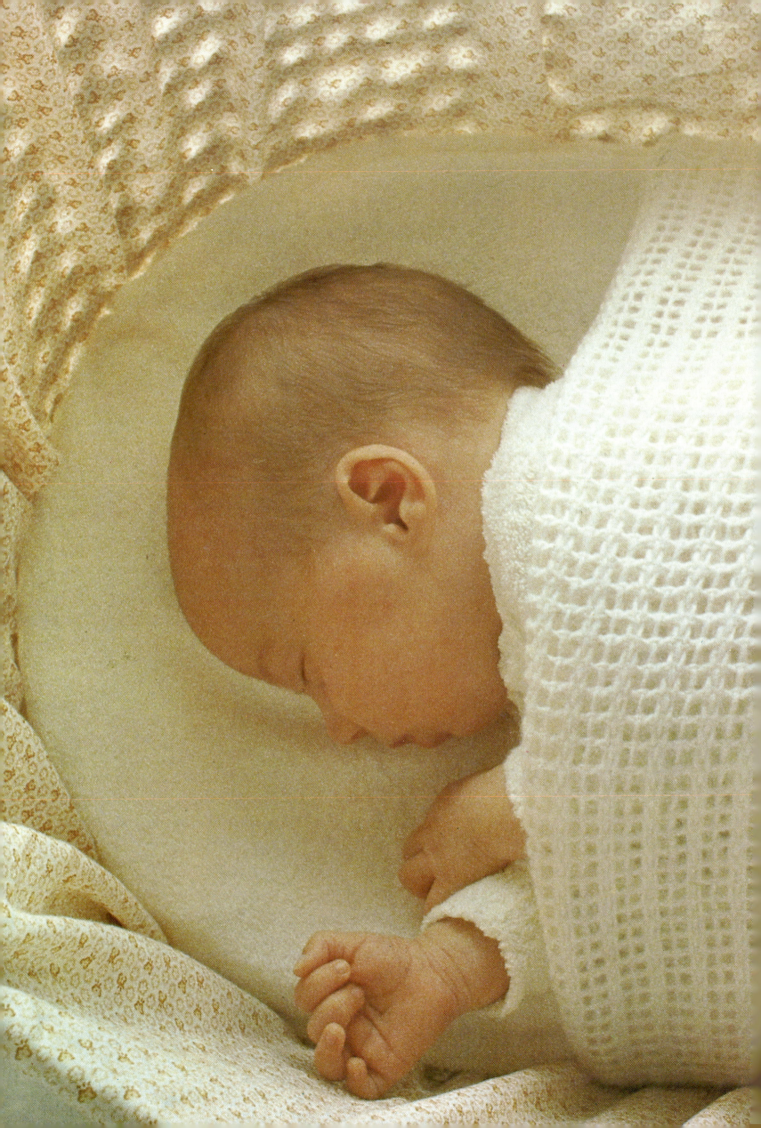

Your baby

You should spend the first few days concentrating on getting to know all about your baby and becoming familiar with all the normal things that newborn babies do that may alarm you when you first see them. For instance, you may notice that your baby suddenly shivers, or that her breathing becomes irregular, or that she makes strange snuffling noises. They may give you a fright when you first notice them but they are all perfectly normal.

Your baby will sleep most of the time during her first few days, so try to spend as much of her waking time with her as you can. Research with monkeys has shown that physical contact during the first few days of life is extremely important.

Research with human babies has given us further clues. It seems that newborn infants require contact with soft objects and also require to be stroked. If they are not stroked they tend to move their own limbs and their bodies so that they rub them against the soft object. Some very interesting work has been done with premature infants. It was found that their daily weight gain was greater if they had been lying on fluffy, soft, flannelette sheets than if they had been on smooth cotton or linen sheets. The reasons put forward by the researchers for this difference was that the premature infant found contact with the soft material more soothing and was therefore more contented and simply did better. Also lying in contact with the soft sheet was similar to being stroked. The babies moved, wriggled and turned less, used less energy and put on more weight. The children who were nursed on smooth, less cosy sheets, moved and turned more, used up more energy and put on less weight.

This research seems to provide a sound basis for really early physical contact of mother and baby, starting as soon after birth as possible (see page 48). Following on from there, you should try to keep your baby in contact with you as much as you possibly can and not just at feeding, bath times or play times. The close physical presence of the mother can be nothing but reassuring to a newborn infant. She is soft and warm. When the baby's head is laid against her mother's body, she can hear again the familiar heart beat which she heard in the womb. That makes her feel at home with her surroundings.

Smell

Furthermore she becomes familiar with her mother's smell and we now know that this is one of the first characteristics of the mother that a baby recognizes. You may have noticed that a stranger, even your husband, can go into your baby's room while she is asleep and she won't stir. But when you go, your baby will more often than not wake up. This is due to a biological response in your baby. In the first weeks of life, her sense of smell is very sensitive to chemicals called pheromones which give you a special scent. She wakes because she recognizes you as her main source of food, comfort and pleasure.

Movements

It is never too early to make your child familiar with physical movement. Newborn infants detest sudden or violent physical movement. Do not forget that for nine months they have been floating, well-supported and cushioned, in a bag of amniotic fluid. When this firm support is removed or seems in jeopardy, they feel very insecure and you probably notice that if you make a sudden movement when you are carrying your baby, she will stretch up her arms and legs in a jerking movement as though to save herself from a fall, so try to avoid this. All movements should be smooth and slow so that she can prepare herself for them.

But I believe that you should get used to moving your baby and help your baby to move, as soon as possible. One of the greatest gifts you can give your baby is confidence about her body and the way she co-ordinates it and uses it. In the early days movement probably only involves you moving her arms and legs, taking hold of her hand, grasping and ungrasping her fingers, bending the knees and elbows etc. but as she grows older and you continue to show her how she can move her body, you can be much more adventurous as long as you do not put your child in any danger.

As long as you feel confident with the manoeuvre, you will find that your baby enjoys being held firmly and carefully under the arms and having her legs swung to and fro. From a very early age she will also love being propped up securely, surrounded by pillows so that she can see you moving about the room and can take an interest in what is going on around her. You will also help to strengthen her muscles and to encourage their development if, when she is lying down, you grasp her fingers and lift her an inch or so from the mattress and let her take her own weight on her arms. This little exercise will strengthen the muscles of the arms, shoulders, back, neck and spine.

(Above and right) Your newborn baby is a source of delight and concern at the same time. He's small but surprisingly strong. He's cuddly to hold but may scare you with jerky movements and irregular breathing. It's never too early to introduce your baby to his world. First of all with you – your chatter, your songs, your feel, your smell. Then your husband. Then to interesting sights, a mobile, a mirror, then to interesting sounds, music, clapping, tapping out rhythms, household noises.

Sound

During the first days, your baby is also becoming used to your voice. Babies do not like loud noises so try always to use a soft, soothing, gentle voice. Interestingly, work at Oxford suggests babies respond better to high-pitched sounds, i.e. to women's voices better than men's. If you do not feel like chatting to your baby, sing or croon to her. Even very young babies seem to enjoy nursery rhymes and simple songs that have a defined rhythm and rhyming sound. Work in child development has also shown that children who are sung to early in their lives seem to develop a facility for words in general and for speaking and reading.

Sight

Eye contact with your baby is also extremely important. The eyes are the focus of emotion in the face and babies seem to be aware of this from their early days, even though they may not be able to focus their eyes for several weeks. It used to be believed that babies could not see properly until they could focus their eyes, which usually does not happen earlier than four weeks. But we now know that your baby can recognize your face much earlier than this and can distinguish it from other faces. The eyes seem to be the part to which they pay most attention. It has been found that newborn animals and human infants will respond to a white disc on which has been painted two round dark circles in a position of the eyes. Studies have shown that women who make early eye contact with their children tend to be gentler, more sympathetic, more understanding mothers who rarely resort to physical punishment.

Proportion of the newborn

Don't worry if your baby seems to have rather odd proportions. His head will seem large for the rest of his body and his abdomen may seem distended. You will also notice that his abdomen moves rather a lot while he is breathing. His arms and legs may appear thin and fragile. All of these things are normal.

The fontanelle

This is a space on the top of a baby's head where the skull bones are not joined and don't join for about two years. A baby's skull bones are soft so that they 'mould' without damage as the baby is delivered. If they are pressed hard together the fontanelle allows the bones quite a lot of freedom to move towards one another without crushing the brain. The skin and hair covering the fontanelle needs no special care.

Breathing

Your baby will almost certainly make strange noises while he is breathing. He also may remain quite quiet for long period of time. If you are in a hospital ward, you will notice other newborn babies behave in exactly the same way. You must remember that your baby's lungs are small and his breathing will seem shallow. In the first few days you may hardly be able to detect his breathing but do not be frightened by this. It gets stronger with each day.

You will also notice that his breathing is irregular. Sometimes it is undetectable and at other times, it is faster and more noisy. Each breath may be accompanied by a strange snuffling noise when he breathes in and out. Sometimes the snuffling noise is so pronounced that you may think he has a cold but this isn't often the case. In most babies the bridge of the nose is low and the snuffling noise is merely the air trying to get through small nasal passages. As he grows older and the bridge of the nose becomes higher, the snuffling gradually stops. The only time snuffling needs treatment is if it interferes with your baby's ability to feed. Tell your doctor and he will probably prescribe some nose drops to use before feeding.

Some babies sneeze at the slightest provocation, very often when they open their eyes and this is due to the brightness of the light stimulating the nerves to the nose. Next time you feel a sneeze coming on, look into a bright light and you will find this will probably precipitate the sneeze. It is caused by nervous impulses passing along the nerves to the eye and escaping along the nerves to the nose. Even if your baby is sneezing quite heavily, it doesn't necessarily mean that he has a cold. The lining of his nose is sensitive and a sneeze may simply mean that he is clearing his nasal passages and preventing dust from getting down into his throat.

Newborn babies also tend to hiccup quite frequently. This does not bother your baby at all and nor should it bother you. Again it is a sign that your baby's breathing is getting stronger and that all the muscles involved in respiration – the diaphragm and the muscles between the ribs – are trying to work in harmony.

The only time that you need be concerned about your baby's breathing is if it becomes very laboured, you notice that his chest is being sharply indrawn with each breath and the rate rises above 60 breaths per minute. At the same time you will probably notice that the breathing becomes more shallow than normal and your baby is obviously having difficulty with breathing. In these circumstances you should call your doctor immediately.

Temperature control

A newborn baby cannot control his body temperature with the same efficiency as an adult. Newborn babies, like small birds, have a large surface area for their body weight and they therefore tend to lose heat rapidly. This is one of the reasons why a baby has to feed frequently in its early days until the ratio of surface area to weight decreases. This rarely can happen before the time a baby reaches 10-12 pounds (4.5–5.5 kg) in weight, regardless of age. So don't expect your baby to be able to go through the night without a feed before this weight is reached.

It is therefore very important that you control the baby's temperature for him. You do this by making sure he is clothed properly, perhaps in a 'baby-grow', and the temperature in the air around him is fairly constant. If possible, his own room should be kept at a temperature of about 22°C (72°F) and he should be wrapped warmly but not so that he perspires. You should not allow him to lie naked for any length of time and when you bath him he should be dried quickly.

Babies who are allowed to get cold tend not to feed satisfactorily and therefore do not gain weight at the rate they should. They are also more prone to infections. Babies who become over heated tend to develop sweat rashes (see page 85). Because over heating irritates them, they also tend not to feed properly. As a general rule, over heating a baby does him as much harm as allowing him to get cold.

The skin

When your baby is first born, his skin will be covered by vernix (a white greasy substance). At one time vernix was meticulously washed off but as it is now thought to provide a barrier against infection, it is very often left on the skin with the exception of the face and hands and in the skin creases where it tends to collect. In many hospitals, babies are not bathed after birth but only topped and tailed (i.e. face, scalp and bottom only are washed).

A newborn baby's skin is soft and delicate and can be easily damaged. Your baby's appearance at birth may come as quite a shock to you. The skin is quite often blotchy and red and may even appear dry and to be peeling. If he has been delivered by forceps or with suction apparatus his skin may be slightly bruised. In nearly all babies these characteristics are temporary and will have disappeared in a few days.

It is not uncommon for there to be small red marks on the baby's skin, on his eyelids, his forehead and if you lift up his hair, at the back of the neck just at the hairline. The old-fashioned name for these marks is 'stork beak marks' and they are due to an enlargement of the tiny blood vessels in the surface of the skin. You should not worry about them because they nearly all disappear by the time the baby is six months old, although some may last as long as eighteen months.

You will notice that your baby's skin is almost translucent and you may be able to see his veins, particularly around the face, chin and neck. This is normal. His skin may still have a fine covering of downy lanugo hair which will be lost in a couple of weeks.

It is quite common for babies to have small white spots (milia) over the bridge of the nose. They are due to blockage of the openings of the sebaceous glands which secrete oil or sebum. You should not interfere with them in any way. They are entirely normal and will disappear in a few weeks. Never squeeze them.

The eyes

Sometimes it is quite difficult to open a baby's eyes but you must never force them. The easiest way is to hold the baby above your head so that he is looking down at you. All babies are born with blue eyes. This is because the skin's natural pigment, melanin, is absent from the eyes. If a baby is going to have brown eyes, the colour will gradually change and they may not have reached their permanent colour until the baby is six months old or so.

You will notice that your newborn baby squints occasionally and this is because he has not learned to use his eyes as a pair to focus on things. By the time he is one or two months old he will be using them together and squinting will become less frequent. If your baby is still squinting after three months you should consult your doctor.

Discharge from the eyes in a newborn baby is always abnormal and should be properly treated (see page 86).

You may be surprised to see that there are no tears when your newborn baby cries. Usually tears do not form until a baby is four or five months old and in a newborn the tear ducts which lead from the corner of the eyes down into the nose can carry away any amount of tears which may be produced by the tear glands.

Reflexes

All babies are born with a set of reflexes or instinctive movements which are usually designed to protect them. Two such reflexes are closing of the eyelids when they are touched and sharp movements of the arms and hands if you gently hold the nose between your finger and thumb. Others are described below.

The grasp reflex

If you press anything into the palm of a newborn baby's hand, she will automatically tighten her fingers around it and grasp it. Immediately after birth this reflex is so strong and powerful that a baby can take her whole weight on her fingers and so can be lifted.

The sucking reflex

A newborn baby will suck automatically if something enters her mouth and presses on the upper palate just behind the gums. Sucking movements may be strong and may last for some time after the pressure has been removed.

The Moro reflex

If your baby is undressed, lying on her back and hears a loud noise nearby, she will throw up her arms and legs, stretch her fingers, then slowly draw her limbs back into her body, bend her knees and clench her fists.

The swallowing reflex

The baby can swallow from birth which means that she can feed and swallow food immediately.

The rooting reflex

If you gently stroke your baby's cheek she will turn her head in the direction of your finger and open her mouth. This is the movement she makes when she is searching for your breast to take milk.

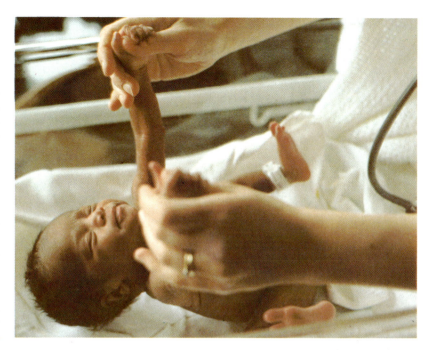

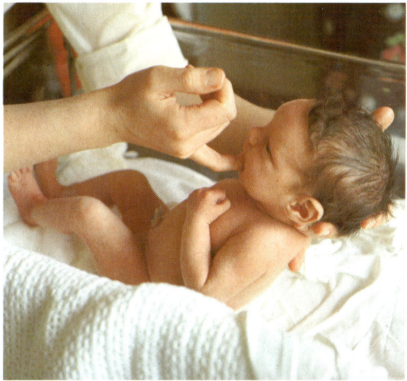

The walking reflex

If you hold your newborn baby upright underneath the arms and let her feet touch a firm surface, she will move her legs in a walking action. This reflex is lost soon after birth and is not a sign that your baby will walk early. She will have to learn the art of walking right from the beginning.

Urine

Don't worry if your baby's nappies are dry for the first 48 hours. It is not uncommon for a baby to pass hardly any urine at all during that time. If you find a pinkish stain on the nappy, do not let this concern you. It is usually due to the formation of uric acid crystals in the urine which is normal.

(Top) Your baby is surprisingly well equipped to survive when he's born. This is mainly due to his reflexes. He can take his entire weight, by hanging on with his fingers due to the grasp reflex.

(Above) She can also suck straightaway, so she can be put to the breast immediately after birth.

Stools and bowel movements

Your baby's first stools consist of meconium and therefore will be dark green and sticky and will have no smell. Meconium is digested mucus from the mucous glands in the bowel. It is usually passed during the first two to three days. For the next three or four days you will notice that the stools change colour and become mustard yellow or buff-coloured due to the residue from milk feeds. The appearance and consistency of your baby's stool will depend on whether she is on breast or cow's milk.

If you breast feed your baby you will notice that the stools are soft, hardly smell at all and rarely irritate your baby's bottom. If you see streaks of green in the stool, ignore the old wives' tale that they are a 'danger sign'. They are not. Nor do they mean that your baby is taking too much, too little, or that your milk does not suit him. The streaks are simply a sign that your baby's digestive system is getting into the swing of things. If she is feeding normally and is happy and contented, the odd bits of slime or mucus in the stool are also normal.

If your baby is being fed on formula (artificial or modified cow's milk), the stools will be firmer and an orangy brown and they will have a stronger smell.

It is usual for most newborn babies to pass several stools a day. In fact they may empty the bowels with every feed. But don't worry if your baby only passes one stool a day or one every few days, especially if you are breast feeding her, because breast milk contains very little waste and there is no stool to pass. The residue from formula is bulkier and there is therefore more stool for the baby to pass. If you are feeding your baby on formula and her stools become hard and she misses a day or so, try giving her a drink of boiled water, cooled to room temperature, once or twice a day to see if the motions become softer and more frequent. If the constipation persists, consult your doctor.

Constipation does not occur in breast fed babies. The stool is acid and therefore does not irritate her skin. On the other hand, the stool of an artificially fed baby is alkaline and this can make the skin of the buttocks rather sore and if this is not attended to, nappy rash may occur. It is therefore quite a good idea to apply a barrier cream to your baby's bottom before putting on her new nappy if you are going to feed her on formulated milk. The sensitivity of your baby's skin to the alkalinity of the stools usually disappears after a few weeks and nappy rash is less likely to occur unless the skin is not properly cleansed and protected.

You

Because of the sudden drop in the level of pregnancy hormones, your body starts to change back to its pre-pregnancy state immediately after delivery. It takes almost nine months for a woman's body to recover fully from the effects of pregnancy. This is not surprising if you remember some of the changes that take place in your body as a result of becoming pregnant.

☐ the womb increases in volume 1,000 times.
☐ the womb increases in weight 30 times.
☐ the individual muscle fibres of the womb increase in length 40 times.
☐ the work done by the mother's heart increases by 50 per cent.
☐ the volume of the mother's blood increases by one third.
☐ the mother's kidneys filter 50 per cent more blood than before.

Your shape

Any weight gain during pregnancy in excess of 18 pounds (8.2 kg) is nearly always caused by the deposition of fat. At one time it used to be acceptable for every woman to gain one stone (6.4 kg) with each baby. Do your utmost during pregnancy to make sure that this does not happen. If you have gained more weight than you should, you should go immediately to your doctor for advice on a sensible slimming diet so that you can get back to your original weight as quickly as possible. This applies whether you are breast feeding or not. Do not be fooled into comforting yourself with the thought that you will go on to a diet when you have finished breast feeding your baby. In six months time you will have become so used to carrying around your excess weight and your large size that you will not have the enthusiasm to try to become slimmer. Women who breast feed and who eat sensibly usually regain their pre-pregnancy weight and shape faster than women who opt for bottle feeding.

Exercises

You will be relieved by the comparative flatness of your abdomen but you should try to start exercises for strengthening and flattening the abdominal muscles as soon as you possibly can so that they will regain their tone. Some women manage to do them the day after their delivery. Above right are two simple exercises, which you can do preferably lying on the floor.
If you can you should perform these exercises twice a day. I am very keen on any exercise which can be done without special preparation and there is an exercise like this which you can do for your abdominal muscles. Wherever you are, whether standing or sitting, pull in sharply your lower abdominal muscles, hold for a count of three and relax. Repeat this 10 times and do it whenever you can remember. You will find that your slack, rotund tummy will soon become flat and firm again.

It may take longer for your waistline to return. Flattening out of the waistline is an early physical effect of pregnancy. Consequently it takes a very long time for your waistline to become trim again, rarely less than three months.

It is essential that you wear a strong, nursing brassière during the period you are breast feeding to give your breasts the support they need.

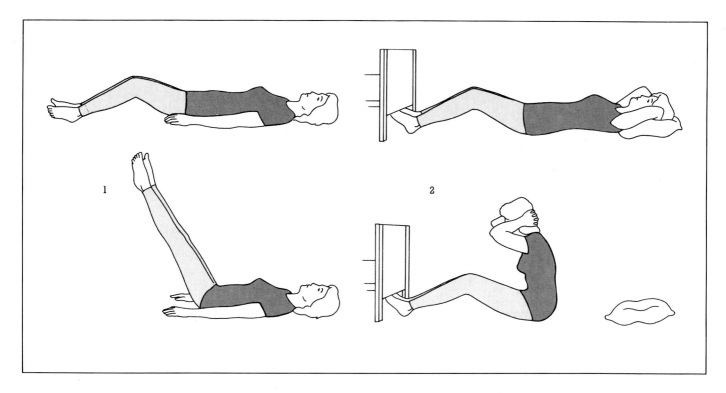

Any swelling of the ankles which you may have experienced during the latter few weeks of pregnancy may take some time to disappear completely. Six weeks is not uncommon.

Your skin

If you have a dry skin, it may have become drier during pregnancy but will gradually return to normal after the baby is delivered. The increased pigmentation which affected many parts of your skin will also gradually fade after delivery, even chloasma (patches of brown skin, usually on the face), though this may take nine months to a year to disappear altogether. Pigmentation on the areola of the breasts (the circular part of the nipple area which surrounds the protuberant part of the nipple itself) on the other hand, is usually permanent.

Stretch marks may have appeared on your breasts during pregnancy because they enlarge rapidly over a short period of time. They quickly become pale after delivery and within a few months they may hardly be noticeable. But stretch marks on the abdomen and thighs take much longer to fade and may never disappear. They nearly always remain as thin, papery scars that have a silvery glint. Unfortunately, once these stretch marks appear, there is nothing that can be done about them (sadly, they cannot be prevented either). If they are very unsightly, they can be removed by plastic surgery.

Your hair

Nearly every woman notices a change in her hair during pregnancy. It is quite often difficult to manage and may occasionally become more sparse. After pregnancy, however, hair fall may be quite alarming and may continue for anything up to 18 months. But this is quite normal and the hair always regrows though it may take two years for you to regain your normal head of hair. When you are not pregnant you can lose up to 100 hairs a day without noticing the loss. This is because hairs are growing and falling at different rates all over the head. Hairs grow for a period and then go into a resting phase. At the end of the resting phase they fall out. Pregnancy makes all the hair go into a resting phase simultaneously. This means that they are lost in large numbers over a fairly short period of time. They are replaced but you may notice that your hair type is different. Someone who has curly or wavy hair may have straight hair when it regrows after pregnancy and this surprisingly can be a permanent change.

Your uterus

Even when your uterus has completely shrunk, it will be slightly larger than it was before you became pregnant. This makes it easier to insert an intra-uterine contraceptive device. There will also be less pain and bleeding than in a woman who has not had a baby. Having contracted rhythmically for a whole nine months, the uterus goes on contracting for a short time after delivery. These contractions may be accompanied by slight discomfort which is more noticeable when you are breast feeding your baby. After pains may last several days but they are perfectly normal and usually can be relieved by analgesics, such as aspirin or paracetamol (see page 84).

Your vagina

If you have an episiotomy during labour, the stitches will be sore for several days after delivery and the whole area around the vagina may be tender for several weeks. This should not stop you doing your post-natal exercises, which will help the muscles of the pelvic floor and your

(Above) Postnatal exercises.
(1) With your knees bent and legs close together, raise your legs from the floor until your hips are at right angles with the rest of your body, then slowly lower the legs down to the floor again. If you gradually increase the number of times you perform the exercise you will simultaneously increase the tone of your muscles.
(2) Tuck your toes under something firm and then pull your trunk into the upright position, then slowly lower it back to the floor. As the muscles become stronger you can get them in tip top shape by placing your hands behind the back of your head as you perform this exercise.

As a precaution to safeguard your spine these exercises should be done with the knees bent. Stop if you feel any discomfort at all.

vagina to regain their tone. There is a simple exercise that you can perform at any time wherever you are. It is best described as a drawing-in movement of the vagina, which contracts the muscles of the pelvic floor sufficiently to stop the flow of urine. You should try to do it the first time you pass urine after delivery and once you have learned how to do it you should repeat it several times whenever you remember. This exercise will help to strengthen and firm up the walls of the vagina which relaxed and stretched during labour.

Lochia

This is the name given to the vaginal discharge, mostly blood, that follows delivery quite normally for up to six weeks, usually for four, sometimes only for two. The discharge quickly becomes brown but occasionally is pink or bright red after exercise. The lochia should never be offensive or irritating. If it is consult your doctor immediately.

(Below) Breast milk is the ideal baby food. All women are equipped to breast feed. Hardly any women can't produce enough milk for their baby's needs. Give your baby a flying start and breast feed him – even two weeks is better than nothing.

Your periods

Once you begin to menstruate again (and if you are breast feeding, the first period may be delayed for several months) you will probably find that your cycle has become more regular than it used to be and that you may bleed for a different number of days and the pattern of blood loss is different. If you are not breast feeding the first period may occur 28 days after delivery. Sufferers from painful periods nearly always benefit from pregnancy, it has an almost 100 per cent cure rate.

Breast or bottle feeding?

The aim of good feeding is to make sure that the baby is fed and this should be your main concern but try not to become obsessed with it.

Most women have decided during pregnancy whether they wish to breast feed or not. If you have opted for bottle feeding but change your mind after delivery, be sure to let your doctors and nurses know as soon as possible, so that they don't give you anything to stop the milk.

You will find that almost without exception, doctors and medical staff advocate breast feeding, even if it is only for a short time. Two weeks on the breast is better than no time at all. Even this short period will give your baby many benefits. A few years ago there was a trend towards bottle feeding. The reverse is now happening to the benefit of all our babies.

The advantages of breast feeding are undeniable. Here are a few of them:

☐ It provides the baby with a food of an ideal composition which is at the correct temperature (no testing is necessary).
☐ The milk is 'sterile'.
☐ Breast fed babies contract infections, particularly gastro-enteritis, less frequently and less severely than bottle fed babies.
☐ It helps the development of a happy relationship between mother and child. The physical nearness of the baby at feeding time helps to cement the bond.
☐ You don't have to mix the feeds or sterilize the bottles and teats and so it is easier than artificial feeding.
☐ You can breast feed whenever the need arises and therefore it is more convenient than artificial feeding.
☐ It helps the uterus to contract to its pre-pregnant size.
☐ It is cheap.

Despite these advantages, the number of women who rely completely on breast feeding is quite low. Some mothers decide that they do not want to breast feed, others abandon it because they experience pain during feeding or they find difficulty in getting the baby to suck properly or because they believe they have too little milk. This is often because the mother's expectations are too high. For 90 out of every 100 women, the first 2 or 3 weeks can be a difficult and worrying time but it is worth persevering.

The most commonly quoted reason for breast feeding is that it is natural which implies that every woman can do it. This is probably true, there are hardly any women who are not physically equipped to breast feed. It is also natural for a mother to feel proud that her baby is being fed on a food which is provided by her.

Human breast milk is tailor-made for the human baby with just the right amount of minerals and proteins. On the other hand, cow's milk has a higher percentage of protein and a high content of casein. Casein is the least digestible part of cow's milk for human babies and it is passed in the stools in the form of curds. The kidneys in a newborn infant are unable to deal with high levels of sodium in the blood. Human milk contains just the right amount of sodium, whereas cow's milk contains a little more. The quantity of fat in both kinds of milk is the same but the droplets of fat in human milk are smaller and therefore more digestible. Also breast milk fat is high in polyunsaturates and low in cholesterol. It may, therefore, protect against heart disease in later life. Breast milk contains more lactose (milk sugar) than cow's milk and, in addition, the mineral and vitamin content is different. Because a human baby cannot digest cow's milk completely, weight for weight human milk contains more calories per ounce, and this is reflected in the baby's stools (see page 70).

A survey done in 1948 showed that breast fed babies were less prone to illness than bottle fed babies. They suffer less from gastro-enteritis, from chest infections and from measles. This is because all of the mother's antibodies to bacteria and viruses are present in the colostrum. In the first few days of life they are probably absorbed straight into the baby's body unchanged and protect the baby against infection. In addition, they may exert a protective local effect in the intestine. If a mother has suffered poliomyelitis, her antibodies will be passed directly into her baby's body from her milk and will protect her baby against infection by the poliomyelitis virus. It is probable that he will never get poliomyelitis while she is breast feeding him. On the other hand, measles and poliomyelitis antibodies will have been passed through the placenta while the baby was still in the womb and so a bottle fed baby will have had an initial protection. Other bonuses of breast feeding include the baby having less wind, sleeping longer, and posset smelling less unpleasant if you breast feed.

As far as the mother is concerned the advantages of breast feeding are numerous. Some are:

☐ It's convenient anywhere, anytime.
☐ The milk is always the right temperature.
☐ It doesn't involve sterilizing bottles and making up feeds.
☐ It 'bonds' you to your baby and encourages mother love.
☐ It brings intense emotional satisfaction.
☐ It helps you to regain your figure.

You are, however, restricted in the amount of time you can spend away from your baby.

By comparison, bottle feeding does not show up as well especially with regard to safety aspects, nutritional value, its overall suitability and amount.

The risk of giving your baby contaminated artificial milk is dependent on a clean water supply, milk which contains no impurities and a good standard of hygiene in the house. In developed countries the risk is very low but infections like gastro-enteritis are still more common amongst bottle fed babies.

As already outlined, formulated cow's milk does not provide as suitable a food for a newborn infant, though there is no reason why a bottle fed baby should not thrive.

Many mothers worry in case the brand of artificial milk which they have chosen does not agree with their baby and they may mistakenly ascribe any minor trouble to the milk.

Closeness to you

Whatever method of feeding you choose, it is only satisfactory if your baby is physically close to you, so that feeding time satisfies your baby's need for comfort and play as well as his hunger. If you bottle feed your baby you should pay particular attention to this.

Naturalness

To many women who live in countries where bottle feeding is widespread, the normal way to feed a baby is by a bottle. A woman who is determined to bottle feed should never be dissuaded as it is probably better for the baby to have a happy mother bottle feeding her than an unhappy mother breast feeding her. Your baby will almost certainly thrive whatever method of feeding you choose as long as you are happy.

Breast feeding

For your baby to successfully breast feed, your nipples should be prominent, see page 22.

Breast size is irrelevant to the amount of milk you can produce. Small breasts contain as many milk glands as large breasts. Women with small breasts therefore have the potential to produce an adequate quantity of milk to breast feed.

With the birth of your baby, certain hormone changes take place in the blood which are a signal to your breasts to start producing milk. This is why it takes two or three days for the milk to 'come in' and replace the highly proteinaceous and nutritious colostrum.

'Let-down' reflex

The 'let down' reflex is under the control of a hormone called 'oxytocin' and regulates the flow of milk out of the breasts. It works like this. The stimulation of your baby sucking at your breast causes a message to be sent to the pituitary gland in the brain which then releases oxytocin into the blood stream. When the hormone

(Top) See this baby looking intently up at his mother. Breastfeeding should be a time for lots of eye contact. It's good for both of you and 'bonds' you tightly together – for life.
(Middle) The contentment on this baby's face is only a reflection of the contentment you'll be feeling too.
(Bottom) When feeding's over, relax together, play gently, get used to one another. You and your baby should look forward to feeding time. Try to keep free of interruptions and devote yourself wholly to enjoying your baby.

reaches the milk glands in the breast, it stimulates the glands to contract, thereby pushing the milk down the milk ducts to the nipple area. Milk will spontaneously flow from both breasts, not just the one that is being sucked. As breast feeding progresses, the let down reflex is caused not only by the sucking of the baby at your breast, it may be caused by his cry or simply by his presence. The let-down reflex is not just a physical reflex, it is an emotional one too. This is one of the arguments in favour of mother and baby being together as soon as possible after delivery.

Oxytocin makes the uterus contract. Sometimes these contractions are painful and more frequent during feeding time. This is why you may feel after pains for the first few days of breast feeding. They are working in your favour however, because they speed up the process by which the womb returns to its normal size. It is important that you should understand the connection between after pains and breast feeding, otherwise you might be put off from breast feeding by the abdominal discomfort.

The let-down reflex only occurs spontaneously if you are relaxed and happy and without tension. It can be inhibited by embarrassment, or anxiety, or fear of after pains or sore nipples. Do whatever you can to reduce your tension. If you are embarrassed, then ask that you be allowed to feed the baby alone. If you are tense, lie down and rest and try to relax a few minutes before the feed is due to begin.

Most women find that their breasts have a tendency to leak. This is quite normal and is the result of your breasts trying to match their supply with the demands of the baby. Once these two things are in line, leaking will stop. If for some reason you want to stop the flow of milk before your baby has finished feeding, push the nipple sharply inwards with one of your fingers and you will find that this will cause the milk flow to cease almost immediately.

Breast enlargement with swelling and tenderness (engorgement) is so common on the second or third day after the birth of your baby as to be considered normal. It is due to the activity of the breasts when the milk starts to come in and once the baby starts to feed they will soon get smaller. It may be necessary for you initially to manually express some of the milk out of your breasts to relieve the tight sensation and get the milk flowing (see page 22). Once this happens, it becomes easier for your baby to take and hold the nipple in his mouth. If your engorged breasts are causing you some discomfort, you can quite often get relief by applying cold compresses or ice cubes. Do not hesitate to call your doctor if your discomfort is prolonged. Engorgement is always a temporary phenomenon.

All babies are born with an enthusiasm for sucking and if this is not encouraged in the first few days, then it may wane and they will have to re-learn how to suck. This can be tedious, so you should really take advantage of your baby's desire to feed. If you see him doing well, you will

(Above) When breast-feeding, make sure the baby's head is held so that the nipple is accessible and he can swallow comfortably. The nipple should touch the roof of your baby's mouth, so aim it upwards. His chin should be firmly against your breast.

(Above) Your position is also important, whether you choose to sit or lie. If you lean back too far you will be pulling against the baby and this can cause sore nipples. You can support him with a cushion or a pillow on your lap. Cradle your baby in your arms so that his back and shoulders are supported and his head is free. If you hold your baby close to you, he will usually lift up his face and bring his mouth up to the nipple.

become more relaxed. As a result, the milk will flow more easily and feeding times will become something to look forward to.

The sucking reflex causes your baby to take into his mouth as much of the breast as possible including the areola which he presses between his gums, squeezing the milk from the breast. Though we call this sucking, it is more of a chomping action and in the first few days you should not allow your baby to suck for longer than a few minutes at each breast at each feed because the chewing action can make the breasts sore. But they soon get used to your baby's chewing and squeezing and develop a resistance to bruising.

There is only one way to establish a feeding routine during the first few days and that is to feed your baby when he is hungry and he should be the one to decide when this is. Your baby's feed times should not be time-tabled by you or anyone else. You should never leave him to cry because you feel it is not yet time for him to be fed and you should not be afraid that you will spoil him by feeding him frequently. If, on the other hand, your baby is asleep when feed time comes around, you can encourage him to go a little longer between feeds by leaving him until he wakes up himself. If you follow such a programme of 'demand' feeding, you will find that your baby will evolve his own routine.

During the first feeds before the milk comes in do not be concerned at all about how much food your baby takes. You should concentrate on getting to know him and finding out the most comfortable way of holding him. By the time your milk does come in, you will be an expert.

Perfecting the technique

Introduce your breasts gradually to the rigours of sucking. The first breast feed should be no longer than one minute at each breast and the feeds should continue for this length of time throughout the first day. On the second day, you can increase the length of the feed to two minutes each breast and on the third day, to three minutes so that by the end of the first week your baby will be feeding for ten minutes on each breast. You should consider that ten minutes is a maximum time for your baby to feed at one breast. If your baby is hungry he will empty the breast in a much shorter time. Most babies take two thirds of their feed in the first five minutes, so you should put your baby on each breast at the beginning of the feed.

It is important in the early days to make sure that your breasts are completely empty after each feed, so it's worth spending a few minutes after feeding is finished to manually express any milk which is left behind. This both stimulates lactation and helps to avoid engorgement. Many authorities believe that this routine of emptying the breast by manual expression is one of the key factors in the successful establishment of lactation. It is almost impossible to overfeed a breast fed baby but under feeding is possible. If the baby appears to be still hungry when the breasts are empty, he can be given a supplementary bottle after the feed. If this is necessary, give your baby unsweetened formula milk or he may develop a preference for the artificial feed. There is no truth in the old wives' tale that once a baby has been fed on a bottle he will refuse to go back to the breast.

Frequency of feeds

Small babies, i.e. those under seven pounds (3 kg), will usually require feeds every three to three and a half hours, while larger babies over seven pounds will probably go four or more hours between feeds. However, demand feeding is sensible feeding. A baby who has taken a full feed is unlikely to need feeding more often than this. If he cries after only two hours try giving him a ½ oz (15 ml) of boiled water, cooled to room temperature, as a drink. One of the reasons why you should not allow your baby to cry if he wakes before a feed is due, is that crying will tire him out so he will not feed well.

Your baby may be a slow feeder to start with. He may seem too lazy or too sleepy to take the breast. Do not try to force him to do so. Stimulate his rooting reflex by stroking his cheek with your nipple and do not be concerned if he does not seem too interested in feeding. Around the second or third day, when the milk starts to come in and engorgement starts to build up, your baby's appetite will probably increase dramatically to create the demand for which your breasts have established the supply. In many cases nature gets it just right so that babies tend to want extra feeds just on the days when the milk flow is becoming established, so it is not uncommon for babies to want perhaps 10 to 12 feeds from the third to the sixth day instead of the usual 6 or 7. Increased frequency of feeding helps to prevent severe breast engorgement. You need not worry that your baby is learning bad habits. On the seventh or eighth day his appetite will settle back to normal and so will your milk production.

Night feeds

As your baby needs feeds at three to four hourly intervals, night feeds are a necessity during the first few weeks. This is just as well because your breast produces milk at a constant rate throughout the 24 hours and if they were not emptied by a feed during the night, you would probably wake in the morning with severe engorgement. In the first few days you may have to feed twice during the night and gradually over the next six to eight weeks, you may be able to encourage your baby to go a little longer between the last feed at night and the next feed. The most that you can hope for is that he will sleep for perhaps five to six hours between one of his feeds and that extended sleep will occur at night. As there is no way you can avoid night feeds in the early weeks, it is better to approach them with a positive attitude. In any case, few mothers can sleep through their baby's cry and your baby

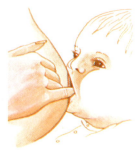

(Above) One of the ways of getting your baby to release the nipple after he has finished feeding, is to insert your little finger into the corner of his mouth. This will let some air in and therefore release the vacuum he has created.

(Above) Another way of easing your baby from your breast is to gently press down on his chin.

will need changing during the night. There are some advantages to having your baby in the room next to yours and not by your bed. Firstly, you will not be disturbed by his every restless movement and you may gain some valuable sleep that you would have lost if you heard his murmurings. Secondly, as he will need changing, you will need quite an assortment of baby equipment and your husband may prefer it if your bedroom does not become a nursery and thirdly, your activities with the baby may wake your husband.

Make the night feed as quiet, relaxed and as short as possible and if your baby is dozy or falls off to sleep again, just place him gently back in his cot without waking him. Do not bother to wind him as it will only make him more wakeful and may awaken you so much that you cannot get off to sleep again. These interrupted nights will make you very tired. This is why a supportive husband is invaluable and why it is such a good idea to have a friend or a relative to stay with you for the first couple of weeks after your return from hospital so that they can take on the day to day chores of running your house for you.

If this is not possible, then you really must let everything but the absolute essentials of your domestic life lapse. Close off all but essential rooms in the house so that they are not used and do the minimum of shopping and cooking. Sleep whenever you can. If the baby goes to sleep and you are feeling tired, drop everything and sleep along with him. Even a snatched few minutes of sleep can be very refreshing. And console yourself with the thought that this very tiring time is a transitory stage of development and does not last more than a few weeks.

From the age of four weeks onward, be on the alert for signs from your baby that he is able to sleep longer between feeds. Most parents make the mistake of thinking that a good feed at 10 p.m. will take the baby through the night and that he will drop the 2 a.m. feed. Quite often however, it is the 10 p.m. feed that the baby will want to drop first. A sign that he is ready to do this is irregular waking for the 2 a.m. feed. When you notice this, try letting your baby sleep on when the 10 p.m. feed is due. You may find that he will sleep on well through the night. Alternatively, he may wake around midnight and take a good feed and then sleep through to 6 a.m. As with early feeding, let your baby give you the lead as to when and which feeds should be dropped.

Some possible difficulties

Sore or cracked nipples are one of the commonest causes for breast feeding being discontinued. There are four common causes.

1. **Chewing** The best thing to do is never to let your baby chew on the nipple. Make sure that whenever he feeds, the whole of the areola of your breast goes in his mouth. Suckling movements will therefore compress the breast tissue itself and not the nipple.

2. **Finishing a feed** Do not pull your baby forcibly off your breast. Ease him off your breast by one of two manoeuvres (see illustrations).

3. **Sucking an empty breast** Take your baby off your breast as soon as you feel there is no milk coming.

4. **Sucking an engorged breast** If the nipple is difficult for him to grasp he will tend to bite on it. If your breasts are engorged, express a little milk to make the skin less taut. Only then, when it is easier for your baby to take the breast into his mouth, should you offer it to him.

The only sure treatment for a cracked nipple is to stop your baby feeding from it for about 48 hours. As soon as you develop a cracked nipple you should consult your midwife or doctor for special applications which will speed up healing. While the breast is being rested, you should express milk from it and give it to your baby from a bottle. As your free breast will be taking the brunt of your baby's feeding, take special care that its nipple does not become damaged. Moisturizing lotion or baby lotion rubbed into your nipple several times a day will help to keep it soft and supple and well moisturized. Another tip is to change the pads in your nursing bra as often as you can. Do not keep a damp pad in contact with your breasts for any length of time. When the skin of the nipple becomes waterlogged it is prone to cracking and infection. If the nipple is sore smearing a moisturizing lotion on the breast pad will help protect the skin.

Breastfeeding twins

The probability is that you will not be able to rely on breastfeeding alone for your twins for longer than a few days, perhaps up to two weeks. As your babies need more milk you will have to use formula to supplement their feeds. Breast feed your twins by whatever routine suits you and them. If they wake separately you can feed one then the other. In the very early days if they wake together it's very pleasant to lie with a baby on either breast and you can continue to do this as they get older and more manageable – as long as you have sufficient help.

When to stop breast feeding

You can stop breast feeding whenever you want to. When you stop, your baby can transfer to cow's milk (provided he is over six months) or formula, from a bottle. It helps the baby to accept a first bottle if you do not give it to him until he is really hungry. But if both you and your baby are happy and contented with breast feeding then you can continue it for nine months or more without either of you coming to any harm. If you do this you will probably miss out the transitional bottle feeding stage and go straight to feeding from a cup and spoon. As your breasts have got used to supplying the right quantity of milk, you can stop gradually by missing out one more feed each week. The last feed to give up is the early morning one, to prevent engorgement.

If you become ill, there is no need to stop feeding your baby unless your illness is very serious.

Bottle feeding

Bottle fed babies can thrive just as satisfactorily as breast fed babies. You need not fear that your baby will not gain enough weight, quite the reverse. Bottle fed babies are more likely to be overweight than breast fed babies.

Most mothers want to prepare the feeds only once a day. This will mean that you need six or eight bottles and teats, and bottle sterilizing equipment which you can purchase from any chemist. It is also a good idea to keep a handy supply of teats so that soft ones can be replaced as soon as they start to perish. You should also have a bottle that can be tightly sealed for travelling and a small bottle for giving your baby drinks between feeds.

Guidelines

Here are some guidelines about bottle feeding:
☐ Do wash the bottle, teat, cap and screw-on top and any other parts of the bottle assembly immediately after each feed.
☐ Do sterilize all the bottle equipment after washing in ordinary washing-up liquid and rinsing. There is a specially designed sterilizing bath which you fill with water and then add a given quantity of sterilizing fluid or crystals.

☐ Do sterilize your bottle equipment until your baby starts to crawl. After that, there is no point. All you need to do is to keep his equipment 'household' clean.
☐ Do prepare enough bottles for a full 24 hours at one time. Fill each bottle with the milk you have prepared and then keep them in the refrigerator until you need them.
☐ Do warm up the bottle before you feed your baby. You can do this by standing the bottle in a jug of hot water but always test the temperature of the milk on the back of your hand just before you start feeding. It is the right temperature if it feels neither hot nor cold.
☐ Do throw away any milk left over in a bottle after a feed. Never save it.
☐ Do make sure that the teat is soft so that it simulates the feeling of the nipple.
☐ Do make sure that the hole is large enough to let through an almost continuous stream of drops when the bottle is held on end. If the hole is too small and your baby has to strain to draw milk through it he may swallow a lot of air with his feed. The act of feeding may also tire him out and he may fall asleep before he has taken sufficient. On the other hand, if the hole is too large, he may have to struggle to keep up with the flow of milk. A bout of coughing may be precipitated which

(Above) Not all mothers will be able to manage feeding twins together like this one. You will work out your own routine – but this delightful set up seems worth emulating, and worth spending time over.

(Above and right) As soon as your baby wants to take an active part in his feeding – like this baby boy holding his bottle – encourage him to do so. It's one of the very first signs of independence and he's learning all the time. But give him a hand when he needs it.

feeding difficulties but if you feel that it does not agree with your baby, consult your midwife or health visitor before you change it.

☐ Do mix your feeds exactly as directed by the manufacturers, mixing them with boiled water which has been allowed to cool down a little.

☐ Do wind your baby if you feel strongly about it, though it is rarely necessary (see page 79). Most authorities recommend that you wind bottle fed babies half way through the feed but this becomes pointless as your baby gets older. To wind your baby, all you have to do is to make sure that her head is upright, either resting on your shoulder or supported on your lap with your hand. If she is upright, the bubble of air in her stomach will rise and she will burp. It is thought that gentle rubbing or patting on the back encourages burping. Never delay a feed because your baby does not bring up wind. Persist for no longer than five minutes and then continue regardless.

☐ Do hold your baby close during feeds. This close physical contact is important to both of you and there is no reason why it should not bring both of you as much satisfaction as the physical closeness of breast feeding.

☐ Do put a little more milk in the bottle than you think your baby will need during the first few days. In the early stages it is almost impossible to overfeed a new baby.

☐ Do give your bottle fed baby a little boiled water (cooled to the right temperature) to drink at least once a day.

What not to do

☐ Don't leave a bottle warming for any length of time, as this will only encourage bacteria to multiply. By all means let the bottle stand so that it is at room temperature when the feed is due. This is all most babies require.

☐ Don't ever keep the remains of an old bottle.

☐ Don't ever add a scoop of powdered milk in the hope that you will be giving your baby a little extra nourishment. In the first few days a baby cannot cope with a mixture which is over-concentrated. If you forget the number of scoops that you have put into the jug, start again.

☐ Don't heap or compress the scoop of milk powder when you are making the feed. Lift a full scoop out of the powder and scrape off any excess by running a clean knife across the top with the blade at right angles to the scoop.

☐ Don't feed your baby when she is lying flat on her back, because swallowing is difficult in this position.

☐ Don't make your baby finish the bottle. When she shows that she has had enough, never force her to take more. Just like you, her appetite varies. If she takes less than you think she should have at one feed, she will almost certainly make it up at the next.

☐ Don't use undiluted, unboiled cow's milk in the first four to six months of your baby's life.

☐ Don't ever leave your baby to feed herself unattended with a bottle propped on a pillow. She may swallow a lot of air but much worse she

may make him vomit. As the teat gets older, the hole gets larger, so test that the milk is coming out of the teat at the correct rate before each feed. If the hole is too small you can enlarge it with a red hot needle. Push the needle through the teat slowly otherwise the hole will be too big and you may waste several teats before you get a hole of the correct size.

☐ Do stick to a brand of food once you have chosen it. If you are in any doubt which brand you should choose, consult your midwife or doctor. Most women continue with the brand which their baby was introduced to while they were in hospital. The brand is rarely to blame for

(Above) You should try to hold your baby in such a position that you can maintain eye contact just as though you were breast feeding. Hold your baby close to you. You can even undress so that your baby's skin is next to yours. This type of bottle has a disposable inner lining, which means it is very hygienic. It also has a specially shaped top, to closely resemble a breast.

Carefree feeding

As with breast feeding, it is best if you feel relaxed and placid when you feed your baby. Make sure to choose a chair in which you can sit comfortably without changing your position for at least half an hour. Sometimes a footstool helps and it will be easier to hold the baby if the chair has a suitable arm-rest for you.

Make sure that her head is tilted slightly upwards so that she is looking up at you and keep the bottle tilted at an angle to ensure the teat is always full of milk. As with breast feeding, some babies are fast feeders, others are slow. On average a baby should take about half an hour to finish her bottle.

Discontinuing the bottle

Babies may sometimes become very attached to their feeding bottles, but make sure that you finish the bottle by the age of twelve months. Continued use of a feeding bottle may result in a particularly bad form of dental decay, sometimes called 'nursing bottle caries'.

The restless feeder

If your baby seems to be one of those excitable restless babies with a tendency to stop and start feeding, try the following routine. While she is still rather dozy at the end of her sleep, wrap her quite tightly in a shawl so that her limbs are held firm, then encircling her securely in your arms, start the feed. Leave all washing, bathing and nappy changing until it is over.

Make sure that you are in a quiet part of the house when you feed your baby and tell everyone that you must not be disturbed. Try and keep the light rather dim so that she is not distracted and never try to hurry a feed. This kind of baby is not only bright and active during feeding, she tends to be wakeful quite a lot of the time and not to need a lot of sleep. This wakefulness is usually a sign of interest in the surroundings and an expression of intelligence.

On the other hand, there are some babies who find feeding so soothing that they may fall asleep during the middle of a feed. If she seems satisfied and quite happy this should be treated as normal but if she wakes a short time after you have completed the feed, it means that she has not taken sufficient. You could try to stimulate her appetite by gradually making the interval between feeds longer.

If you follow the traditional instructions for winding' or 'burping' your baby, you may waste a lot of time because she will not necessarily bring up wind during and after feeds. You and she may become impatient and frustrated with the delay and you may prevent her from finishing off the feed or falling asleep contentedly at the end of it. Babies do swallow air while they are feeding but there is no evidence that this gives rise to digestive problems or causes any discomfort. Making a special routine of winding the baby is an unnecessary ritual.

may gag on a mouthful of milk and vomit. She may even choke.

☐ Don't let the first feed you prepare be the one which your baby needs on returning from hospital. Practise making feeds so that the whole routine is familiar by the time you come home.

☐ Don't add sugar.

How much and how many

If you're going to make up enough bottles for 24 hours, you need to calculate how much food your baby will require in that time. The standard rule of thumb is that most babies need 2½ fluid ounces (71 ml) per pound (0.45 kg) of body weight. A 10 pound (4.5 kg) baby would therefore need 25 fluid ounces (710 ml) of formulated milk in a day. Divide the milk between the number of bottles you think your baby will take, then seal them, cap them and when cool, place them in the fridge.

Every ingredient and every utensil used in the preparation of the bottles should be kept scrupulously clean and sterile. Your hands should be scrubbed clean for about half a minute before you begin preparing the bottles, the water should be just off boiling when you make the mixture and the jug you use to make up the milk should have been sterilized along with all of your bottles. Try not to let your fingers come into contact with those parts of the bottles which will be in contact with the milk.

A baby is usually offered her first bottle feed between four and eight hours after delivery because it is about this time after birth that she needs food. It is quite normal for newborn infants to take very little in the first few days (see page 75). Your baby's appetite will pick up quite suddenly and quickly around the second, third or fourth day and she will start to feed more consistently. Be flexible about the frequency of feeds. Most young infants require feeding every three to four hours but you should follow your baby's needs in setting up a feeding routine.

Routine care: hairwashing and bathing.

A full bath is only needed every 2 or 3 days, in between you can just 'top and tail' (see pages 82-83). Time the bathtime to coincide with when your baby is awake but not too hungry. Get everything ready beforehand and put on a waterproof apron. The bath water should not be too hot or too cold, test it with your elbow.

1. Wrap your baby's body firmly in a towel, cradle her head in your hand and hold it over the bath.

2. Dip two pieces of cotton wool in the water, squeeze them dry and then use one to clean first the right eye, moving from the inside corner to the outer one, then the right ear. Use the second piece for left eye and ear.

3. Wash the rest of her face with plain water using cotton wool starting at the middle and gently wiping out towards the sides. Never cover your baby's face with a flannel as this will frighten her. Don't wash the inside of her mouth and do not poke anything up her nose or into her ear.

4. Now wash your baby's scalp with water, use soap only once a week. Make sure that none of the soap goes near her eye and keep her head tilted downwards for rinsing. Rinse thoroughly.

5. Dry her head and hair.

6. Now take off vest and nappy.

7. When you're inexperienced you might find it easier to soap your baby with a flannel while she is still on your knee or, even easier, use a special baby bathing liquid in the water. Put a nappy into the bottom of the bath to stop your baby sliding. Now with your right arm round the baby's back, holding her right upper arm, supporting her bottom with your left hand, gently lower her into the water.

8. Rinse your baby's skin all over with the bath water containing the cleansing agent. Take care with the skin creases in neck, thighs and underarm. If you have not soaped the baby on your knee, wash her front first and then gently turn her over and wash her back and bottom.

9. Lift your baby out of the bath, wrap her in the towel and gently pat, not rub, her skin dry.

10. Put on a vest to keep her warm.

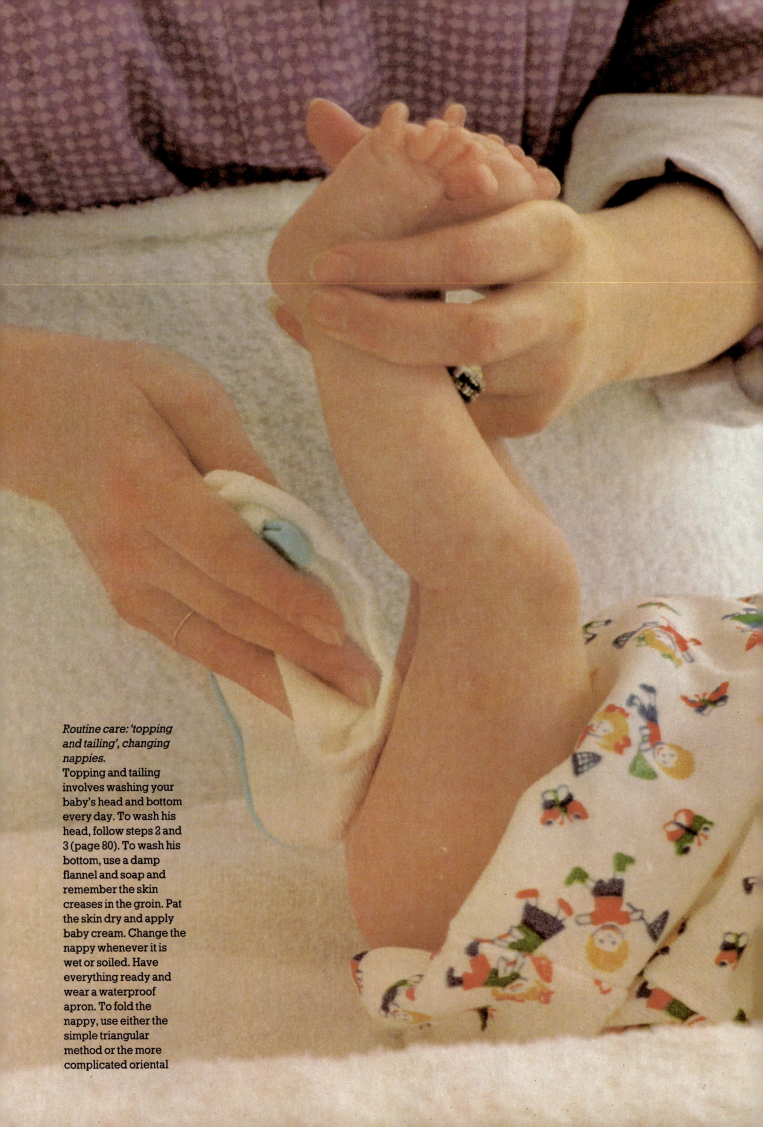

Routine care: 'topping and tailing', changing nappies.
Topping and tailing involves washing your baby's head and bottom every day. To wash his head, follow steps 2 and 3 (page 80). To wash his bottom, use a damp flannel and soap and remember the skin creases in the groin. Pat the skin dry and apply baby cream. Change the nappy whenever it is wet or soiled. Have everything ready and wear a waterproof apron. To fold the nappy, use either the simple triangular method or the more complicated oriental

method, especially suitable for boys, as shown in the diagram. Lay your baby on a plastic sheet with a nappy over the bottom half. Remove the soiled nappy. If his bottom is soiled, wash it with dampened cotton wool and dry as above. Put on the folded nappy with the straight edge under his back and the point between his legs. Fold the two ends over his tummy and bring up the point of the 'triangle' to meet. Keep your hand between the three points of the nappy and the baby, whilst pinning through all three layers, to avoid pricking him. To clean nappies: 1. Scrape off any solid pieces. 2. Discard nappy liner (if using). 3. Rub under running water. 4. Soak in bucket with water and sterilizing powder. 5. Wring out, then wash normally and dry.

oriental

fold

fold

turn over

fold

pin

triangular

fold

pin

(Above) If your baby is in the special care unit you may feel afraid to handle him as he seems so tiny. Try to hold your baby as soon after birth as you can. Ask if you can help with the care of your baby.

The low birth weight baby

Most low birth weight babies are nursed on special hospital units which are designed to look after their health and comfort. Many are nursed in incubators so that the baby is kept at an optimum temperature, which is meticulously controlled. If your baby has to be nursed in an incubator you may find the first few days disappointing and you will miss the close physical contact that the other mothers enjoy with their babies. You need not miss out altogether. Medical and nursing staff will probably go out of their way to encourage you to have as much contact with your baby as you possibly can. Don't worry that you may not be developing physical and emotional ties with your baby as these will develop quite normally once you are able to look after him completely by yourself.

Once a low birth weight baby has reached five and a half pounds (2.5 kg) it is usually possible to take him home. In addition to the routine daily care that has already been described, there are one or two special points that you should pay particular attention to.

Feeding
A small baby needs feeding more often than a large one and you will probably have to feed your baby every three hours. Also, a pre-term baby cannot be relied upon to wake up when he is hungry. They tend to sleep more than full term babies and may sleep straight through a feed time. It is important for a small baby not to go very long without food and so you must make it a rule during the first few weeks at home to wake your baby when a feed is due.

Keeping warm
All babies lose heat quickly but a pre-term or low birth weight baby is especially prone to do so. It is therefore of great importance that you guard against this by never leaving your infant uncovered and never allowing the temperature of his room to drop sharply.

After a few weeks your pre-term infant will be thriving and gaining weight at the same rate as other babies. Once he has reached this stage and is progressing normally resist the temptation to be over-protective and coddle him. Even though he may be physically smaller than other babies of the same age until he is two years old, never allow him to be labelled as a special care baby, he is not.

Postnatal discomforts

During the first few days you may suffer various discomforts which can be treated efficiently with simple medicine.

After pains

After pains are the continuation of Braxton Hicks contractions of the uterus which have been present right through pregnancy and last for a few days after delivery. They aid the womb to shrink. After pains are very easy to treat and usually respond to simple analgesics such as aspirin and paracetamol. Additionally, they very rarely last more than three or four days.

Constipation

Many women suffer from constipation during pregnancy and quite a number rely on purgatives to keep their bowels regular. As soon as pregnancy is over, you must try to stop taking purgatives as soon as possible. Start by relearning the old habits, see page 28.

Stopping the milk supply

If you have decided that you do not wish to breast feed your baby, your doctor will advise you on the best way to stop your breasts producing milk. About two days after the birth when milk normally comes in, your breasts may feel swollen and uncomfortable. You can relieve the discomfort by simple remedies like cold compresses, or analgesics such as aspirin yourself. If however the discomfort is severe, call a doctor who may prescribe a diuretic. This can bring great relief.

Episiotomy stitches

If you have had an episiotomy the skin stitches will cause you some soreness for four or five days. The stitches may give you a twinge of discomfort with any movement of the lower half of your body. You can help to minimize this while you are sitting by using a rubber ring cushion.

Minor illnesses in the newborn
Birth marks

Most birth marks are nothing more than a small collection of blood vessels just beneath the surface of the skin. They may be found on any part of the baby and the majority of them fade and disappear completely in a few weeks. Nearly all are gone by the time the baby is eighteen months. There are, however, some rare ones that may remain.

Temporary birth marks are merely discolorations of the skin usually found on the face and neck (see page 68).

The strawberry mark or naevus is a bright-red, usually raised area, varying in size from a pin head to several inches. It will often shrink and disappear completely in early childhood, sometimes leaving a patch of pale skin. If you are worried, ask to see a dermatologist.

The larger reddish or purplish birth marks do not disappear as quickly but don't be upset. Even if they affect your baby's face, modern techniques by dermatologists and plastic surgeons can remove most of them almost without trace.

A fourth type of birth mark contains brown pigment. It may be a flat patch in the skin or raised like a mole. They are nearly always pale and may grow slightly bigger as your child gets older. They are rarely unsightly but unless they are in an area which may be chronically irritated, most doctors would recommend leaving them alone.

Various swellings

Most babies are born with the head slightly misshapen. This does not indicate that they have suffered any damage during birth. It simply means that the part of the head which is swollen was subject to pressure as it moved down the birth canal, resulting in the collection of a little fluid. This will disappear in two or three days and the shape of your baby's head will be perfectly normal.

Occasionally extra pressure can result in minor bruising which may take a little longer to disappear. But it still does not mean that your baby has suffered any damage during delivery.

Many of the proportions in a newborn baby's body are different from those in an adult. The genital organs in both male and female infants appear proportionately larger. This is due to the high circulating levels of hormones in the mother's blood which cross the placenta to the baby. For the same reason a female child may have a whitish discharge from the vagina and even menstruate for a couple of days. The effect of the mother's hormones lasts only a few days after birth.

Maternal hormones crossing the placenta may be responsible for enlargement of the breasts in both male and female children which occurs usually around the fourth day. Do not interfere with the breasts in any way and they will return to normal size in a very short time as the level of hormones in the baby's blood returns to normal.

Rashes

One of the commonest rashes is heat rash. This is a red rash, each spot being about the size of a pin head. It appears in the skin where the baby is hottest and sweats most and is due to over-heating. The remedy is to let him cool off. Taking off a layer of clothing will help, as will using one less blanket. Never cover your baby in a waterproof coverlet that stops the air from getting to his body and letting the sweat evaporate.

Another common rash in newborn infants is a red, blotchy, raised rash with small white bumps like nettlerash (urticaria). This is a transient rash and never lasts longer than 10 minutes. It needs no treatment and you should not worry about it.

Babies get an assortment of rashes on the face, quite unpredictably. Most newborn babies have tiny white spots over the bridge of the nose and cheeks called milia. These spots are due to blockage of the oil and sweat glands and disappear of their own accord. They need no treatment and you should never squeeze them.

You should take any septic spot on your baby's skin seriously, because newborn babies have a low resistance to infection and it can spread. Tell your doctor, midwife or health visitor. Do not try proprietary products yourself.

Nappy rash

Nappy rash is better prevented than cured. You will minimize the chances of your baby developing nappy rash if you do the following:

1. Always clean your baby's skin gently with plain water. Only use soap at bathtime or when you top and tail him.
2. As soon as your baby's skin begins to look sore, stop using water and soap and use baby oil or baby lotion.
3. Never let your baby stay in a wet or soiled nappy.
4. If your baby's bottom begins to look sore, let him lie without a nappy for as long as possible so that the air gets to his skin. This allows the skin to dry out and regain its integrity.
5. If the skin appears red and sore, change over to a disposable nappy whose inner lining is one way and presents a dry surface to the baby's skin, or use one way nappy liners with your terry towelling nappies.
6. At each nappy change apply a thick, heavy baby barrier cream to the whole nappy area, taking care to include skin creases.
7. Minimize chafing by keeping your nappies thoroughly clean and soft. Wash them in soap powders and avoid detergents and enzyme cleaners.
8. Make sure the nappies are thoroughly rinsed.

If the rash does not respond to the above

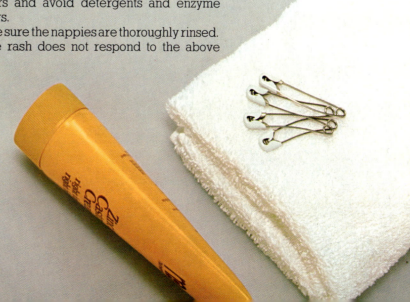

remedies, consult your midwife or health visitor as it may need more specialized treatment.

Ammonia dermatitis is a special form of nappy rash. It is caused by the presence of ammonia which results from the bacterial breakdown of urea. Urea is contained in your baby's urine and the bacteria are present in his stool. Obviously it can only happen if the stool and the urine are present on the skin for some time. You may find that when you change your baby's nappy after a night's sleep, it smells very strongly of ammonia but this does not mean that his diet disagrees with him or that his urine is 'strong'. You may also notice that the skin around the genital area is starting to get red. Typically in ammonia dermatitis the skin's creases are spared. If you do not treat the rash promptly it may spread to the whole of the nappy area. The skin may peel at the edges and shallow ulcers may form.

You should treat ammonia dermatitis in the way outlined for nappy rash, with one additional remedy. In the final rinsing water of your nappies, add one fluid ounce of vinegar to a gallon (30 ml to 5 l) of water. This will make the nappy slightly acid and inhibit the breakdown of urea to ammonia. The stools in bottle fed babies are alkaline and this helps the formation of ammonia. This is why ammonia dermatitis is more common in bottle fed babies than in breast fed babies.

Occasionally nappy rash may be caused by thrush which is a yeast. The infection usually starts in the baby's mouth where it appears as white patches on the cheeks, tongue and palate. It resembles milk curd but can be distinguished because it does not wipe off easily. As a result of the mouth infection, the yeast contaminates the stool and a rash may appear round the anus which spreads to involve the buttocks. It can be distinguished from ammonia dermatitis because it affects different areas. It is treated with a special ointment which eradicates fungus.

Cradle cap

Cradle cap is caused by oily scales piling up on the scalp, making the skin look greasy and crusty. It usually starts on the front of the head or the fontanelle and if left untreated may spread to involve large areas of the scalp, so it needs prompt treatment. It is caused by the tendency in most babies to produce a lot of grease on the scalp. One of the best remedies is to massage the scalp with a piece of cotton wool, soaked in baby oil. The scales will soften, loosen and slide off the baby's skin after a few minutes gentle

rubbing. Never try to lift an unsoftened scale with your finger nail or a comb. If the scales persist or leave a red patch see your health visitor.

Jaundice

One in three healthy newborn babies develops jaundice. This lasts a few days, then disappears and they are perfectly normal. It occurs if your baby's liver has not quite reached its peak efficiency and disappears when the liver matures – usually in 10 days.

The jaundice may be due to rhesus incompatibility (see page 31). If it is severe at birth, an exchange transfusion may be necessary to wash out all the mother's antibodies, the excessive bilirubin and to treat the baby's anaemia.

Sticky eye

Sticky eye is quite common in the first 48 hours of a baby's life and is nearly always due to some foreign substance getting into the eye during delivery. It could be just a drop of amniotic fluid or blood. Very often careful cleansing with a wet cotton wool swab will cure the condition. Start with the swab on the inside corner of the eye and move outwards. Then throw the swab away. Use a new swab for the other eye. You should always consult your doctor about sticky eye as a special antibiotic cream may be necessary if there is an infection. When your baby has sticky eye never lay her down on the side where the eye is affected as the unaffected eye could be contaminated from the mattress when she turns over. Treatment for sticky eye is always immediately effective.

Possetting and vomiting

Possetting is the regurgitation of a mouthful of food either during or just after a feed. Some babies posset quite often and some not at all. The ones who do posset do not seem to mind it, so you do not need to worry about it.

Some babies go a little further than possetting and tend to vomit from very early in their lives. If you watch your baby carefully you can tell if her vomiting is a sign of something serious. If she does not seem upset, if it doesn't cause a change in her normal behaviour, if she smiles and goes to sleep, then do not be concerned. Usually a baby only vomits that amount of feed which she has taken in excess of her needs. A baby rarely vomits a whole feed and can easily make up any deficit in the next 24 hours. With a bottle fed baby, always check the size of the hole in the teat if she starts to vomit. If the hole is too large she is probably getting too much milk too quickly; if the hole is too small, she will have to suck very hard to get her milk and may be swallowing a large quantity of air with it.

If vomiting is serious your baby will probably seem ill, miserable, lethargic and whimpering. She may have obvious spasms of pain when she screams and draws up her legs. She may refuse food, sleep a lot and resent being disturbed. As vomiting can quickly lead to dehydration if it is accompanied by diarrhoea, call your doctor immediately. Vomiting in a small baby always warrants immediate medical attention.

Other minor causes of worry

Epithelial pearls are two white spots on either side of the baby's hard palate. They are simply harmless collections of trapped skin cells. If you see them, do not worry, they are normal.

If your baby's cord does not separate in the first week, do not worry, keep it dry and dab with surgical spirit at each nappy change. Very few cords have not separated by three weeks. If you are worried consult your midwife.

You may notice that it is difficult for you to straighten your baby's legs. This is because she has been in a tightly curled up ball for some months inside your abdomen and for the first week or so she cannot straighten her legs because she needs time to unwind.

A small bulge or hernia may appear around your baby's umbilicus when she coughs or cries. This is a small split in the muscles of the abdomen but it is harmless and will probably close up before she is six months old. If you notice a hernia in the region of the scrotum or labium draw it to your doctor's attention immediately as it may need treatment later.

Most babies have some degree of tongue tie. This is due to the incomplete development of the tip of the tongue. It will eventually grow. Meanwhile it hardly ever interferes with sucking or speech development.

Babies' nails grow very quickly. During the first few days you should cut her nails straight across with a pair of scissors while she is asleep as it causes less disturbance to both of you. Keep your baby's nails well trimmed as she may scratch herself accidentally if they are too long.

To the mothers of most male children the foreskin seems tight and it is not unnatural to think of the troubles that may lie ahead for your son. However, what is a tiny hole at birth, grows, lengthens and widens over the next three or four years and it is rarely necessary to resort to surgery to enlarge it. Never try to force the foreskin back in a newborn baby. This will tear the skin and cause bleeding. Practically the only reason for circumcision during the first few days of a baby's life is religious. It is a common practice amongst Jewish and Muslim families. After your baby has been circumcised, a gauze dressing will be put round the end of the penis and you will be told how to remove the dressing, clean the wound and put on a new dressing. You should report any signs of infection or bleeding to your doctor.

First Aid
Giving a baby medicine

If your baby needs medicine, it will come in liquid form to be taken from a spoon or dropper. Whatever you use, make sure that it has been sterilized. With a dropper, take up the required amount into the glass tube. Insert the dropper in the corner of your baby's mouth and gently compress the rubber teat so that the medicine runs down the inside of your baby's cheek. Never do this while he is lying flat because swallowing will be difficult. If possible, cradle your baby in the crook of your left arm so that his head is at an angle and he is looking up at you.

With a spoon, if you gently open his mouth and slowly let the contents of the spoon flow into his mouth you should have no difficulty.

If you find both of these methods difficult, you might try dipping your clean little finger into the medicine and letting your baby suck on it.

Taking a temperature

If your new baby is feverish you should always consult your doctor. While he is visiting, take the opportunity to ask him to show you how to take your baby's temperature.

One of the ways of taking a baby's temperature is in his rectum but you need confidence and a co-operative baby for this. You may find it easier and it is just as efficient to take it in his armpit or groin, see illustration (below).

You can buy a thermometer that takes only thirty seconds to register the temperature accurately, so hold the thermometer in place for this length of time.

Babies frequently have a lower temperature than normal when they are ill. As you'd expect, a baby's normal temperature is the same as her mother's, i.e. 98.4 degrees Fahrenheit (36.9 degrees Centigrade) and it should remain so.

A new type of forehead thermometer consists of a strip of heat sensitive material which is held flush against the forehead for just fifteen seconds to obtain a reading. However, it should be used with caution as it does not give a precise reading.

(Below) There are two ways of taking your baby's temperature.
(1) To take it in his armpit, lay him on his back, without his vest, and insert the thermometer with one hand, whilst keeping it in place by holding down his arm with your other hand.
(2) To take it in his rectum, you really need two people. Lie him face downwards on the other person's lap. Make sure that you have a soft warm towel to lie him on and remove his nappy but leave his vest and top clothes on, so that he will not get cold. Lubricate the thermometer bulb with a little water or cream and then gently insert it into the rectum, for about 1 inch (2 cm). Keep your baby still with your left hand and hold the thermometer securely with your right hand.

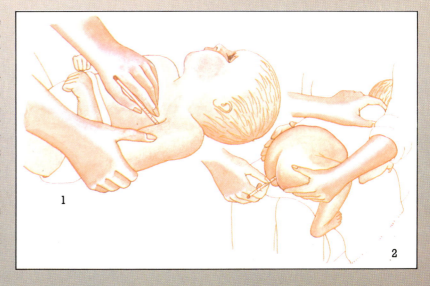

1

2

Father

No matter how good you are at making your husband feel included and at maintaining the closeness of your relationship, most husbands feel a bit left out. This is entirely understandable. Before the arrival of the baby, your relationship with your husband was the most important one in your life but now you feel yourself more as a mother than as a wife. This is biological and entirely to be expected.

Right from the moment you bring the baby home, you should try to make your husband feel included. He should be an active participant, not an observer. As far as his working timetable will allow he should be present at least one feed and bathtime and he should get used to bathing the baby himself, in the first few weeks if possible.

For a while at least, he should be patient if the house is not as tidy as it was, if his meals are not punctual and if you aren't your usual bright and breezy self.

You should set aside some time each day to spend alone with your husband. Be prepared to leave your baby occasionally in the evening to go out with your husband. If not, he may go without you.

You

Even if you are not the worrying kind, there are many things which happen in the first few days after your baby is born which may cause you concern. In the rather unstable emotional state most women find themselves in immediately after birth small worries can become artificially magnified.

In the first place, you may not experience that flush of mother love that you expected. Mother love may take some time to develop and you should certainly not feel you are emotionally inadequate if it is not instantaneous. In truth you may not be in control of your maternal responses to your baby. There is a sharp fall off in the level of circulating hormones in the body after delivery. This is a shock to the system which can take quite a long time to stabilize and to adjust to the low pre-pregnancy level of hormones. As part of this disturbance your maternal feelings may suffer. Be reassured that this is not uncommon and is natural.

Secondly, you may well be overawed with the responsibility of caring for such a small helpless human being. It takes time to get used to his needs and how to satisfy them.

(Below) Your partner should be an *active* father not one who just looks on. Most men, if encouraged, are keen to be involved in bringing up their baby and want to do everything you do for their new child. So include him, amd make sure he knows how much you value his participation.

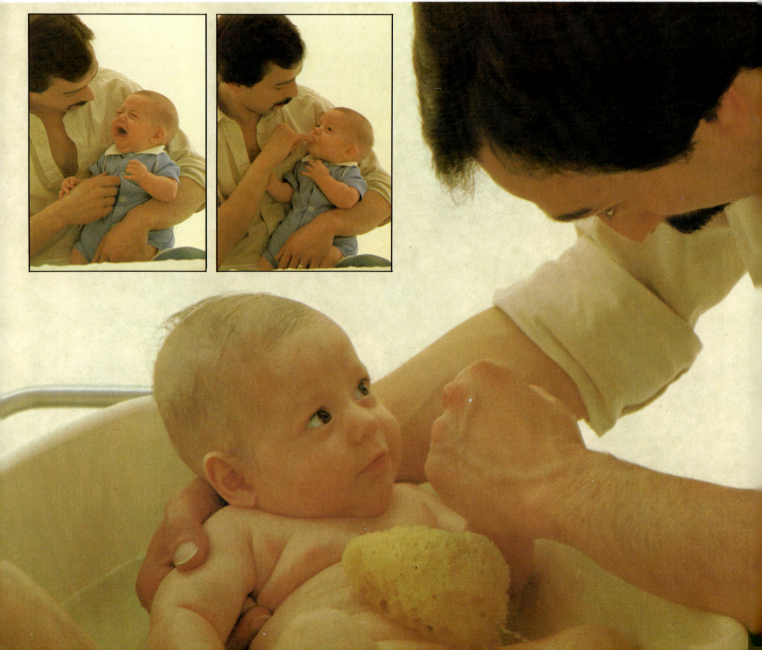

Anxiety

Probably the commonest anxiety felt by a new mother is whether she will be able to produce sufficient milk for her baby. Many hospitals are aware of this and are trying to overcome it. Some have a breastfeeding counsellor, so enquire about it. This anxiety usually begins as a lack of self-confidence, so that the mother goes into breast feeding already doubting that she can produce enough milk to satisfy her baby.

In an attempt to get the baby on to a settled feeding regime in the short time that he and his mother will be on the hospital ward, the nursing staff suggest a complementary feed with artificial milk from a bottle. This only worsens a woman's feelings of inadequacy. She comes to rely on the complementary feeds and suddenly they seem an attractive and easy way out. She abandons her breast feeding.

Problems which may seem insurmountable to you are often quite common, so it is a good idea to have a heart to heart chat with your midwife or health visitor to discuss the whole subject. They have helped many mothers through the early difficult stages and will often give you useful tips and emotional support that will keep you going.

One of the most useful pieces of advice is to stop test weighing. This involves weighing the baby on accurate scales before and after a feed. The difference between the two weighings is the number of ounces of milk he has taken. One test weighing is worthless and it can unnecessarily increase your anxiety. Before any useful conclusions can be drawn it should continue throughout 24 hours. Unless there is good reason for suspecting the baby is a poor feeder it should be avoided. You will also probably be told to take no notice of so-called 'average' weight gains. Every baby gains weight differently and many do not conform to the average. For every baby who gains weight faster than average, there is one who gains weight more slowly.

Anxiety about feeding and looking after your baby when you first get back home from hospital plus lack of sleep and fatigue, may result in a temporary fall-off of your milk supply. And if your well-behaved baby becomes more fretful when you get home you may be all too quick to blame it on your lack of milk.

To be positive, there are other things you can do to stimulate your own milk supply besides expressing milk from your breast.
□ Try to rest and relax as much as possible.
□ Eat a varied and well-balanced diet. If you like milk, drink a pint a day, though it is not necessary to do so. You can eat dairy products in whatever form you like.
□ Make sure that you take plenty of fluids and do not allow yourself to become thirsty. Before you start the feed, make sure that you have a drink by you, so if you become thirsty during the course of it you do not have to interrupt your baby's feeding by stopping to get a drink.

Do not worry about being tied to your baby's feeding times. There is no reason why you should not go out on your own to relax and enjoy yourself and let your baby have the occasional bottle. It is best if this can be your own expressed breast milk put into a bottle. Try not to give your baby a regular bottle, particularly in the first three weeks of breast feeding because your breasts need the constant stimulation of being completely emptied several times a day. There is no reason however why your baby should not have one artificial milk bottle each day.

Some women have a frank distaste for breast feeding and they may have difficulty in coming to terms with this without feeling guilty. There is absolutely no need to feel guilty. A woman's preference must be respected and she should never be forced to breast feed against her will. A loving mother feeding by bottle is far superior to an unhappy mother who breast feeds her baby with distaste.

Depression

With so many profound changes taking place in your life and inside your body, added to the sense of anti-climax which most women feel after their baby is born, it would be surprising if you did not feel a little depressed during the first few days. Nearly every woman is tearful some time during the first week after delivery and around the third day when the milk comes in there is a great tendency to break down and weep. The reason is that the hormonal changes taking place in your body make you emotionally very fragile. The irritability, tearfulness and depression you feel is not dissimilar from the mood change that many women experience in the week before menstruation. Considering that the hormonal changes which occur during the monthly menstrual cycle are fairly small in comparison, it is not surprising that you become easily upset.

The sense of anti-climax is one of the most important contributing factors. Nine months is a long time to wait, rehearse and build up to a grand event and suddenly it is all over. On the one hand you feel over-awed by the prospect of having a small, defenceless human being relying on you for everything and on the other you may feel no strong maternal instincts towards it. Perhaps you hoped for a boy and you had a girl. Your baby may not even seem attractive to look at. You may feel resentful of your husband who can escape the monotony of the day to day routine care of the baby by going off to work and only comes home for the best part. Any fatigue you feel can be exaggerated by dull, repetitive household chores like washing nappies and preparing feeds. You may resent the lack of intellectual challenges and the adult company you enjoyed in your job. In the early days, these routine chores which later become automatic and quickly completed, can take up so much of the day that there is no time left over for relaxation and distraction and you may feel that you are tethered to the house.

Fortunately, the attacks of depression which are common during the first few days after delivery, last a short time and can be explained. There is a light at the end of the tunnel for all

(Above) Everyone in the family should be your baby's friend. A sister can help to broaden her world and teach her many things you can't.

It's good for both of your children to have a loving person close to them other than you and your partner.

mothers and it is not so far away. At the end of two weeks you will probably be back to your normal self. Try not to think in the long term. Just deal with each day as it comes and forget about the problems that tomorrow may bring.

If you feel very strongly that you do not want to leave your baby, then invite friends to come and see you at home so that you do not feel that life is passing you by. It is even better for you if you can get a baby sitter so that you can spend several hours at a stretch away from home on your own, doing your own thing. If your husband is sensitive to your needs, he will encourage you to do this. It is very important when your life is so taken up with looking after the baby that you have a period when your privacy is not invaded.

A woman who does not find that her spirits are lightening at the end of two weeks but who continues to be always tired, easily upset, anxious about the baby and depressed about the future, is suffering from more than the typical post-natal blues. It means that she is severely depressed and should seek immediate medical help and treatment.

Your instinct

There are many babycare books that will tell you how to look after your baby. Much has been written as the result of years of experience and acquired wisdom. But remember that you are

the only expert about your baby. Before he is a month old, you will know things about him that no book can tell you. Information about baby care shouldn't restrict the way you look after your baby. It should liberate you to use your own maternal instincts and your own common sense, for which there is no substitute.

A new baby in the family

If you already have children, it is very important that you prepare them properly for the arrival of the new baby (see page 175).

Do not be upset if your children react in a rather disappointing way and avoid trying to force a reaction from them. There is plenty of time for them to get to know the baby and you should allow things to take their natural course. Remember that a small child may not have any idea how to react to a stranger in the house. You can be sure that he is feeling somewhat uncertain about his own place in your affections so you should try to make him feel secure by giving him an equal amount of attention to the baby when they are with you. Do not be surprised if your small child seems to treat the baby like a toy. Do not jump on him angrily for doing this but explain carefully that small babies are delicate and have to be treated gently. You will be surprised how quickly most children respond to this and become protective, quiet and very careful.

Help
Friends

Do not hesitate to call upon the services of a friend. Most friends are only too delighted to help out especially if your immediate family is not living close by. If your friend has a family of her own, all the better. She will be familiar with most of the things that are going to happen during the first few days and will not only be able to prepare you for them but will build up your confidence by telling you how to cope and reassuring you that most things work out in the end. Most women welcome the opportunity to help with looking after a new baby. Even with a grown up family, no woman loses her maternal instinct. What is more, her experience in bringing up her own children will minimize the minor hiccups and obstacles that you encounter and it will help you to get a more sensible perspective on your problems.

Midwife

There is quite an army of medical and ancillary medical help that you can call upon. The mainstay of this group is your midwife. She will probably call on you very regularly during the first week to ten days after your return from hospital. If you are having any problems, she will continue to call until she is satisfied that you are managing well. Never be afraid to discuss your fears and anxieties with your midwife. She is so experienced that she will very often give you a simple explanation which will immediately clarify and reassure. She will also be able to give you many practical tips which will make your routine more efficient, less repetitive and monotonous. If your midwife feels that you are not ready to take on the full burden of looking after your house and family, then she can arrange for a home help to come in and tide you over the early weeks, until your baby has settled down.

Relatives

The birth of a new baby is a very special circumstance and it puts special strains and burdens on you, your husband and children if you have any. You should not be afraid to seek help from whatever source you can. Your own mother will be the mainstay of this help and possibly your mother-in-law or other relatives. But before inviting a parent or relative to stay in your home, be sure that you get on with them and that your husband not only agrees but fully supports their coming to stay with you. Having help is important but it would be a pity if it formed the basis of a rift between you and your husband. Most women like to have their mothers with them at this time but do not invite your mother to stay without having a full discussion with your husband. As long as he finds it acceptable, your own wishes should prevail but he may wonder why you do not want his mother to stay. If it makes him feel better, suggest that his mother does come to stay but not immediately after you return home from hospital; a few weeks later. It is fair to give both grandparents the opportunity of looking after their new grandchild.

(Below) if you get on with your parents and parents-in-law, they can be a source of valuable help and advice (yes, sometimes it's useful), especially in sharing the work-load with twins. They widen your baby's circle of friends, too, and often have patience to spare when yours is exhausted.

Health visitor

A health visitor will take over visiting you when the midwife stops. You will not have to get in touch with her, she will be informed of your baby's birth and she will automatically come to see you about ten days after your discharge from hospital. With your first baby she will call regularly several times a week for three or four weeks and she will almost certainly leave you her 'phone number so that you can contact her between visits if you need her help. The health visitor is usually a nurse with a qualification in midwifery and training in child development. Her job is to look after the health and progress of you and your baby. She is very experienced in dealing with the problems of new mothers, so do not be shy and embarrassed to tell her about your problems and anxieties. No enquiry is too trivial or silly for her.

But try to be honest with your health visitor and do not be afraid to speak up if you disagree with her views. Most health visitors are very flexible and would not want to force you to do something which you instinctively felt was wrong. It is up to you not to give your health visitor misleading information. If you are worried about your milk supply, do not give the impression that you wish to start bottle feeding if all that you are asking for is moral support in continuing to breast feed. Be honest and you will get the best advice.

Baby sitters

Though you may be tired and have no desire at all to go out of the house during your first days home from hospital, it is important that you do. You need some time to yourself, a break in the routine of daily care of your baby which can be repetitive and sometimes monotonous. You also need to enjoy other people's company because you are on your own with the baby most of the time and while you love her, you may feel lonely and crave adult conversation.

If you do not have a relative or friend staying with you, you will want a baby sitter. It will be better for both if you give her a really good briefing. You should:
□ show her where all the baby equipment is for nappy changing, etc.
□ show her where the next feed and the bottle warmer is.
□ show her the general layout of your house so that she knows the location of the bathroom, kitchen and the baby's room.
□ tell her about any of the baby's peculiar likes, dislikes or individual habits.
□ warn the baby sitter if your baby tends to cry a lot. Most baby sitters do not mind walking up and down for an hour nursing your baby if they are warned about it.
□ try and have a conversation with your baby sitter before you actually fix a date and time. Make sure that you like the person and that you feel confident in her. It also gives your baby sitter a chance to refuse if she does not really wish to take your baby sitting on.
□ Remember that looking after a baby for only one evening is not as tedious for a baby sitter as it is for you who normally have to look after the baby 24 hours a day.
□ Remember that your baby comes to no harm whatsoever by your evening's absence.
□ Once you have decided on the baby sitter, have confidence that she will be able to deal satisfactorily with your baby no matter how fretful he is.

Being with your baby

Most women feel drawn to their babies most of the time. Even when the baby is asleep, it is irresistible not to peep at her sleeping in her cot. One of the handiest ways to have your baby with you most of the time is to carry her around from room to room in a carry cot or a Moses basket.

Some mothers crave closer contact than this and want to be nursing and carrying their babies much of the time. After all, in primitive tribes, a baby is carried around strapped to her mother's

(Below) A baby who's close to you for much of the day is often a contented baby. One of these baby carriers (there's another type that goes on your back) makes it easy to get on with chores while still holding your baby near to you.

body from the moment she's born. It is a perfectly natural thing to do and if you want to do it, buy a special baby sling which you wear around your trunk like a harness with your baby tucked safely inside it. It is probably safer and more enjoyable for the baby to be carried on the front, as she will be able to hear the reassuring sound of your heart beating.

You should not carry your baby around in a sling when you are working, or where there is the possibility you may bump or knock her, or where an accident might happen.

Even if you don't like the idea of a baby sling, you should look upon nursing times as very special. In the first few days nursing times are those hours whenever your baby is awake because she will probably sleep 16 out of the 24. Use these times to really get to know each other.

A baby is never too young to participate in games. In the first few days, these can be songs, rhymes, tickling, patting, rubbing. The important thing is for your baby to associate you with pleasure and diverting activities. These very early games if continued will become learning times for your baby.

The first game your baby ever plays with you is feeding. You will notice after a few days that the baby does more than suck at your breast. It is obviously bringing her pleasurable sensations and very soon she starts to explore these with her fingers and hands. She may push and knead your breasts. You will notice that this helps the let down reflex of the milk. She quickly learns

this and does some more kneading. So she is not only playing rather a rewarding game, she is taking her first steps in learning.

Registration

There is a certain amount of official red tape that you have to deal with as a result of your baby's birth. The birth must be notified to the local medical officer of health within 36 hours. This is done by the hospital authorities, or if you have your baby at home, it is usually done by your doctor of midwife.

Every birth must be registered. Some hospitals arrange for this to be done through the local Registrar, so ask if your baby has been registered before you go home. If your baby is born at home, your husband must go to the Registrar's office within six weeks of the birth. However, the time limit allowed varies from country to country so consult your health visitor who will be able to advise you.

Once your baby has been registered, you will receive a copy of her birth certificate, plus a card to take along to your general practitioner so that she can be added to your doctor's list as a National Health Service patient.

You will get a second card from the Department of Health and Social Security which allows you to buy baby foods cheaply and get free vitamins from your local child health clinic.

You may qualify for milk at a cheap price but you should check this at your local post office.

(Above) You are your baby's first and most important playmate. Time spent just enjoying yourselves together is time well spent. It will increase your sense of fulfilment and give your baby a sense of his own self. It will cement your relationship with your baby and provide a firm foundation for the future.

LOOKING AND LEARNING

Crying

Most new babies seem to cry a lot. No one knows why but it is not surprising, since crying is their only way of communicating. Most cries mean that a baby wants comfort of some sort and you should always give him the comfort he needs. For the first few months of life you must not worry if you will be encouraging bad habits or spoiling your baby by picking him up when he cries. Instead you should ask yourself what he needs and then try to satisfy him. If you ignore his cries you will never understand what his needs are but by answering them you will gradually get to know his likes and dislikes, what pleases and displeases him, how much cuddling he needs, if he likes sucking a great deal, etc. Probably most important of all, if you answer his cries he learns that help is near at hand and you are the person who helps him. In this way, you will start building up a relationship together and you will be teaching your son patterns of behaviour that will form the basis for relationships with other people in later life.

A newborn baby has a very restricted pattern of behaviour. He can be awake and quiet, awake and crying, or asleep. It is as well to be prepared for your newborn baby to cry quite a lot. If you are lucky, yours may not and you will have an easier time than you expected but most do cry and it is normal. If you expect it and treat it as normal, you will be less concerned and worried about the cause. Consequently, you will find it easier to cope with.

Usually within a couple of days, a mother will become attuned to her own baby's cry. She learns to recognize a range of different cries, each with a different meaning. Within the first two weeks she will be familiar with the cry for hunger, the cry which signals discomfort, the cry for pain, the cry for irritation and the cry that simply means bad temper. If you are an observant mother, you and your child can carry on this dialogue quite efficiently.

You should not expect your baby to have acclimatized or to have developed any sort of routine for three or four weeks and it will take you at least this long to discover what sort of person he is. Round about this time, the frequency with which a baby cries usually diminishes. Most mothers find it easy to cope with a crying baby during the day when they are feeling strong and sympathetic. It is much more difficult if your sleep is interrupted. Few babies under six weeks of age sleep through the night and you should be prepared to lose quite a lot of sleep in comforting your baby.

If you have a baby who wakes between feeds during the night, you may find that you cope better if the baby's cot is right next to your bed. This way you will be spared having to stumble half asleep several times during the night to where your baby is sleeping (see page 76).

It is not uncommon for babies to have one long crying spell, anything up to a few hours a day. Sometimes this occurs in the early evening, just before or after the evening feed but sometimes

(Below) Attention from you is a panacea for most of your baby's distress. Genuine sympathy, sincere interest and the obvious desire to make things better for her, do more to calm and comfort your baby than anything else. A cuddle, a gentle word, a soothing hand and a kiss are often tantamount to magic. You have it, so use it.

it can occur during the night. Once you have made sure that your baby is dry, comfortable and not hungry, the remedy is simply to nurse him. Never let your young baby cry for a long time unattended.

It is very difficult for a mother to accept that there is not always a cause for crying. Many understandably assume that if a baby is crying there is something seriously wrong but you will find that after countless occasions when you have excluded the common causes of crying, you are forced to conclude that your baby just feels like it.

Causes

There are several common causes for crying in the first few months. Crying is often attributed to wind but I am not convinced that the reasoning behind this is sound (see page 79). It is possible however that as the baby's digestive system starts to get going, things will occasionally go less smoothly.

A bubble of air when trapped in an adult's intestine may cause spasm of the section of muscle behind it, as the muscle contracts down hard in an effort to push the air along the intestine. This spasm of intestinal muscle gives rise to intestinal colic. Colic is a pain which comes in waves, beginning with slight pain which rises to a crescendo and then dies away. In a lesser way, this type of pain may occur in babies. If the baby periodically draws up his legs sharply to his abdomen, it could suggest a coincidental spasm of pain. However, not too much importance should be attached to this because drawing up his legs is the natural thing for a baby to do while he is screaming.

Occasionally, crying bouts can take a more severe and prolonged form during which the baby draws up his legs as described and positively screams without any apparent reason. As it is thought to be due to wind in the bowel and it usually stops quite suddenly when the baby reaches three months of age, it has been termed 'three month colic'. You can obtain a special medicine from your doctor but it will end and usually quite dramatically at three months.

Most babies, of course, cry when they are hungry. If your baby is crying for his food, then you should feed him. One of the dangers of leaving your baby to cry when he is hungry is that while he is crying he will inevitably swallow air. This will cause discomfort and will prevent him from taking a full feed. He will, therefore, wake up early and cry for the next one. Also, prolonged crying will exhaust him and he may be too tired to feed properly by the time you feel it suits you. You will then be in the vicious circle of him taking too little food to satisfy him until the next feed, early waking and further crying.

Being flexible does not mean that you should feed your baby every time he cries. If he cries after a feed, the probability is that he wants you to nurse him. After all, babies like company just as much as we do. He may be thirsty rather than hungry in which case he will enjoy a drink. Try half to one ounce (15-30 ml) of plain boiled water. Alternatively, the feed may not have fully satisfied his desire to suck, in which case a dummy will comfort him. Do not worry about using a dummy, particularly at night. Your baby's happiness and comfort and your sleep count for more than disapproving comments about the use of dummies. If your baby seems happy sucking one, keep several in the sterilizing unit so that you always have a clean one ready and never leave home without one. Resist the temptation to use a reservoir dummy filled with a sweet drink. It encourages a sweet tooth and later on when your baby develops teeth, it may contribute to tooth decay.

Tiredness is a common cause of crying. Many babies keep the habit of crying when they are tired until they are four or five years old. It can be very difficult to calm an overtired baby despite your crooning, walking and rhythmic nursing. He may try to tell you that he simply wants to lie down by wriggling in your arms. When he is a bit older he will arch his back. Once he is laid down still, after gentle singing and patting to calm him down, he will fall asleep with relief.

It is said that babies cry when they are wet and dirty. As your baby gets older you may find that he is fastidious and cries even only when slightly soiled. On the other hand, some babies seem not to notice at all. However, lying in a wet or soiled nappy will encourage nappy rash and ammonia dermatitis (see page 85).

Dealing with crying

A commonly quoted philosophy is – if a baby is clean, dry, well fed and winded, then he is all right, so let him cry. I cannot stress how strongly I am against this philosophy. In my opinion a baby should never be left to cry. Babies learn lessons very quickly, especially unpleasant ones. It will not take your baby long to learn that no-one takes any notice of his pleas for attention and that there is no loving response when he asks for it. If love and care and later, friendship, are denied him then he will stop asking for them. A baby's pattern of behaviour towards mother, father, family and friends is probably determined in the first year of life and his ability to form relationships with others may be seriously damaged by what has happened to him in the early months. If friendship and affection is denied him, you may be encouraging him to grow up to be withdrawn and shy. He may be repulsed by displays of affection and overtures of friendship. The model for behaviour that your baby will remember for the rest of his life is his early relationship with you. A child under one year old cannot be spoiled enough. He is not being spoiled, on the contrary, he is learning about loving human behaviour.

Beyond this natural desire for mother love, there are some babies who can only be described as over-demanding, so demanding that their mothers eventually become short-tempered, fatigued and resentful. If you have an over-demanding baby, there will certainly be some occasions when you will gladly do anything to stop him crying and you should not consider it abnormal if you nearly get to the point of doing so. It is particularly important for mothers of such babies to have some time on their own. You must get a baby sitter or a friend or relative to look after your baby for at least one half day a week so that you 'get away from it all'.

If you are not careful, an over-demanding baby who wants to play with you more during the night than during the day may so disturb your sleep that you find yourself going through your daily routine in a daze. If this is the case, it is essential you take a break. You should arrange for your husband to do a night duty for you and you should have a lie-in on a regular basis. If your husband's work makes this difficult, have someone who can give you a few nights off to stay for a few days. If there is no other way, arrange for a relative to come and live in while you go and stay with friends, although this alternative is, of course, not open to you if you are breast feeding.

It should not surprise you if a child demands more of your attention than usual when he is ill. Most sick babies need more nursing and comfort than usual. You are quite right to respond to his increased demands.

Difficult babies

There are some babies who are more than over-demanding. They are bright, active and sleep very little. They are classically intelligent, interested in everything that is going on around them and very affectionate. You may pay the penalty of losing a great deal of sleep at night but you will be more than rewarded during the day.

I think it must be said that the standard advice given in baby books about bedtime routines with a feed, a drink, a story, a game or a song, putting the baby down in her cot, saying goodnight and leaving will almost certainly not work for this kind of active child. If you are prepared for this, you will feel less frustrated and inadequate. You must make getting sufficient sleep for yourself one of your priorities. Many baby books seem loath to give advice that puts the parents before the baby but if you are having recurrent sleepless nights you really must start thinking about yourself or you may crack up.

One of the reasons why there seem to be more and more babies who are wakeful at night is that there are more mothers working. Because of his mother's day time absence the baby wants to take advantage of her presence at night. If this is your problem, do not be too rigid about the time your baby goes to sleep. There is a certain amount of contact that he wants with you and he will not sleep happily until he has had it. Also, let your child go to sleep where he is happiest and most comfortable. This may be lying on the couch next to you. I cannot see any reason why this is wrong. There is nothing magical about bedrooms or beds.

If your child is awake much of the night, do not feel pressurized into doing what you think you ought to do. Do what your instincts tell you. If you are distressed by hearing your child cry for any length of time, try taking him into bed with you. Most children fall asleep within minutes if they can feel and smell the closeness of their parents. Your child will come to no harm and the whole family will get more sleep. I really do not think you should worry about forming bad habits in this case. Sleepless nights are much too high a price to pay for having a well-trained baby.

So while interrupted sleep may temporarily become a way of life, minimize your suffering. Your baby may demand a lot from you but he is not abnormal. He is one of a great number of demanding but very loving babies. You may find things very hard at the time and very wearing but as your baby grows up you will get back all the love that you lavished on him in more than full measure.

Sleeping

There is no standard sleep pattern for a baby. After the age of about one month, when she is eating larger meals, you may find that your baby sleeps for longer periods of time at one stretch, even that she sleeps for more hours out of 24 than she did when she was younger. Conversely, your baby may sleep less and less as she grows older. By the time she is six or eight months old, you may find that she can stay awake most of the day without apparent tiredness and get by on one or two short sleeps. Your baby will sleep as long as she needs to and you need have no fears about your baby not getting enough sleep, or about sleeping too much. Nor should you listen to the old wives' tale that a baby needs to sleep to grow and if she does not sleep her brain will become tired. There is no truth in either belief. There is no way that a baby will stay awake when she needs sleep. She will go to sleep anywhere.

During the first month, it sometimes helps your baby to settle down to sleep if you wrap her fairly tightly in a shawl or a blanket so that her arms and legs are held securely before putting her down in the cot. This is logical because when she was in your uterus, your baby's body was firmly swathed in a strong bag of muscle. Most babies are comforted if they experience a similar sensation for the few weeks after birth. Later on your baby will find this swaddling frustrating because she will want to move her arms and legs freely. In the early stages, your baby will not be physically equipped to move or turn over into the position which she finds most comfortable. To begin with try laying your baby down on her side. Later, when her arms and legs are freely mobile, you should lay her down on her front or her back. There is a general preference for laying a baby down on her stomach so that any posset will run out of her mouth rather than running back down her throat, which might make her gag or choke. Whatever position you lay your baby down in, the chances of her suffocating are virtually nil. A baby will always move her head from a position in which she finds breathing difficult to one in which breathing is

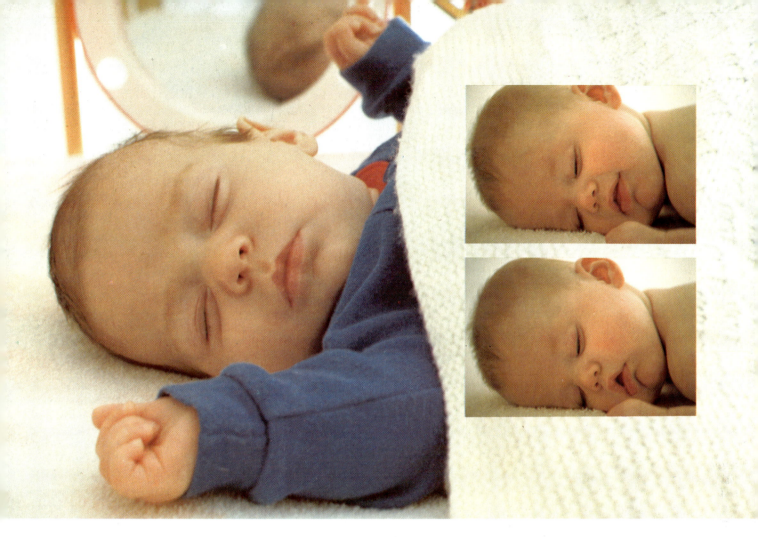

easy. For the first few months it is as well not to use a pillow in case her head sinks in and she finds it difficult to move it.

While you may feel safer with your baby lying on her stomach, look forward to the time when your baby may lie awake for quite a long time. If she is lying on her stomach and has not yet learned to turn herself over, she will have less interesting things to look at and absorb her attention than if she were lying on her back. So if your baby is contentedly lying awake, she will be even more contented lying on her back when her field of vision will be wider. At this stage you should try putting toys of interesting colour, shape and noise on the side of the cot and mobiles suspended from the ceiling above it.

Choosing the place where your baby sleeps should be entirely a matter for your own taste and convenience. There is no absolute need for a baby to have a room of her own. On the other hand, the house will be a tidier place if you keep most of her clothes and equipment in one place. Another advantage is that with your baby sleeping in a separate room from you, her minor disturbances of sleep will not wake you.

But many parents find it easier during the first few months of a baby's life to have her sleeping in a cot in their own room. This allows you to feed and nurse your baby during the night with the least possible disturbance to you and your husband. If you are breast feeding and keep your baby's cot by your bed, you need not even get out of bed unless you have to change her nappy.

At one time, breast feeding your baby in bed during the night was frowned upon, mainly because of the possible danger of overlying. Over-lying is the term used for a mother lying against her baby's face and preventing her from breathing. But most infants in the less sophisticated countries have been fed this way for thousands of years without coming to harm so it is obviously not a real hazard. There is absolutely no reason why you should not do it, especially if it gives you both a comfortable night's sleep.

Try not to be an obsessive parent at night, lying awake for your baby's every snuffle. Babies make lots of odd noises during the night and may even cry for a short while but try to wait a minute or two to see if the disturbance is a temporary one. After a short time, her crying may stop and she will go back to sleep. This not only has the advantage of letting you continue your rest but helps her to go for longer periods between feeds.

Also, do not be too fanatical about where your baby goes to sleep. There is absolutely no reason why she should have to go to sleep in one place every night. This is particularly applicable to babies who are wakeful and cry for long periods if left alone. If necessary let them stay with you but do not let this stop you from doing what you want to do or being where you want to be. Be flexible.

One of the good things about this flexible attitude to sleeping is that it gets your baby used to household disturbances. If you want to spend an evening watching television and you have the baby in the carrycot with you, you should not turn down the sound for fear of disturbing her. Start like this and your baby will grow accustomed to going to sleep even when surrounded by quite a lot of noise.

(Above) Babies are happy lying on their back or their front to sleep but they do not need a pillow. They vary in the length and type of sleep they need and may, just like adults, have dreams, as the inset pictures show.

Mixed feeding

There is no fixed time for all babies to start mixed feeding but it is rarely necessary before four months. Every baby is different and there is no rule which can apply to your baby. As with every other aspect of baby development, you must let your baby give you the lead and your response should be tailored to fit your baby's needs alone. Go into this phase of your baby's development with an experimental attitude. Be prepared to try different things before you find out what works best. On the subject of food your baby will not be slow to show you strong likes and dislikes. Follow the direction in which she leads you but do not expect too much from her.

How and when to begin

Start slowly and only introduce one new food at a time. You should give your baby a few days breathing space on one new food before you start another. You should proceed along these lines for a month or so until your baby gets used to mixed feeding. If a new food brings your baby out in a rash, or obviously does not suit her, then leave it out of her diet and go on to another. Never, however, blame a new food for a worrying illness in your child. It is unlikely to be the cause and you should consult your doctor so that your baby's illness can be properly diagnosed. If for any reason your baby seems fractious, or not her usual self, wait until she is well again before you give her another food.

In the beginning, a teaspoonful or two of solid food such as cereal may be all your baby wants, so always start with small quantities. You can increase the amount as your baby gets used to the taste and feel of solid food. She will almost certainly indicate in some way when she is ready for more, so gradually increase the quantities you give her. Do not hurry this process. Babies should never be given or forced to take large quantities of food of any kind, especially fattening starchy foods such as cereals. The result will be a fat baby and you should do your utmost to avoid this. Fat babies become fat children and later, fat adults. A baby rarely gets fat on a milk diet but the danger time is when you start to introduce solid food. Your baby may show a preference for fattening foods but do not be tempted to give her more than she needs. Give second helpings of vegetables and fruit and meat, fish, eggs and cheese but not of cereal, bread and biscuits. A baby does not need any added sugar or salt.

Many babies take their food slowly when they go on to mixed feeding. This is because feeding is pleasant and babies are inclined to make it into a playtime. Food is lovely and messy to play with and spoons banged on plates make interesting noises. Your baby's tardiness may irritate you if you have another job to go on to. Plan your day so that meal times can be extended and once your baby has got the hang of feeding herself, let her take as long as she likes. At the beginning, you can speed things up by giving your baby a spoon to feed herself while you have another spoon with which you get most of the food into her while she is amusing herself.

You can start giving solid food at any of the feeds in the 24 hours as a baby has no sense of time, be it night or day. Many mothers like to start with the 10 a.m. feed because the house is quiet and they can give the baby their full attention. It is better to give the new food in the middle or at the end of the feed. It is quite a good idea to take the edge off your baby's hunger before you start feeding her solids, otherwise she may become frustrated because she cannot get food down into her stomach fast enough. Thus many babies will refuse food from a spoon at the beginning of a feed, whereas they will take it quite greedily in the middle or the end.

As your aim is to have your baby eating the same meals as your family, it seems sensible to start off by giving her foods which correspond with normal mealtimes.

The baby who is thriving on milk (and if they are being bottle fed on formulated cow's milk they will be having vitamin supplements from the age of one month, see page 102) can start on mixed feeding at any age between four and six months. You should not leave it later than this because neither breast nor cow's milk will give the baby sufficient iron. If you go on feeding her on milk alone after six months, she runs the risk of becoming anaemic. Foods rich in iron are egg yolk, meat, liver and green vegetables.

With a breast fed baby, a little boiled formula thickened with no more than half a teaspoonful of cereal is a good way to start supplementing breast feeds if your baby still seems hungry after a feed. The general principle for starting on new foods is to try one teaspoonful of solids after one feed only per day. Do not think of this supplementary food as in any way replacing your breast milk. It is not. It is to keep your baby happy while your milk supplies are increasing. A bottle fed baby should start receiving solid food at about the same time as a breast fed baby and at first you can simply give a milk bottle which is slightly thickened as mentioned above by the addition of cereal, then go on to solids. Alternatively, you can add one teaspoonful of cereal to formula in a bowl at the end of a feed.

Preparing your baby's food

When your baby first goes on to solids, the food should be the texture of a thick cream. Avoid the cloying mixture of thick mashed potatoes as this may make your baby gag and cough. Babies tend to be particular at the weaning stage and once they have had an unpleasant experience with food, they will refuse it for a long time. Always examine the food for lumps and remove them if your baby finds them unpleasant or difficult to swallow. Try not to use foods that contain skins unless they can be puréed down to a fine mush. A baby may refuse food that contains the skin of peas.

To prepare your baby's food you can use a liquidizer or a Mouli. A liquidizer will give you a purée, the thickness of which you can adjust by

(Below) The priorities at mealtimes are that the baby should be fed and that you should both enjoy it. Messiness really doesn't matter. Let your baby feel the food and play with it. As long as some of it reaches his mouth you can finish the job off when he's done.

adding water, gravy or milk. You should take the precaution of sieving fibrous or stringy foods such as meat, or the stalks of green vegetables.

If you use tinned foods, wash the top of the can with boiling water first and use a clean tin opener. Always wash your hands before you start and use a clean surface. If you use leftover food make sure that it is resterilized by reheating it to full boiling point. You need not sterilize plates, dishes, cups and spoons. They can be washed along with your other dishes and left to drip dry. Do not use a tea towel as it may harbour germs. If you are using a beaker with a lid, make sure that you clean the spout and lid very carefully and sterilize them once a day.

If you have not already started mixed feeding, you will notice that around four months your baby will start to chomp and bite on anything which is put into his mouth. He starts making real chewing movements at about the age of six months. This means that he is ready to have foods that are more interesting than liquids. He will probably welcome foods of varying textures (but without lumps) from a spoon and also foods that he can bite and chew on such as crusts and rusks, or a piece of peeled apple or pear. This is quite an important part of his development. By

(Left) As soon as your baby is moving around you can relax your sterilizing routine and work on 'domestic cleanliness'. This means your baby can be much more active about feeding.

It's important to encourage this phase of his development, even if he's only holding on to the spoon, so don't be fussy.

gnawing and chewing on hard foods, he is exercising his jaw and making sure that the muscles of chewing are well developed. By about six months your baby will be able to hold a crust in his hand and guide it into his mouth. Once he has reached this stage, never leave him eating alone in case he bites off a large lump and gags or chokes.

A baby does not develop a sense of taste before the age of about six months. If you introduce mixed feeding at three or four months, you are in a position to guide him towards tastes of foods that are good for him. These include proteins (meat, fish, cheese and eggs) and fresh fruit and vegetables. A baby does not need any added sugar or salt. Do not add these to foods because you think it will taste better and try not to introduce foods which contain sugar such as biscuits, cakes, fruit syrups, chocolate or sweets. Your baby does not need them and it will help you to control sugar when your child is older. Choose a brand of rusks which have no sugar and get into the habit of checking food labels for sugar content.

You will probably also notice that your baby's appetite seems to slow down after the age of six months. This is because his rate of growth diminishes at this time and his appetite reflects his rate of growth. A baby's appetite is greatest during the first six months of his life, when he needs more calories per pound of body weight than a man doing heavy physical work.

Here is a run-down of the vitamins your baby will need according to what milk he is taking and where they can be obtained from:

Breast milk – contains sufficient vitamin A, B and C but insufficient vitamin D. Your baby should be given vitamin D supplement in the form of cod or halibut liver oil or concentrated vitamin drops as soon as your doctor advises.

Cow's milk – contains enough vitamin A and B, but insufficient vitamin C and D. Should not be given to babies under 6 months. Vitamin drops can be obtained from your health centre and provide all the extra vitamins that your baby is likely to need. When giving fruit and vegetable juice:

☐ never give in the concentrated state. Always dilute with water.

☐ never boil as it destroys the vitamin C.

☐ never prepare before you are going to use it because vitamin C is destroyed very quickly if it is exposed to air.

☐ never give rose hip syrup undiluted or in a miniature feeder as it contains a lot of sugar which can weaken your baby's teeth.

Formula – contains enough vitamin A, B and C and may contain sufficient vitamin D. Check with your health visitor whether you should be giving vitamin D supplement.

There is no need to continue giving your child vitamin supplements once he is eating a fully balanced diet, e.g. one pint of milk a day, fresh fruit, meat, fish, egg or cheese daily and fruit juices or fresh vegetables. Your baby will only be having his full quota of vitamins if these foods are freshly prepared. A baby who is weaned on to tinned, strained foods is not taking a really balanced diet and will need extra vitamins. Do not overdose your child with vitamins, give exactly the manufacturers' recommended dose. If you miss giving a dose on one day, do not double up on the next. This is particularly important with vitamin D as it is possible to give a baby too much and make him ill.

If your tap water is not fluoridated, fluoride drops can be given at around six months as an early start in preventing tooth decay. Give ¼ mg daily but don't worry if a dose is missed.

Completion of weaning

The first step you and your baby will take towards complete weaning is the introduction of food containing lumps. Lumpy foods are only intended for the second six months of your baby's first year.

Don't worry if your baby refuses lumpy food at the first try. This is quite natural. You should leave it for a day or two and then have another go. Each time he refuses, leave it for a short interval and then try again. Be patient and keep trying until he starts to enjoy champing on the lumps in his food.

At about nine months your baby will become a very active participant at feed times, so do give him his own spoon as soon as he shows that he wants to take one from you. It does not matter if he does not use it to feed himself, let him just hold it and bang it on his high chair. He is becoming familiar with it and after watching you feed him with a second spoon he will soon realise what it is for and try to imitate you.

There are special baby spoons, which have the bowl at right angles to the handle but they are only an in-between stage and he can learn to use an ordinary spoon properly without them.

As soon as you start to introduce solid food you should encourage your baby to use his hands as feeding implements. Even if he just paddles about in the food and then puts his fingers into his mouth he is learning about feeding himself.

A little later, introduce him to 'finger foods'. To make the food easy to pick up, cut it into cubes or squares, or dice and grate it. He will find his mealtimes varied and exciting if you offer squares of cheese, cubes of bread and butter, shredded carrot, pieces of peeled apple or pear, or slices of banana. While your child is interested and absorbed in these easy-to-grasp solid foods, you can feed him the puréed or mashed food from a spoon.

Never try to make your baby eat anything that he does not want. He will probably refuse many foods which you know to be good for him but there is always an alternative which is just as nutritious. Never try to force your baby to finish up the last morsel in the dish because you think it is the correct amount he should have. If your baby is finished and will not eat any more, take the plate away and never force your baby to sit in the hope that he will eat the last little bit.

Do not try to make your baby eat what you think are suitable food combinations. You may

(Right and below) Finger foods are a good way to introduce your baby to feeding herself.

This means you have to prepare her food so that she can pick it up easily with her fingers – cubes of apple, slices of cheese, 'soldiers' of bread, etc.

put his first course and his pudding in the different compartments of his feeding dish but he may eat his pudding first and then his first course, or he may even mix the two. There is no reason why he should not. The important considerations are that he gets the food and he is happy while he is getting it. Always expect your baby to make a mess and take the precaution of covering areas that you do not want soiled, then turn a blind eye to any mess he makes.

Some schedules and guides

☐ Rice can be given as early as 2 months if you really want to (Chinese children are given rice this early)
☐ Barley at 3 months
☐ Soft fruits at 4 months
☐ Vegetables at 5 months
☐ Meat, eggs, citrus fruit, wheat at 6 months

Suggestions for a 6 month old (in addition to regular milk feeds)

Morning: infant cereal mixed with milk (usually about 2 tbsp)
Midday: mashed banana or puréed apple (2-3 tbsp)
Afternoon: mashed or strained vegetables (2-3 tbsp)

Suggested feeding for a 12 month old
Morning: cereal mixed with milk; ½ slice toast; 2-3 tbsp fruit
Snack: ¼ cup fruit juice
Midday: 1-2 oz hamburger chopped up; 2 tbsp green beans; 1-2 tbsp mashed potato; milk
Snack: small glass of milk; rusk
Evening: ¼ cup cottage cheese or yogurt; ½ slice of bread; slice of fresh fruit; milk

Hair washing

Most babies develop a profound dislike of hair washing when they are about nine months old and unless handled successfully, this can remain a problem for many months to come.

What parents usually do not understand is that babies are afraid of getting water, rather than soap, into their eyes, so you should never splash your baby's face with water. A baby is usually afraid of having water poured directly on to her head and never try by force to show her that there is nothing to be afraid of. If she is crying and thrashing about, there is a good chance that you will get soap and water in her eyes and you will have confirmed her worst fears. Once she has started to struggle, give up. Leave shampooing for three or four weeks. You can keep her hair quite clean enough by removing bits of food from it with a flannel or sponge and brushing it with a soft brush dampened in water to stop it looking greasy.

To avoid these problems, try sitting your baby with her back towards the basin. She will be happiest sitting on your lap. Wet a flannel with warm water from the basin and then wet her hair by wiping the flannel over it. Pour a little non-sting baby shampoo in your hand and then rub it into her head to get a lather. Rinse the shampoo off her hair with the wet flannel and with her head tilted back, no water need ever go over any part of her face. If by chance it does, have a dry towel by you to wipe it away immediately. Shampoo guards which fit over the head and provide a barrier against water and shampoo can be bought.

You could try making hair washing into a game by lathering the hair into funny shapes and then showing them to your child in the mirror. She may well want to join in the fun herself. However, if she really hates it, it is best not to do too much touching or rinsing.

(Below) The charts show the average weight and height gains for a child during the first 12 months. The three bands are for small, medium and large babies. These are average measurements. They have been calculated from statistics of the fastest growing and the slowest growing children and the range of 'normal' is very wide. In fact, the 'average' child does not exist. It is dangerous to compare your child with the average and while it is said that on average a child should have doubled her birth weight at six months and trebled it at a year, we must remember that it is only true for the child of average birth weight.

Growth and development

Growth and development are two entirely different processes. Growth simply means an increase in size. Development means an increase in complexity. It is obvious therefore that growth is easier to measure than development. So wide is the range of normal development that very few doctors would be prepared to define what normality is.

Growth

Different parts of your baby's body grow at different rates. At birth the head is large in proportion to the rest of the body and during the first 12 months its circumference increases around 5 inches (12.7 cm). During the next 11 years, it will only increase about 3 inches (7.6 cm). In parallel with the rapid rate of growth during the first six months, your baby will increase rapidly in length and then will gradually slow down. The proportions of your baby's body, however, will change markedly during her first 18 months and continue to do so until they reach their final adult proportions at about 18 years of age.

If your child is eating well and does not contract a severe illness, there is nothing you can do to affect her rate of growth as it is controlled by hormone glands and her potential size is genetically determined.

A severe illness or gross under-nourishment will slow down your child's rate of growth. Temporary interruptions of eating will not harm your child at all. She will make up her losses very quickly. This also applies to growth rate.

As the growth rate is faster in the spring and slower in the autumn, so you must study a child over a period of a year to see if it has been changed.

Weight gain

It is possible to construct a weight gain chart which plots the weight of a child against its age in weeks and length in inches (see left). However, I should like to stress that regularity of weight gain is more important than the amount so you should not be distressed if your baby's weight gain does not correspond exactly with the chart. Much more important is a sudden change in the slope of the curve. For instance, it may suddenly flatten off and this suggests that your baby is being underfed. Changes in the long term are more important than short term changes. In other words, it is the trend that you should note.

Development

No two babies develop at the same rate or in the same way. It follows that the rate of development of different babies should not be compared. Your baby is not abnormal because she is not developing as fast as another baby of the same age. She may be developing quite normally for herself. Your baby's development depends on many unique inter-related factors.

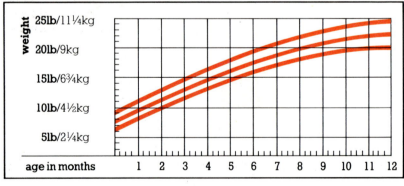

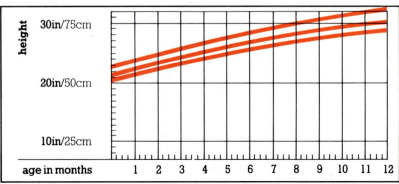

However, there are certain general principles which can be applied to development process in all babies:

☐ while babies develop at different rates, milestones are reached in the same order.

☐ development does not proceed at a constant pace. It is continuous but it slows down and speeds up. All children experience developmental spurts when they may take great leaps forward. These spurts may be followed by periods of slow development.

☐ a child makes progress not only in what she does, but how she does it. In other words, her degree of skill may increase.

☐ a baby develops as fast as the brain and nervous system are developing and no faster. So walking can only be learned when the parts of the brain associated with walking are mature.

☐ as a general rule, a baby has to lose a primitive reflex movement before she can acquire a skill. In other words, she must lose the grasp reflex before she can voluntarily grasp an object.

☐ a baby develops from head to toe. Development of control starts at the head and progresses down the body to the arms, then the trunk and lastly the legs.

☐ movements are jerky and primitive at first and gradually become more refined.

☐ progress to a specific activity is quite often made from a generalized activity. For instance, walking is a refinement of the purposeless leg movements of a six month old baby.

☐ when a baby is concentrating on the acquisition of a new and difficult skill, other previously learned skills may suffer. They are not lost or forgotten but will return when the new skill is mastered.

☐ a child's personality can affect the age at which milestones are reached. As a general rule, independent, determined children are more likely to practise new activities than timid children and therefore master them earlier. Outgoing, gregarious children often have a strong desire to communicate and develop speech earlier than others.

Learning to control the head

If a newborn baby is held horizontally, the head drops. When she is lifted, the neck stays relaxed because she cannot control it at all.

At six weeks, when lifted from a supine position (lying on her back in bed) the baby can just about raise her head from the bed.

As the neck muscles get stronger, at about eight weeks, she can hold her head slightly above the plane of the rest of her body if she is held in a horizontal position.

By twelve weeks the neck muscles are usually strong enough and the baby's co-ordination good enough to allow the head to be held quite clear of and higher than the rest of the body.

With the increasing strength of the neck and back muscles and improving control of the head, it is possible for a baby to raise the chest and head off the bed when lying in the prone position, by the time she is sixteen weeks old.

(Above) We all had to walk before we could run. A baby has to control her head before she can sit up.

Placed on her stomach she'll be trying, with studied concentration, to use her neck muscles to lift her head and see about her.

Learning to use the hands

Your baby is born with a strong grip and will hold on tightly to anything which is pressed into his palm. This is the primitive grasp reflex.

From three to four months old your baby will be holding his hands open most of the time. He will study them and examine the movements of his fingers. If an object is put in his hand he is quite likely to wave it about but may drop it involuntarily.

Between five and six months he will be grasping most things with the whole hand, holding it in the palm. At this age he loves feeling different shapes and textures. He puts objects in his mouth. He may even hold his bottle. When he is lying on his back he may grasp his toes and pull them up to his mouth. He will drop one toy if offered another. He will transfer objects from one hand to the other.

He may try to feed himself with a rusk or a piece of fruit at eight or nine months. He likes to hold a spoon and will probably enjoy banging it on the plate.

When your baby reaches out for something at ten or eleven months old, he will be leading with the index finger as though pointing at it. He will be starting to play the game of dropping things on purpose so that you will pick them up for him. His co-ordination may be such that he is able to pick up something quite small like a button or a crumb with the finger and thumb instead of with the whole hand.

Control of arms and legs

If placed on his stomach, your newborn baby will lie with his bottom in the air, his legs drawn up under him and his head to one side.

At four weeks his chin is just barely coming off the bed. His bottom is still in the air but the legs are beginning to stretch out behind.

By eight weeks your baby will be trying to straighten out both legs and to lean on his arms to just lift his head.

He will probably be able to kick his legs up and down by the time he is sixteen weeks old and will be pushing on his arms to hold his chest and head off the bed.

By the time he reaches six months, your baby will be holding his chest and head off the floor by supporting his arms, at the same time, bending his knees up jerkily.

At about seven to eight months, your baby will have learned to take his weight on only one outstretched arm. At about this time he shows signs of wanting to crawl.

During the next two months, with his head held quite erect, he will be trying to pull himself forward with his tummy still on the floor. He will be making kicking movements with his legs.

Learning to sit up

When your baby is first born, she cannot sit at all without support. She is wobbly and will collapse in a few seconds. If held, her back is round and her head lolls forward.

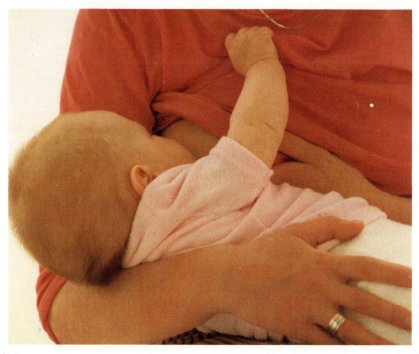

As soon as your baby can sit up unaided, encourage the next stage of controlling his balance by placing a favourite toy in front of him, so that he has to reach out for it (top left). Before that stage is reached he may only manage to sit up momentarily before toppling over backwards (above).

Babies at this age are constantly exploring the use of their hands and legs (middle and bottom left) and their finger control is becoming more delicate (right).

If you hold your baby in a sitting position when she is four weeks old, she is a little steadier but her back is still well rounded.

At sixteen weeks, if you support your baby's arms she will probably manage to sit with her head held up. By now, the upper part of her back is almost straight when she is sitting but the lower part is still rounded.

By the time she is six months your baby will be able to sit up without support for a few moments. She will really enjoy sitting up in a chair surrounded by cushions to support her.

By seven months she is starting to sit on her own, though she needs the support of her own hands. She often braces herself by placing her hands in front of her on the floor.

In another month, your baby will almost certainly be sitting occasionally quite straight without support.

At nine months your baby will not only be sitting straight and unsupported, she may even be well enough co-ordinated to reach out for something in front of her.

During the next three months, your baby sits up straight with confidence and is learning to swivel around the waist, so that she can keep her balance while she twists to see about her.

Learning to stand

It is not until your baby is 10 or 11 months old that she has control over the muscles in her knees, lower legs and feet. By that time she can take her whole weight on her feet and stand squarely, keeping her knees stiff. She can stand but she finds balancing very difficult.

Most six-month-old babies love to be held supported 'standing' on your lap and they will make jumping movements by bending and straightening the knee. A month later 'dancing' has overtaken jumping, and now your baby will hop from foot to foot if supported on your lap. In this dancing movement she may hop from one foot to another, or she may place one foot on top of the other pulling out the underneath one to make the next movement.

At 9 or 10 months, your baby will start to place one foot in front of the other and, if well supported, may try to take one or two steps forward on your lap. Once she has accomplished this, you can try letting her stand on the floor with your hands under her arms, securely supporting and balancing her and with you taking most of her weight she may try to take a few steps.

When your baby can take her full weight on her feet, she will start pulling herself up on pieces of furniture, even though her balance is imperfect. It is therefore essential that any furniture in the room which she is likely to use as a ladder should be solid and unlikely to topple over. Once your baby has pulled herself into a standing position, it may take her a few weeks to learn to sit herself back down.

She will be delighted once she is standing up and then she will shout out for help because she cannot let go and get down on to the floor again. It may be wearisome for you but you should come to her aid each time she calls and lower her gently to the floor until she learns the knack.

Here are a few tips to help your baby:

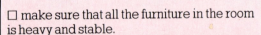

☐ make sure that all the furniture in the room is heavy and stable.
☐ do not leave any knick-knacks that can be knocked over or cloths that can be pulled, on top of the furniture.
☐ never try to hurry your baby with standing or walking. While her balance is imperfect, removing support will frighten her and put her back several weeks.
☐ never try to fool a baby by giving her your support and then withdrawing it suddenly; she must be able to trust you.
☐ do not dress her in shoes and socks. Socks can make standing more difficult on slippery floors and shoes are only needed when your baby starts to walk outside. Both cut down the sensations that your baby feels in the soles of her feet, all of which provide her with valuable information in learning to balance.
☐ do not dress her in restrictive clothing. It will only make falling more likely.

The age at which any child acquires skills is not simply a matter of her own aptitude but depends very much on the behaviour of the other people around her and on her environment. Like adults, a baby acquires skills more easily and quickly if encouraged and given a chance to practise. If her efforts are applauded she will quickly develop a sense of achievement which will spur her on to greater efforts. Lack of opportunity and encouragement largely account for the retarded physical, intellectual and social development of children brought up in institutions. This slowness may be evident as early as three months old and contributes to lateness in speaking. The use of educational toys (see page 140) can make a tremendous difference to the rate of progress in certain areas of development. With the interesting toys specially devised for young babies, your baby will become able to amuse herself earlier and achieve a higher level of manual dexterity than she would without them.

Whilst you should always encourage your baby and try to provide as interesting an environment as you can, do not make the mistake of confusing her by too many distractions. Try only one activity at a time. To a baby, over stimulation becomes a blur and she will miss everything.

(Above) Your baby will stand with confidence more quickly if she has something to hang on to.

You are the best thing she has to hang on to. You can respond to her tugging hands, her bendy knees, and unsteady feet.

You'll bring her on that little bit faster if you build her self-assurance so that she knows she can trust you.

Common baby illnesses
Infections

Some antibodies, for example those to measles are passed from mother to the baby in the womb via the placenta. The baby is thus temporarily immune to measles for about the first six months.

The young baby has very little resistance to infections until he is about six months old. His resistance is weak because the system which protects the body from infection by manufacturing antibodies to germs, is still in a primitive state. A breast fed baby will be protected from infections by maternal antibodies which he takes in with his mother's milk during feeding.

You must take certain precautions to protect your baby from contact with germs. Essentials would be taking meticulous care in preparing bottle feeds, sterilizing all utensils and making sure that your hands are clean. In the very early weeks you should wash your hands before you handle your baby, taking particular care if you yourself have an infection such as diarrhoea, or a skin infection, even something such as a whitlow. There is no need to be obsessive and there is absolutely no point in wearing a mask if you have a cold or a sore throat because your baby has almost certainly come in contact with your germs before you feel any signs of illness.

There are three general signs of infection in a young baby and they may be present with any infection regardless of its site.

Fever
Your baby may have a fever if he has an infection (see page 87 for taking the baby's temperature) but the temperature alone should not be relied upon as an accurate guide of your child's state of health. A baby can have a severe infection and show no change in temperature.

Loss of appetite
Loss of appetite almost invariably accompanies infections in young babies and is the most important sign. If his pattern of eating is regular and he takes food well, sudden loss of appetite should raise an alarm. In an otherwise perfectly healthy baby, a refusal to take more than two feeds should prompt you to call your doctor. Loss of appetite is so common with an infection that infection is considered the cause until proved otherwise.

Vomiting
Vomiting by definition is the forcible expulsion of the stomach contents. Possetting or the effortless regurgitation of milk is not vomiting (see page 86).

In young babies vomiting is the frequent accompaniment of an infection, for example, of the ear, the tonsils, or simply a cold. It is not necessarily related to stomach trouble. Very forcible violent vomiting may be symptomatic of pyloric stenosis (see below).

If your child vomits and seems perfectly well and happy, there is probably no serious cause for his upset. As long as he does not go on being sick, he will probably come to no harm and there is no need to call the doctor. Let him eat whatever and whenever he wants to.

The slightest thing seems to make some children sick, a cough or a tickle in the throat, or a hair or a piece of fluff on the tongue. Other babies are rarely sick. Sensitive children sometimes vomit if they are emotionally disturbed. A bout of crying can become so upsetting that it precipitates vomiting and some children will vomit with fear.

Travel sickness rarely begins before the age of six months and is easily diagnosed because of the circumstances in which it happens.

Repeated vomiting in a young baby can quickly lead to dehydration and this is something that you should prevent. Initially, if your baby is becoming dehydrated, he will not settle easily and will cry and whimper a lot. At a later stage he will become lifeless and sleepy. But if your baby is vomiting you should never wait for this to happen. There are three instances in which vomiting should make you call the doctor:
☐ If your child feels unwell afterwards.
☐ If your child vomits more than twice.
☐ If your child's sickness is accompanied by abdominal pain, diarrhoea or fever.

Severe vomiting can make a child very ill in a matter of a few hours, so do not wait to seek medical help.

Pyloric stenosis

This is a condition which usually occurs in boys and statistically more often affects first born children. It tends to run in families.

The condition usually occurs at the age of two or three weeks when your baby will start to vomit. This vomiting quickly becomes violent, or as it is often described, projectile. So forcible is the expulsion of the contents from the stomach that the vomit may shoot right across the room. This kind of vomiting can be a sympton of pyloric stenosis.

The tendency to develop pyloric stenosis is hereditary and for some reason which we do not know, the condition is triggered off in the second or third week of life. It is thought that in a baby who is predisposed to pyloric stenosis feeding may cause thickening of the pylorus which is just at the exit to the stomach. This prevents the stomach from emptying efficiently and eventually it becomes full and overdistended. The projectile vomiting is the result.

You can distinguish pyloric stenosis from other causes of vomiting because despite the projectile nature of your baby's vomit, he may have a good appetite and otherwise seem well.

The treatment is a very simple surgical operation. Your baby will recover quickly and will be feeding normally in a very short time.

Diarrhoea

With diarrhoea the stools contain more fluid than they should, which means they become loose and frequent. As the normal contractions of the intestine are geared to allow maximum absorption of water from the stool, diarrhoea means that food is passing through the intestine faster than normal. It is usually due to an increase in the number of intestinal contractions, thereby hurrying the food through the intestine. Intestinal 'hurry' can be caused by an infection, by an irritant and by emotional stress.

As with vomiting, if your baby has diarrhoea but retains his appetite and otherwise seems perfectly well, then you should probably ignore it as long as he is eating and drinking normally. It is a mistake to think that a child is ill simply because his stools are loose. It may be that for him, loose stools are normal. However, if the stools are green, this means an infection is present. His general state of health will tell you whether or not there is any cause for concern. However, if looseness continues after three days, consult a doctor for reassurance.

Even if the diarrhoea is accompanied by loss of appetite but your child is taking plenty of fluids and there is no fever or abdominal pain, then you need not worry unduly but check with your doctor.

But whenever diarrhoea is accompanied by vomiting, you should not hesitate to call for medical help, as the combination of vomiting and diarrhoea will quickly dehydrate your child. To help your doctor make a diagnosis, save one of your baby's stools for his examination. He can then make accurate diagnosis and treatment, which may be a kaolin or codeine preparation which dries up the diarrhoea, or antibiotics if laboratory tests show that an infection is present. The rate of dehydration with severe diarrhoea and vomiting is so fast that if your child cannot take sufficient fluids by mouth, your doctor will probably have him admitted to hospital so that he can be rehydrated and fed via a drip in a vein.

Constipation

Constipation means the infrequent passage of hard stools. You should remember that 'hard' means uncomfortably hard, not firm, and 'infrequent' means less than twice a week. If your child does not experience any discomfort in passing the stool and she seems otherwise happy, there is no need for you to worry.

The first thing that you should consider if your child does appear to be constipated is her diet. Most babies, given a diet which contains roughage, in the form of bran cereals, fresh fruit, green vegetables and wholemeal bread, should have no difficulty with bowel movement. If your

baby is not having a full range of these fibrous foods, then you should step up the quantity that you give her.

Never give your baby a laxative before consulting the doctor. It is appalling to give laxatives to a young baby as there is hardly ever any need. Laxatives make the bowel lazy. The natural emptying reflexes go unheeded and you may make a bowel reliant on laxatives to achieve a bowel movement.

Also, remember to expect a short period of constipation if your child has been off her food and not drinking, or has had a bout of diarrhoea or vomiting. When your child has a fever, there is excess sweating. The body therefore conserves water by absorbing every scrap from the stool and in these circumstances, the stool may become very dry and hard. When this happens it is best to give your child's bowel the opportunity to return to a normal rhythm.

Abdominal pain

The only way you can tell if a young baby has abdominal pain is because he is crying. The fact that he draws up his legs at the same time may be a sign but cannot be relied on. Most babies when they cry, for whatever reason, draw up their legs. This is a natural thing to do during a crying spell.

The main things that you should look for are signs of general illness, fever, diarrhoea and vomiting, see above. If your baby's appetite is good and he is feeding well, there is probably nothing seriously wrong with him. If he stops crying when you pick him up and nurse him, the same applies.

Acute intussusception

This is one rather serious cause of abdominal pain in babies between the ages of 3 and 12 months which needs immediate treatment. It is caused by one part of the intestine telescoping into the part immediately in front of it. This causes a blockage in the intestine which may lead to vomiting and to severe colicky abdominal pain which comes in regular spasms. The pain starts in a mild form, builds to a crescendo and then dies away. The baby becomes pale and screams with pain. Sometimes between spasms, his colour returns and he may lie contented. He may even go to sleep for a few moments between spasms from sheer exhaustion, but the pain will, unfortunately, return.

The stools in this condition contain blood and slime, which make them resemble redcurrant jelly.

It is essential that you contact your doctor as soon as possible if you suspect that your baby has this condition. It is easily remedied by surgery.

The surgeon will unkink or cut out the small piece of intestine which has become blocked and then restitch the ends together. It is usually a straightforward procedure and your baby will be well and feeding normally within a short time.

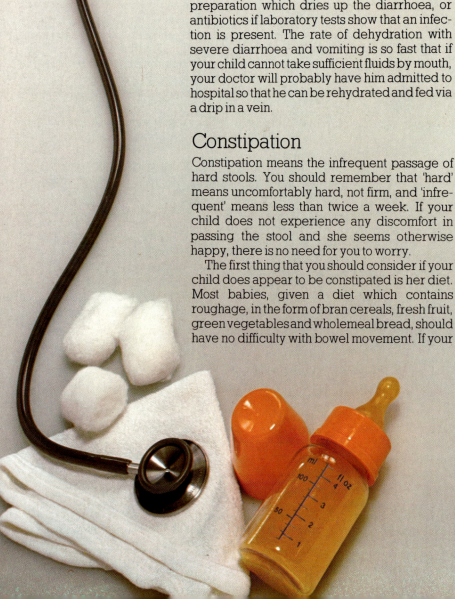

Acute appendicitis

This is one of the commonest causes of abdominal pain. Typically the pain starts in the middle of the abdomen around the navel, then moves out to the right side. This is because initially, an inflamed appendix causes spasm of the bowel and it is not until it is well advanced that the pain centres over the appendix itself. In children, however, the symptoms are somewhat different. The pain may remain in the navel area throughout the entire illness so you should not wait for it to move out to the right side. The pain will start suddenly. Your child will probably have no appetite and refuse food. He may have vomiting and diarrhoea but his temperature may remain normal. If you suspect appendicitis, call your doctor who will make the diagnosis on examining your child's abdomen. The treatment for this condition is surgical removal of the appendix which is simple and straightforward and your child will be eating normally and on his feet again in two or three days.

Convulsions

A convulsion is a fit which may be anything from jerking of the body lasting several minutes to just periods of blankness lasting only seconds. Young babies with high temperatures are prone to convulsions which are due entirely to the fever and have no other significance. Some convulsions have no cause at all. Others are symptomatic of epilepsy and any recurrent fits (more than two) should be fully investigated. If your child has a fit put her somewhere where she cannot hurt herself, don't move her, loosen tight clothing and never try to get anything between her teeth. If she vomits turn her over on her side with her mouth downwards so that the vomit runs out. Don't leave her for a moment. Then call the doctor if you're alone, or someone else can as soon as the fit starts.

Nosebleeds

There is a patch of thin skin just inside the nostril where tiny blood vessels run near the surface. If the nose is hurt as in rough games or picked this area can bleed quite profusely. If this happens don't panic; calmly hold your child's head forward (never backwards – swallowed blood can irritate the stomach and cause vomiting) and apply gentle firm pressure on either side of the nose until bleeding stops, usually not more than a couple of minutes. Troublesome recurrent nose bleeds can be treated by a specialist who will cauterize the delicate areas.

Coughs and colds

In children, the nose, sinuses, throat, ears and upper chest are closely connected and they may be considered members of one system (termed the upper respiratory tract), whereas in adults the various parts remain separate. Thus, in a child, an infection in one area is quite likely to spread to another.

Colds

A cold (sometimes loosely called a chill) is not caused by going outside with wet hair, wearing too little clothing on a cold day, or being soaked to the skin in a rain storm. These are old wives' tales. A cold is caused by a virus infection. Doctors still have no way of killing off viruses, which is why, despite continuing research, there is no cure for the common cold.

The familiar symptoms of runny nose and sore throat are caused by a virus infecting and inflaming the membranes of the nasal passages and throat. The effects are likely to be felt for ten days whilst the body's own defences are fighting the virus. In children, the cold virus can weaken the body and allow secondary bacteria to multiply. When this happens the clear nasal discharge becomes yellow. The tonsils and adenoids may be affected. They may swell up and become septic and your child will develop swollen glands in the neck.

A cough is also likely to develop with a cold. It is caused by mucus dripping down the back of the nose and irritating the throat. The natural reaction is to cough to get rid of it (see below). Colds are more upsetting for young babies as a blocked nose prevents them from breathing whilst feeding. The solution is to give nose drops which clear the nasal passages long enough for them to feed comfortably. But nose drops should never be used frequently over long periods because they can damage the lining of the nose.

As there is a delay between catching the virus and the outbreak of symptoms, you are likely to have passed on the cold to your baby without realising it. So once you or any member of your family shows signs of having a cold, there is very little chance of keeping it away from the baby. However, visitors with colds should be asked not to handle the baby or go into her room.

The body is usually able to overcome a cold infection on its own. However, if your child has a high temperature, develops an earache or a sore throat or generally seems ill, do call your doctor. Apart from breast or bottle feeding babies, children take less notice of the discomforts of a cold than adults and so there is no need to give them the proprietary cold cures that adults use. Never give your child an aspirin at night to help her to sleep, as aspirin has serious side effects. It should not be used on a regular basis unless prescribed by a doctor.

Coughs

Coughing is often part of an upper respiratory tract infection. There are two types, the productive cough and the unproductive cough. With a productive cough, your child is using her cough reflex to clear mucus coming up from the chest or down from the back of her nose. It is therefore a useful cough and is one of the body's best protective devices. An unproductive cough, however, is nothing but a dry, irritating cough with no mucus which is a nuisance that may prevent your child from sleeping at night. It serves no useful purpose. It is important to make a distinction between a productive and an unproductive cough because a productive cough must never be suppressed with cough medicine. If a small baby has a persistent productive cough, however, it is worth talking to your doctor to see what can be done to help. On the other hand, an unproductive cough can cause great distress to a child and a prolonged bout may even make her vomit. It makes good sense to suppress an unproductive cough. Your doctor will prescribe a cough suppressant linctus, safe for children.

One of the most common causes of night coughing is when fluid from the nose drips into the back of the throat, irritates it and sets off the cough reflex. You can avoid this by turning your child on to her side or her front.

Tonsils and adenoids

The tonsils trap bacteria and viruses and therefore localize throat infections. They also warn the rest of the body when an infection is present, so that it can prepare its defences. The adenoids are at the back of the nose and perform the same function, so in medical terms they are often thought of together. They are most important to children up to ten years old, when they are likely to meet most infectious illnesses and their defences must be strongest.

Despite their useful function, it used to be a common policy to remove them, because they often became infected. Nowadays most specialists will only agree to take out the 't's and 'a's' if your child is suffering from recurrent attacks of severe tonsillitis associated with ear infections and deafness. Even so, the tonsils are rarely removed before the age of four.

Surprisingly, even severe tonsillitis may only be discovered during a routine examination of your child's throat by a doctor. She is unlikely to complain of a sore throat beforehand. But with acute tonsillitis (caused by a virulent form of streptococcus bacterium) your child may have a high, swinging temperature, stop eating, have a bad cough, be unable to sleep and need a lot of attention. In this instance you should consult your doctor to see if antibiotics are needed.

With recurrent tonsillitis there is the danger of a further complication: otitis media, an infection of the middle ear, which occurs when germs make their way up the Eustachian tube connecting the throat with the middle ear. It should be treated immediately, see page 172.

Earache

An earache does not automatically stem from a problem in the ears, since pain from the throat, the teeth and the sinuses can be transferred to the ears. As mentioned earlier any infection of the upper respiratory tract in a small child may lead to ear trouble. If your child has a persistent earache, seems a little deaf or has pus in her ears, you should consult a doctor straightaway. The trouble may be caused by enlarged or infected tonsils or adenoids (see above).

Sometimes the general signs of an infection, i.e. fever, loss of appetite and even vomiting and diarrhoea may indicate a severe ear infection. Your doctor will almost certainly prescribe antibiotics, possibly with nose drops to help to drain the infection. Ear drops have no effect as it is impossible for them to penetrate the ear drum and reach the seat of the infection.

Bronchitis

Healthy children quite commonly get nose and throat infections which may go on to bronchitis, an inflammation of the air passages inside the lung. This inflammation usually results in the secretion of large amounts of mucus, which builds up in the bronchial tubes, narrowing them and causing your child to wheeze. As the mucus is cleared from the lungs it causes a productive cough. This type of wheezing, accompanying a chest infection, does not automatically mean your child is asthmatic. A real attack of asthma comes on suddenly whether an infection is present or not.

Some very young babies (between 4 and 10 per cent) will wheeze even with a minor chest infection, but they will grow out of this tendency by the time they are 5 years old. A child with bronchitis should be encouraged to cough, though he cannot be expected to spit up phlegm like an adult. He will almost certainly swallow it. This won't harm him but it may make him sick. Antibiotics and anti-spasmodics may be given to children by the doctor to open up the narrow bronchial tubes and stop wheezing.

Deafness

A baby who is deaf at birth will make sounds at six months like a normal baby, although they may not be quite so tuneful. It is only later that a deaf child becomes quiet and does not vocalize in the way that a normal child does. This is because the child has not been stimulated with outside noises, nor can he hear his own voice. It is essential to discover and treat deafness at the earliest possible age, usually this is during routine testing at eight months at the baby clinic, because vocalizing, babbling, hearing and learning to listen are important preparations for speech. If a baby misses out on these early experiences, learning to talk will be a much more difficult task. The longer a child remains unable to hear, the greater will be the delay in his ability to discriminate between sounds. As this ability diminishes with age it is essential that he has help as soon as possible. If you suspect a hearing difficulty in your baby, you should ask your family doctor to arrange for him to have audio-metric tests from an ear, nose and throat specialist between six and eight months. Once diagnosed, a baby can wear a hearing aid as early as six months and preferably on both ears rather than just one. You may find that there is a lag of up to one year from the time that your child starts to wear a hearing aid before he starts to use what he has been hearing in vocalizing.

Squint (lazy eye)

Beyond the age of three months a squint is most commonly caused by an imbalance of the muscles of the eye. You should take your child to see the family doctor who will probably want to refer him to an eye specialist. At three months old treatment may be unnecessary, or the eye specialist may suggest that it starts later. It is absolutely essential however that you have your baby's eyes checked at three months.

The usual treatment for a squint is to black out one of your baby's eyes with a pad which forces him to use the muscles of his weaker eye and they become efficient through being exercised.

Infantile eczema

Infantile eczema can affect very young babies in the first few months of life. It produces a fairly generalized rash on the face, the inner sides of the arms and behind the knees. The rash is red, dry and scaly and feels itchy. It varies in intensity and may be brought on by a cold or if your baby has a sleepless night. Infantile eczema is nearly always associated with an allergy and is usually hereditary. Other members of the family may not have eczema but may suffer from related conditions such as allergies to drugs or certain foods, asthma, migraine or even travel sickness.

Your doctor will give you specially soothing and healing creams and medicines to control itching. If your baby is scratching a great deal it may be necessary to put his hands in mittens.

Fortunately, the problem may only last until your child is two years old and many children are clear by the age of seven.

The everyday care of an eczematous skin is fairly simple:

☐ Meticulous attention to cleanliness.
☐ Avoid overbathing.
☐ Do not use soap for cleansing, baby lotion on cotton wool will do the same job.
☐ Rub in soft, bland creams and ointments as frequently as prescribed.
☐ Avoid wool next to the skin as it can be irritating.

If necessary, your doctor will ensure that both you and your baby are sleeping properly by prescribing a sleeping draught for the baby.

Immunization

Immunization is one of the most successful forms of preventive medicine ever practised.

Immunization prepares the body to repel infection. Under ordinary circumstances, when a germ enters the body for the first time, the body responds by forming antibodies to that germ or anti-toxins that will neutralize the poisons produced by the germ. When the germ attacks for a second time, the body is prepared and can protect itself. By means of injections (measles) or drops by mouth (polio), we can help our children to achieve immunity to a number of the common childhood infectious diseases. Although the protection may not be absolute it will greatly lessen the severity of the infection.

There has been a considerable amount of discussion about the whooping cough vaccine, since the discovery of an association between the immunization and a small but significant number of cases of encephalitis (inflammation of the brain). The consensus of medical opinion at present however suggests that it is still better for your baby and for the community to have the vaccination against whooping cough. It is wise, however, for babies who have had a convulsion or whose immediate family has a member who suffers from fits not to be immunized against whooping cough. If your baby has a convulsion or develops a high-pitched scream or you notice anything unusual after the whooping cough vaccination, inform your doctor immediately (see page 134).

You may notice a small red bump at the site of your baby's injection. This is quite normal but if he develops a fever or becomes irritable, get in touch with your doctor.

Your baby's vaccination programme will probably start at four months but you need not worry if arrangements are different in your area because your baby's name will automatically come up on a computer well ahead of the time when his immunization programme should start. You will then be sent a card which gives you good warning of where and when you should take your baby for the first injection. It is important to keep a record of the dates of his injections and the types of vaccine he has received. This will remind you when you need to take your baby for his next dose and also help your doctor to complete the programme.

Below is an example of the sort of record you might use to help you keep track of the injections each child has had.

(Below) This is a family record chart. It is important to keep a record such as this for each child, to show the type of vaccine he has received and the date of the injection. It will remind you when he will need his next dose and also will help your doctor to complete the programme.

Name .... Born	Tick square after each injection		Date of each injection
Triple injections at 4, 6, 10 months (diphtheria, whooping cough [please see paragraph about whooping cough above] tetanus) and diphtheria and tetanus pre-school	1st 2nd 3rd 4th	☐ ☐ ☐ ☐	....
Poliomyelitis Drops at 4, 6, 10 months and pre-school	1st 2nd 3rd 4th	☐ ☐ ☐ ☐	....
Measles during second year (single injection)		☐	....
BCG (anti-tuberculosis) offered between ages of 10 and 13 if testing shows they have no immunity		☐	....
German measles (Rubella) at about 12, to girls		☐	....

When to call your doctor

If in doubt, you should always consult your doctor if one of the following warning signs appears:

☐ Loss of appetite if your child is normally a good, regular eater. In a very young baby it needs your doctor's immediate attention.

☐ Vomiting if it is excessive, violent or prolonged, or if it is causing your child obvious discomfort.

☐ Diarrhoea. Should be treated very promptly in a young baby as it can lead to dehydration. With older children, consult your doctor if it is accompanied by a temperature, abdominal pain and obvious illness.

☐ Difficulty in breathing. Warrants immediate medical attention whatever the hour.

☐ Temperature. If it rises above 37.8°C (100°F) and is accompanied by obvious signs of illness; or 39.4°C (103°F) whether showing signs of illness or not. Babies may be very ill indeed with a temperature that is lower than normal.

☐ Emergencies. Any serious accident, particularly if your child loses consciousness, or has eaten or drunk something poisonous. Your doctor may well refer you to a hospital casualty department. If you cannot contact him quickly, do not hesitate to take your child there immediately yourself.

☐ When you are concerned. Doctors will take a mother's suspicions seriously, and do not mind if you go to them for reassurance.

Well baby clinics

You will probably find that there at least two child health clinics in your area; a local authority child health clinic and possibly a child health clinic run by your own GP. These clinics are usually held at regular times on the same day of each week. Usually you do not need an appointment and you can go as often as you like.

These clinics are run primarily for babies that are well. They are there to answer your questions, to reassure you and to clarify small points about your baby's development and behaviour that may be worrying you. They fill the gap that is left when your midwife and health visitor are no longer there for consultation. But if your baby is ill, you should consult your doctor.

The main advantage of your own family doctor's clinic is that it provides continuity of care.

The Well Baby Clinic will keep an eye on the progress of your baby. Part of this assessment, and only part of it, is weighing your baby. If you are concerned about your baby's weight gain, you can discuss it with the health visitor who is usually in attendance at these clinics but it is not the be-all and end-all of your visit to the clinic and you should not worry unnecessarily about it. You should look upon weighing as an occasional interesting way of recording the progress of your baby but do not forget that there are other just as important aspects, such as her energy, her curiosity, her interest in things which are going on around her, her progressive development and her appearance. The chart on page 104 gives an indication of the rate of growth.

(Below) As long as you're realistic about your baby's health, growth and development, baby clinics can be a useful source of advice, reassurance and help with filling in forms and getting your allowances. They will also make sure your baby gets immunized at the right time and will give you useful hints on everyday care and first-aid.

Post-partum clinic

At six weeks after delivery, all women should attend the post-partum clinic. The purpose is to make sure that everything is going normally and well. Doctors will ask you about vaginal blood loss or vaginal discharge and make sure this is normal. They will also examine your breasts whether you are breast or bottle feeding to make sure they are in a healthy condition. They will probably take a cervical smear as part of the routine check up. They will also enquire about your mood and how you are coping with things. They are there to give special advice and help if you need it, so do ask.

They will also want to examine your baby to make sure that his progress is satisfactory. Your post-natal examination can be done either at the hospital where you were delivered, or by your own doctor.

Contraception

Though it's best to wait until the episiotomy scar is completely healed, you and your husband can have sex at any time you feel like it after delivery. Most women find that it is uncomfortable until about 10 days after delivery but this is an entirely personal choice. There is no harm in having intercourse earlier. You should not hesitate to ask your husband to be gentle.

The subject of contraception is always raised during your post-natal visit. Normal menstruation may be inhibited by breast feeding and you may go several weeks or months without a period while you are breast feeding your baby. As it is impossible to anticipate exactly when you will start to ovulate again, it is better to take contraceptive precautions from at least six weeks if you are breast feeding and probably earlier if you are bottle feeding your baby and you are sexually active. In this case, you should discuss contraception before you leave hospital. Below is an outline of the various methods of contraception that are available to you and this is followed by a comparison of their rate of efficiency. You should not make a hasty decision.

Your choice will be influenced by a combination of circumstances, medical reasons and personal preference. For instance the oral contraceptive pill is virtually totally effective but has important side effects, whereas the sheath or diaphragm are less effective than the pill but are also less hazardous to health. Therefore you have to weigh up whether you are just wishing to space your family and consequently do not mind a higher failure rate method against the various side effects of the more reliable contraceptives.

The various methods available can be grouped according to the way they work:
Natural (no outside agent): rhythm method
Mechanical (a device which must be fitted): sheath, diaphragm, intra-uterine device (IUD)
Chemical (chemicals to immobilize or kill sperm): spermicidal jellies and cream
Hormonal (hormones within a pill): oestrogen/progestogen oral contraceptive, progestogen-only oral contraceptive

Natural (rhythm) method

This method involves a close observation of the menstrual cycle to discover on which day you normally ovulate. The cycle begins on the first day of bleeding and for most women ovulation occurs about the 14th day. To find out if this is true for you, you should take your temperature once a day first thing in the morning before getting out of bed. You will see that on the 14th day it drops slightly indicating ovulation. It then shows a distinct rise and remains raised for the rest of the month. After a few months a pattern or rhythm will emerge. However, since the egg can be fertilized for at least two days after it is released and the male sperm may live for five days, you

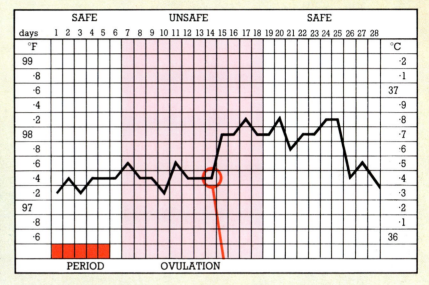

should not have intercourse for over a week in the middle of the menstrual cycle, i.e from the 7th to the 18th day. Keeping a chart like the one above will confirm your own pattern of ovulation.

You may also notice other symptoms of ovulation such as a slight headache.

Mechanical methods

Sheath
This and the diaphragm physically prevent the sperm from reaching the egg, so that fertilization cannot take place. With the sheath worn over the penis, the sperm never even enter the woman's body. For some couples, however, this method is uncomfortable.

Diaphragm or 'cap'
A diaphragm fitted in the vagina traps sperm, preventing them from entering the cervical canal and reaching the ovum. As an extra precaution it is a good idea to add spermicidal cream or jelly to the diaphragm. Spread it thinly round the rim and use a generous amount on the middle of the cap, on the surface which touches the cervix. Its efficiency relies on careful use. It must be refitted before each intercourse. The cervical cap works the same way but fits over the cervix and also is made safer with a spermicide. It takes practice to fit it properly.

Intra-uterine device (IUD)
The intra-uterine device (sometimes called the coil or loop) differs from the sheath and the

(Above) Your temperature chart over the normal menstrual cycle will look something like this. The days on which you are likely to conceive (marked unsafe) are in the middle of the cycle covering the time of ovulation.

diaphragm in that it actually allows fertilization to take place but, because it irritates the womb, it prevents the egg from becoming inplanted. The egg dies and is expelled at the end of the cycle in the menstrual flow. It is a small device made either of flexible plastic or of copper and is fitted in the uterus by an expert in a family planning clinic, or hospital or doctor's surgery. It does not have any direct effect on the functioning of the uterus. Not all women are happy with IUDs, some find them painful either during or after insertion, or on intercourse, others find that it makes their periods much heavier; still others expel the device; vaginal discharge is quite common and very rarely an ectopic pregnancy (the baby develops in a Fallopian tube and this pregnancy must be terminated by a surgical operation) occurs. Women who have not had children are not normally recommended to have an IUD and they are not suitable for those who already have very heavy periods or an infection of the uterus. You should see your doctor once a year for a check up.

Chemical methods

There is a variety of foaming tablets, films, jellies, pastes, creams and aerosol foams available from the chemist. They are used in the vagina just before intercourse and form a chemical barrier to kill sperm. Spermicides may either be used alone (but see 'efficiency table'), or as a supplement to other methods, for instance with the cap or sheath. If intercourse is repeated more of the spermicide should be used.

The 'C-film' is the latest type of spermicide. It is a square of water-soluble plastic which has been impregnated with a potent spermicide. Laboratory trials have proved satisfactory. It can be used by either partner.

Hormonal methods

The hormones are contained in a pill which has to be taken by a woman on a regular basis. It must be taken whether or not you are having intercourse. Many couples find it the most aesthetically acceptable method of contraception. Its almost 100 per cent effectiveness relies, of course, on you taking it exactly according to instructions. There are two main types: the 'combined' pill which contains a synthetic form of both female hormones (oestrogen and progestogen) and the progestogen-only ('mini') pill. They work in different ways and have slightly different failure rates.

The combined pills work by suppressing ovulation. As an egg is not dropped and therefore is not available for fertilization each month, this method has the lowest failure rate. The course of tablets is usually started on the fifth day of bleeding and is taken each day for 21 days. A period usually follows in three to four days.

The progestogen-only pill has, as its name implies, only one hormone and is virtually free of the side effects associated with taking oestrogens. It is therefore suitable for someone who wants to take the pill but is anxious about the risks involved with oestrogens or who is medically unfitted to the combined pill.

The progestogen-only pill works in quite a different way and its success rate is more dependent on how carefully you take it. It has an effect on the mucus in the cervical canal making it so thick and hostile that sperm cannot penetrate it to reach the body of the uterus. It also acts on the lining of the womb, to make it reject the ovum if it does by chance get fertilized. Thirdly, it probably has a direct effect on the sperm itself, making it less capable of fertilizing an ovum.

This pill is not free of side effects. In the first few months you may have irregular bleeding and after that you may sometimes miss a period but this should not be a permanent change. Nevertheless the progestogen-only pill is a good alternative for women who cannot take the combined oral contraceptive.

Whatever method of contraception you and your partner are considering, try to go along to a family planning clinic or discuss the implications with your doctor who will give you individual advice. If you opt for the contraceptive pill make sure you fully understand its drawbacks. And remember, no one should take the pill without her doctor knowing about it, both because of the side effects and because of the necessity of finding which of the many options is the right one. You should have a routine check three months after starting an oral contraceptive, another check at six months and then every six months after that.

Breast feeding and the pill

The quantity of milk may be very slightly less with the combined pill but is rarely affected by the mini-pill. Small quantities of the hormones may come out in the milk. They have never been shown to harm the baby.

Comparative efficiency

Probably the most important factor in deciding which method you and your husband wish to use will be how effective it is.

The efficiency of a method has been calculated statistically over a period of time. The figures given indicate the number of pregnancies per hundred woman years of use. Therefore, if the failure rate of a method is one, this means that of 100 women using that method for a year one will become pregnant.

Method	Failure rate (average)
Oral contraceptives:	
a) oestrogen containing	less than one
b) oestrogen-free	2.0
Intra-Uterine Device (IUD)	2.4
Sheath	up to 7.5
Rhythm (by temperature chart)	6.0
Diaphragm and spermicide	7.2
Spermicides alone	23.5

Just as there are physical milestones which can be used as a rough guideline to chart your baby's physical development, so there are intellectual and psychological milestones by which your baby's progress can be assessed. Do remember that these milestones are a rough guide only. Do not overinterpret them and do not become obsessive about comparing your baby to the average. Many babies who do not conform to the average are nonetheless normal.

Learning to talk

Newborn – six months

As early as four, five or six weeks old, your baby will watch you when you speak to him and may open and close his mouth as though attempting to make a responsive sound to your approach and your conversation. At about eight weeks he responds to your friendly greetings with smiles and jerking hand and arm movements. By 12 weeks, most babies show particular pleasure with squeals and gurgles. At 16 weeks a baby laughs when pleased. At about six months he starts trying to imitate speech by blowing bubbles and pushing out his tongue. He may even try to imitate simple vowel sounds like 'oo and 'ee'.

Seven – eight months

Occasionally, and not always meaningfully, he may come out with simple syllables like 'ga', 'da', 'ba'. He will also playfully try to attract your attention by making a noise like coughing. He becomes very sensitive to any sounds which resemble speech. If someone is speaking on the television or radio, he will look enquiringly in the direction of the sound. If you call his name he will turn in your direction and look around for you.

Nine – twelve months

The simple syllables are now joined up, which makes 'Da-da' an easy word to say. By the end of a year he will be able to repeat a word spoken to him, usually the most commonly heard.

Next you will find that your baby is trying to take an active part in a conversation which is going on in front of him. He will turn from side to side as each person speaks and after watching several exchanges will almost certainly interrupt with a noise or 'word' of his own, so that he becomes an active participant.

A little later your baby may make up all the different sounds he knows into one long 'sentence'. This is technically called 'jargoning' or 'babbling' and means your baby is very close to speaking real words with meaning.

Learning and understanding

Newborn

Even at birth a baby has certain likes and dislikes: mainly those things which increase or disturb his comfort. He soon learns to distinguish your voice from all others and his unfocused eyes may move at the sound of your voice or attempt to follow your face.

Four weeks

Though his eyes have not yet learned to work together, he will watch you. He well appreciates the comfort of physical contact with you and will stop crying when you pick him up.

Six weeks

He starts to make definite responses to his external environment by smiles. His eyes are beginning to focus and will follow you or a moving toy.

Eight weeks

If you hold an object above him it takes him a few seconds to see it but then his eyes will follow it from side to side if it is moved.

Three months

By the time he has reached this age, he will notice a brightly coloured toy immediately. He smiles readily when you speak and sometimes squeals with pleasure. Curiosity, concentration and interest are becoming obvious.

Four months

Some things such as the bottle, breast or a toy make him visibly excited. He laughs and chuckles. He likes to be able to see what is going on around him and he will turn his head at a sound.

Six months

He is starting to take an interest in his mirror image. He reaches out for things. He is begin-

(Below) Your baby tries to talk and communicate from a very early age.

It's thought by some experts that the mouthing and waving movements at 6-8 weeks are your baby's attempt to hold a conversation. Encourage speech and understanding by keeping up a running commentary, and by introducing her to everyday household objects such as this mirror.

ning to show definite preferences for certain foods.

Eight months
He now recognizes his name and understands the meaning of the word 'no'. He reaches out rather haphazardly for things he wants.

Nine months
He may show you quite clearly what he doesn't like, e.g. having his face washed. He is starting to concentrate on games and toys and will handle toys very carefully, turning them over and over, discovering their size, shape and texture. If he drops something he looks for it.

Ten months
He responds to clapping games and easily learns to clap his hands and wave 'bye-bye'. He is beginning to show understanding of several words run together and simple statements.

Eleven months
He loves simple games he can play with you, like 'peep-bo'. He greatly enjoys dropping things so that you have to pick them up.

One year
He loves a happy two-way exchange with you and will repeat anything that makes you laugh. He enjoys looking at simple books with you. He joins in everyday routines by perhaps lifting his arms when being undressed.

Encouraging and amusing

Though most babies cannot sit up unsupported until they are seven or eight months old, most of them enjoy being propped up long before then. As soon as your baby is wakeful for more than an hour at a time, you should try propping her up, well supported by cushions, in a baby bouncer or similar type of comfortable baby chair, which can be safely placed near you on the ground. This introduction to the outside world is so much more valuable for a baby than lying looking at the side of her cot or the ceiling of her room.

It is never too early to start with songs, rhymes and simple games. They are teaching your baby about sounds, physical movements, co-ordination and communication. Best of all, they are teaching her how a loving, human relationship is formed and this stands as the blueprint for all future human relationships.

You should not be afraid to introduce physical movement quite early into your baby's life. From the age of three months, most babies are able to take their weight momentarily if you hold them and let their feet touch the ground. You will find they have great fun and obvious enjoyment from being swung so that their feet kick a large coloured ball.

It has been shown that babies who are sung to tend to have a facility with speech and words. Baby songs and lullabies should start right from day one. Babies seem to gain pleasure from and are comforted by repetitive rhythms and repetitive sounds. This is why nursery rhymes are so attractive to them. Long before you ever think your baby can possibly know what is going on she will enjoy a story read from a book, especially if you point out coloured pictures and repeat the names of simple familiar objects such as 'cat', 'dog', 'ball' and then gradually introduce the names of specific colours.

Another way of making your baby's life interesting is to introduce people and things beyond her immediate family. She is going to have to get used to strangers and to your leaving her and the best way of giving her the confidence to cope with this is to make her familiar with people she does not know whilst she is still on her own home ground.

Most children instinctively love animals and you can encourage this early if you have a pet. Of course, in the very early days, your pet should be kept away from your baby and her room. But once she is sitting up and taking notice and is mobile she will be delighted to see the dog or the cat and to discover how different he is from herself. You will both encourage her curiosity and help her to accept newness and change if you are the person who introduces her to it.

You are her first and most trusted playmate. You can help her over almost any obstacle. One of the greatest ways of helping her is to talk to her. Tell her what you are doing, how you are going to do it, what it will mean, and stimulate responses from her by asking questions.

Games and educational toys can greatly help your baby to widen her horizon and learn new skills. In the early months, one of the most important skills she will be learning is to co-ordinate the movements of her hands with what she sees through her eyes. In the beginning, you need only have toys which encourage her to see and are interesting to look at. These need not be expensive, you can make them yourself by threading interesting objects on to a string which you clip at her eyeline above the cot or pram. You can make a very cheap, pretty mobile out of aluminium foil and balloons.

As your baby gets slightly older, you should try to design toys which she will want to reach out for and grasp. These can be cheap household objects strung firmly across her cot or pram and could include brightly coloured balls of wool or a bobbin of cotton, some plastic measuring spoons and something shiny which might tinkle like a bell when touched.

As her co-ordination and accuracy improves, you can amuse her with toys that she can actually get hold of, like rings, or rattles, balls and cubes suspended across the cot.

As your baby grows older, every day activities like feeding, being warm and comfortable matter less to her and attention, chat, games and entertainment become more important. This is the time that the father can start to build a very special relationship with his child. Just because he is not around all day but is at home for bath time and bed time which are special playtimes, he and your baby can look forward to the social contact which they both crave. You should encourage your husband to have special times with the baby. He is your baby's second most important playmate and with the right sort of encouragement from you, may have a very special place in your baby's affection.

Comfort habits

A comfort habit is basically one which brings a child comfort from herself rather than relying on comfort from you or the outside world. They are often used to bring comfort when you are not there, particularly at bedtime.

From an early age a child may acquire the most common of all comfort habits, of sucking her thumb when you say goodnight and leave the room. But as she grows older, sucking becomes a support. Your baby may only let you leave if she is sucking her thumb and as you leave you will see her sucking harder. The sucking action is a substitute for crying. This comfort habit may later be combined with others such as the carrying of a soft toy, a rag or a piece of blanket.

Never discourage your baby from using a comfort habit. Make sure that her comforter is always on hand and that you have several spares, because she will be loathe to give it up even for washing.

The comforter rapidly becomes one of the child's most important possessions and you should realise this. Never scoff or scold her about it. Never play games of refusing it to her. Never allow one to become lost without there being an immediate replacement.

Be especially careful about your baby having her comforter if she has to leave you for some reason, such as staying with a friend, or has to go into hospital, as it will reassure her that all is well and that she will safely be returned to you.

Rocking and head banging

Young children usually rock themselves rhythmically because they feel deprived of that same rocking movement which they should experience in their mother's arms, in a rocking cradle, or in a gently bouncing pram. For nine months they have jogged and swayed inside their mother's abdomen. They have been programmed to a life which is hardly ever still, so it is not surprising that they feel unhappy when the movement stops. Even being carried around is often sufficient. Some children if left to lie still for long periods will try to comfort themselves with rocking movements as soon as they are physically strong enough, rarely before five or six months. They may start rolling from side to side which is not too worrying. Banging one side of the head against the cot, or making very strenuous movements when they lift the whole of the top half of their bodies almost upright and bring their heads down is a different matter.

It is a serious warning sign because it means that the child has been starved of comfort and physical contact in the early months. It should be corrected at all costs, or the child may grow up expecting affection from no-one and looking only to herself for comfort. Head banging once established may be impossible to stop. Children not only waste valuable time and energy which could be spent widening their learning experience but they may disturb other children who share the same bedroom. If you are worried, see your doctor or Health Visitor.

(Above) Children will quickly become used to animals and their ways, particularly if you already have a family pet. The animal will amuse and delight her and may well help calm her in unhappy moments.

Equipment

The high chair

You can buy a high chair quite cheaply which is light, stable, easy to clean, comes with its own stand and a detachable chair that can be used on its own if you like. From the time that you first clip the harness to the chair, never remove it so that as soon as your baby is placed in the chair you will automatically strap him in. Because all babies drop food on the floor, spread a few sheets of newspaper underneath to catch the mess. These can be thrown away as soon as the meal is over.

Dishes

There are several models of baby dish available. My own favourite was one with a divider in the centre so that you could serve two kinds of food but keep them separate, with a compartment underneath that could be filled with water to keep the food warm. It had a rubber suction pad on the bottom so that it could be firmly fixed to the table of the high chair.

Cup

Make sure that your baby's first cup has a lid. If it doesn't he will find it more entertaining to pour the drink out than to drink it.

Your baby will probably find a beaker easier to hold and the 'teacher beaker' with a perforated spout helps to make an easy transition from sucking the nipple or the teat to drinking from a cup. Make sure that your baby's cup is not too heavy for him to hold comfortably.

Bibs

By far the best bib is made of stiff plastic with no strings which clips comfortably around the back of your baby's neck and is moulded into a tray which catches spills. The danger with thin plastic bibs which have strings is that your baby might smother himself by putting the bib over his head and the strings may tangle. While towelling or fabric bibs may look very pretty, they soil quickly and have to be washed after every meal.

Tins or home cooking?

With the exception of vitamins, there is very little to choose between good tinned baby food and the home prepared equivalent in terms of quantity, number of ounces of protein and number of calories per meal. They are just about equivalent but vitamin supplements will probably be needed with tins (see page 102) and check that sugar has not been added.

As your eventual aim is to have your baby on the same food as the rest of the family, you will probably find the most convenient way of feeding him is to mix home prepared and tinned food. Advantages of home prepared foods are that you easily vary your baby's diet and you can also adapt your baby's meals to suit his individual taste. The food is also freshly cooked. As your baby becomes older, you can start giving him his favourite food in 'finger' form, such as cubes of cheese, diced vegetable, pieces of apples or oblongs of toast.

On the other hand, tinned foods are never any

A high chair (above left) is a useful piece of equipment at this stage, so that your child can sit at table with you.

Babies can be stimulated by light, colour, patterns and sounds much earlier than we ever thought. Decorate the cot with interesting shapes and colours. Copy this clever mother who's used simple kitchen equipment (above).

Whether the toys are specially bought (below left) or part of the household equipment (above right) babies will spend a long time working them out.

trouble to prepare and you can carry them with you and serve them anywhere. They cost more but they are more convenient. They are usually just the right consistency and you can rely on their contents which are standard. However, they are difficult to adapt. Mixtures do not seem to work and they cannot be made into finger foods for your baby to eat independently.

Toys

While you can buy toys that are specifically designed to encourage the development of natural skills which appear as your baby grows older, there are lots of household objects which make very good toys. Here are some of them:
☐ Any kind of circular object like a ball – apples, oranges, balls of wool, tennis balls, rubber balls, ping pong balls.
☐ Anything which will roll across a surface but is not spherical – used plastic bottles, cardboard tubes, toilet roll inners, cotton reels.
☐ Any kind of paper which babies love to crumple, crunch and tear.

☐ Anything with an interesting shape – cardboard egg cartons.
☐ Things which are squashy – sponge.
☐ Things which stretch – elastic or rubber.
☐ Things which a baby might put her hand through – rings and handles.
☐ Anything which is light – a balloon, polystyrene.
☐ Anything which can be safely stacked or fitted inside one another – plastic jars, plastic boxes, with or without lids, yogurt cartons.
☐ Anything which can be safely banged – plastic cups, spoons, plates, wooden spoons, small saucepans and lids.
☐ Anything with holes in it like a sieve.
☐ Anything which is large and rather heavy but nonetheless safe – a cushion or pillow, a large soft cuddly toy, a loaf of bread.

Going into the big bath

Before your baby is six months old you will find that her small baby bath will no longer accommodate her. It will be time for her to go into the big bath. Do not introduce her suddenly to this great white towering object.

You might start by having a few of her baths in her old baby bath in the bathroom where she can look at the bath and become familiar with it. If you have other children, put them in the bath at the same time as you are bathing the baby so that she will see what it is used for and see them having fun. If you do not have other children, you might half fill the bath and float some of your baby's favourite toys on the water so that she is eager to go and join them. Here are a few tips that make the transition from baby bath to big bath more comfortable for you both.

1. Put an old towel or a rubber mat in the bottom of the bath to stop the baby from slipping away from you. This will make you both feel more secure.

2. Make sure that the water is shallow (four to five inches or 20-22 centimetres deep). The deeper it is the more easily she will float and the less securely you will be able to hold her. If she slips from your grasp her face may be covered with water. This fright may set you both back several weeks.

3. Test the hot tap to make sure that it is fully turned off before you put your baby into the bath.

4. Always hold your baby so that you can grasp her shoulder with your fingers and support her head on your wrist. This way she will not roll over and get her face wet.

5. Let your baby do all the splashing, never splash her.

6. Do your best to avoid soap getting into her eyes. If it does, lick it out.

7. As soon as your baby has had enough, lift her out of the water into a large, warm, soft towel.

Working mother

If you have made the decision to return to work while your baby is still young, good expert help is essential. The person who takes care of your baby must be someone you can trust. A relative you get on with is probably best, a good reliable friend with children of her own second best. If it's going to be a stranger, investigate your child minder exhaustively (see page 181). When your child is old enough and is ready for a day nursery investigate it just as thoroughly and make sure it's registered (see page 180).

Travelling

There is no reason at all why you should not embark on quite adventurous journeys, even holidays abroad, with a small baby, as long as you make sufficient preparations and are well organized.

Most babies find the movement of a car or train soothing and often sleep soundly throughout most of the journey, waking more refreshed than you. As your child gets older however, he is not content to sit quietly in your lap and watch the scenery go by. If you are in a plane there may be very little scenery and you will have to think of ways to keep him occupied and diverted. If you are going to share an aeroplane cabin with a hundred or more strangers, you will have to make sure that your children are kept occupied without disturbing others by making a noise.

You will feel less harassed and anxious about the journey if you have made detailed plans as to how you are going to feed, clean, clothe, rest and amuse your baby. If you are travelling by air, check with the airline that they provide a cot in the bulkhead of the plane for small babies and that they will help with the preparation of your baby's feeds. If they do not provide these services, change to an airline that does.

A small child should travel in the back seat of a car. If he is still in a carry cot, make sure the cot is tethered to the back seat. When he is older he should be secured in a safety harness. Carry on using this harness until he is at least four years old, that is when he has good co-ordination.

With a small child you will need to break your journey if you are motoring. As a general rule it is better to have fewer but longer stops than frequent short stops, so that your child has a chance to run around and play and forget the claustrophobic atmosphere of the car. Try to stop at a place where it is safe for your children to play.

You will need food to nibble between meals like fruit and cheese and a proper picnic meal. Always take more to drink than you think you will need. Your child will inevitably be thirstier than you think.

The easiest way to feed a small baby while you are travelling is to breast feed and you may have to find a quiet corner to do this. If you are taking your bottle fed baby on a long journey, it is best to take sterile, pre-packed feeds in disposable bottles. These feeds are not available everywhere, so the alternative is to prepare several bottles in the usual way, seal them so that they are sterile and watertight and take them with you in your baby bag. There is no need to warm your baby's milk or solid food while travelling. In the summer you can keep a bottle of either pasteurized milk or powdered milk unrefrigerated for up to about four hours and in the winter up to about eight. Be sure to take plenty of boiled water or diluted fruit juice for your small baby to drink between feeds.

While you are travelling do not attempt to wash your baby all over, just top and tail. Be sure that you have taken along everything that you normally use during your changing routine and a plastic bag for soiled articles. I would suggest that you use disposable nappies for travelling if you do not use them generally.

Here are some of the things which I found indispensable when I took a baby on a journey:

☐ Plastic baby holdall with pockets and zip compartments in which to place all items.
☐ A complete change of outer and under clothing.
☐ Half a dozen nappies.
☐ Small box of tissues.
☐ Baby lotion or baby oil and baby cream.
☐ Several pre-prepared bottles of milk according to the length of the journey or outing.
☐ A bottle filled with boiled water or diluted fruit juice for drinks.
☐ A flannel.
☐ A waterproof sheet.
☐ A few rusks.
☐ A spare baby comforter.
☐ Paracetamol elixir, dropper and measuring spoon.
☐ Plastic bib.
☐ Plastic feeding dish and two spoons.
☐ Plastic drinking cup.

You should never feel that the presence of a small baby restricts your movements. On the contrary, you should take steps to ensure you are mobile. There is absolutely no reason why a small baby should not accompany you on an outing as long as your friends are prepared for a third visitor. Most families are only too happy to accommodate the needs of a new baby and will make you feel welcome.

You should also bring up your baby to be adaptable. Travelling is a normal part of every day life and your baby should accept it as such. If you look upon it as normal without becoming panicky about it, your baby will almost certainly grow up with the same attitude. Whatever happens while you are travelling, try to remain calm. If you do not, your anxiety will be quickly communicated to your baby and will probably upset him, so that he takes a dislike to travelling.

Safety procedures

As your baby gets older some of the lightweight equipment that was once quite safe now becomes a hazard. Where once your small baby sat firmly in a lightweight pram or a lightweight high chair, she is now able to reach forward quite strongly, rock backwards and forwards and use various parts of her equipment as a lever to sit herself up or turn herself over.

If you want to go on using a pram, you will have to exchange your lightweight newborn baby's pram for something steadier that has strong brakes and a good chassis. As far as the baby's chair is concerned, you will have to replace the rather flimsy stand with a stronger one or buy the tougher, more stable high chair which can be adapted to a low seat and a large table.

Whenever your baby is seated, whether in a chair, pushchair, pram or car seat, use a safety harness. The only exceptions are a dropsided cot or a playpen. Because a safety harness is easy to forget, try to have one already attached to every article in which you place your baby to sit. If there is not a safety harness readily available when you come to sit the baby down, you will be tempted to leave her unharnessed. That is when accidents happen.

Never leave your baby alone on a chair, a sofa or a bed. In the early stages she is bound to fall over, and a fall from any height is worse than a tumble on a floor. Only ever put your child down on the floor.

Never ever leave your baby alone on the floor even if she is surrounded and well-supported by cushions. If she toppled over so that her face was covered by a cushion, she could get a nasty fright. If her arms were trapped she could also smother. It is never worth the risk of leaving her sitting alone in a room.

(Below) In many circumstances, most often in a car, your baby's life is literally in your hands. Never take short cuts, never pinch pennies. Buy the safest equipment and always follow a strict safety routine. Your baby is safest strapped into a proper car-seat firmly anchored to the back seat.

Weaning to household diet

As babies reach the end of their first year, their growth rate begins to slow down. Their appetite and their food intake reduce in line with this diminishing rate of growth and you should not worry about this. Do not expect your baby to take four good meals a day. Your appetite is not constant and neither is your baby's. If he takes one small meal, he will almost certainly make it up at the next meal and if he eats badly for a day he will make it up very quickly the next day. If your baby only likes milk but is taking 40 oz (1 litre) a day, is growing steadily and has plenty of energy, then the amount of solid food that he takes should not worry you. This applies until he is walking.

Until your baby is well over a year you will probably have to use a mixture of home cooked and tinned foods.

It is best not to spend hours preparing your child's food. The trouble you take is directly proportional to your anger if he refuses it. Never ever use food as a bribe, a threat, a punishment or a reward.

A definite policy about sweets is useful. You may decide for the sake of your child's teeth that you are not going to provide him with sweets. On the other hand, you may decide that your child can have sweets whenever he asks for them as life is easier that way. But it is best to take a middle course. Decide which kind of sweets you think a child should have and then control the manner in which he eats them. It is helpful to discuss with the rest of the family and other friends and relatives how you will tackle the problem of sweets. It is very difficult if grandparents constantly bring sweets as gifts and rewards. Try asking them to bring some alternative gifts, such as small toys or books, or save up money for a bigger present. Many dentist's families decide to have sweets on one day of the week only, perhaps on a Saturday.

Snacks are best treated as food and not treats. Because snack foods are usually eaten in circumstances outside of meal times they become more desirable than ordinary food. If chosen badly they are nearly always fattening. You will make snacks less 'sensitive' if you offer your child the kind of food he likes best as part of ordinary meals and keep simple foods freely available for eating as snacks. The majority of snacks contain sugar, such as biscuits, orange squash, ice cream. Constant eating between meals will make your children more likely to get tooth decay. So limit snacks to savoury items.

Of course children can be happily weaned on to diets other than a 'western one', for instance Indian, Mexican, Arabic, etc, with their own special foods. Research has shown that young children, once they are feeding themselves, prefer bland foods to highly spiced ones, and food that they can identify, e.g. meat, vegetables, not anonymous mixtures. So introduce spicy food gradually and if your child refuses it don't try to force her, and don't offer it to her again for several weeks or months, she will only refuse it again.

Especially nutritious foods

By the time your baby is one year old, her daily dietary requirements are as described in the list below. However, it is not necessary to stick rigidly to these figures each day but make sure that this balance is achieved on a weekly basis. The weights are given in metric only as the units are so small. One gram = 0.035 ounces

Energy	1,200 k Cal
Protein	30 grams
Calcium	500 milligrams
Iron	7 milligrams
Vitamin A	300 micrograms
Vitamin D	10 micrograms
Vitamin B_1 (thiamin)	0.5 milligrams
Vitamin B_2 (riboflavin)	0.6 milligrams
Nicotinic acid (Vitamin B) (niacin)	7 milligrams
Ascorbic acid (Vitamin C)	20 milligrams

(Above) Whilst your child has got the hang of using a spoon by now, his aim may not always be perfect. He may well take quite a while over his food, but will enjoy it all the more because he has fed himself.

Fat, saturated or unsaturated is a normal part of a child's diet but need not necessarily be added. She will get fat soluble vitamins from the fat in milk, cheese, meat, etc.

All foods contain calories, though some have more than others. Fats have the most and contain about 200 calories per ounce (29 g). An ounce of first class protein like beef, contains about 80 calories per ounce, while bread contains 70 calories per ounce, boiled potatoes 20 calories per ounce and green vegetables such as cabbage, 2 calories per ounce.

Good sources of protein include meat, liver, fish, eggs, cheese and milk. Milk is especially nutritious as it contains one gram of protein per fluid ounce (28 ml). As your one year old needs no more than 0.9 ounces (25 g) of protein a day, he will get all his protein if he drinks about 20 fluid ounces (0.56 litres) of milk. The following quantities of food contain one third of your baby's daily protein requirements:

1 tablespoon of minced beef
1 tablespoon of minced liver
1 tablespoon white fish
1 tablespoon grated cheese
1 2 oz (60 g) egg
1½ large sausages
2 slices of ham
24 oz (120 g) pots of natural yogurt
as first class protein
or 3 slices of cut white or brown bread
1 heaped tablespoon peanut butter
6 level tablespoons baked beans
4 medium sized potatoes
8 biscuits
4 bags of potato crisps
as second class protein.

As far as the B vitamins are concerned, almost every fruit she eats will contribute to her daily requirements, as will meat, especially chicken, and wholemeal bread. Sufficient vitamin A is contained in one pint (half litre) of milk, or 2 oz (60 g) of butter, or one egg, or one ounce (30 g) of cheddar cheese, or one small carrot. The juice of one orange provides sufficient vitamin C and she will have her daily dose of vitamin D in one egg, one ounce (30 g) of fortified margarine and in one ounce (30 g) of herrings or sardines. Her calcium requirements are satisfied by one pint (half litre) of milk, one ounce (30 g) of cheese, one ounce (30 g) of white bread or one ounce (30 g) of white flour and she will get her daily iron if she takes one tablespoon of minced beef, or one small slice of liver, one egg yolk and one slice of bread.

Remember that there is no food which is absolutely necessary for a baby to have. Even milk, which is the staple diet of all babies, is not necessary. Simply make sure that your baby eats her ration of protein, some carbohydrates and fresh fruit and vegetables every day and nothing will go wrong.

Physical development
Crawling

A baby may learn to crawl at any time after he has learned to sit alone, see page 106, a very few at the same time and some even before. There are many forms of 'crawling' and there are many times to start crawling, all of which are normal. Your baby may continue to stay sitting quite still at a year but this is entirely normal as long as he is taking an interest in what is going on around him and is making some attempts to stand.

Crawling really means any movement or combination of movements which propels your baby across the floor, either forwards or backwards. Many babies do indeed start moving backwards because once in a crawling position they find that their arms and hands are stronger and better co-ordinated than their legs and

(Below) Not all babies crawl and many adopt odd ways of moving across the floor, often spider fashion.

It doesn't matter how he moves. It's his first step to real freedom. The world is opening. He can explore. He's learning to propel his body. Beware furniture with sharp corners and priceless ornaments!

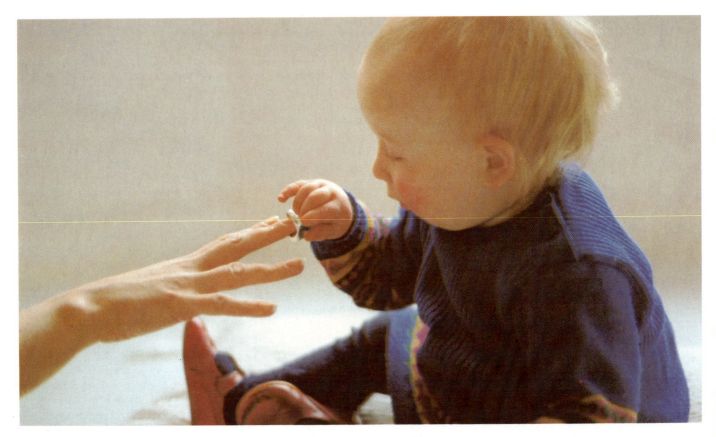

pushing makes them go backwards. Other forms of crawling are shuffling along on the bottom, rolling over and over and of course some babies crawl in the traditional way on their hands and knees.

Signs of wanting to crawl usually show in the seventh and eighth month. Most babies spend a frustrating few weeks rocking backwards and forwards, turning round and round, slithering crab like across the floor, until they eventually learn the knack of propelling themselves in the direction in which they want to go.

There are several things that you can do to encourage your baby to crawl:
□ you can start by putting him on the floor with his toys. He will soon want to investigate all this space around him and to try to reach toys at the other side of the room.
□ try to make crawling space safe by protecting him from hidden steps, floor surfaces that might scratch or hurt and small hard objects that are painful to kneel on. Remove any furniture with sharp corners.
□ make sure your baby's knees are protected by trousers or dungarees unless he is crawling on a very soft carpet.
□ do not dress your baby in pretty clothes if you are going to let him play and crawl about the floor and do not be fussy about trying to keep him clean. Ordinary household dirt will not do him any harm.
□ never leave your baby alone in a room. Even in a few seconds he may crawl to a dangerous spot that you never considered accessible to him.
□ your baby will want to move towards toys and attractive objects. His enthusiasm for moving will be greater if you give him a goal to aim for.

Using the hands

At 12 months your baby will be able to pick up something as small as a pea or a button with her thumb and forefinger, and if you give her a pencil or a crayon to play with, she will try to imitate the marks you have made on the paper.

At about this time your baby will give you something if you ask for it, particularly if you put out your hand, palm upwards, at the same time. She will also be prepared to roll a ball across the room to you. A month or so later your baby will have learned to hold two small objects in one hand and will be trying to put one brick on top of another. She may also be attempting to take off her shoes to help you.

Try to give her lots of varied opportunities for using her hands, like pulling a toy on a piece of string, hammering one object on another to make an interesting noise, and fitting different shapes into holes.

By 15 months your child will almost certainly show that she wants to feed herself and brush her hair. She will also probably kiss on request and enjoy new skills like drinking from a cup. She will try to imitate your daily household chores like sweeping and dusting.

Before your baby can learn the adult grasp, she has to learn to let go of things and you can encourage her to do this by placing your flat hand underneath hers and asking her for the objects she is holding. Once she has let go of it you can reward her by giving it back and this can turn into a very enjoyable game between mother and child. Around the end of her first year, dropping things gives way to throwing things deliberately and you should provide your baby with lots of small soft things that won't break or cause damage.

(Above) The use of forefinger and thumb is a very precise movement and it takes your child six months to go from picking up a pea with her whole fist to precisely nipping a small object between finger and thumb.

(Above and right) Try to get toys which help your child's development. This one improves judgement because the tubes need to be fitted into the appropriate holes. It also develops coordination, strength and aim. And it makes a lovely noise, too. (Below) This diagram shows the order in which your children's teeth will grow.

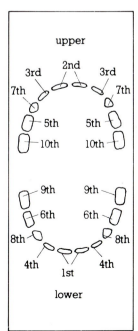

upper

3rd 2nd 3rd
7th   7th
    5th   5th
    10th   10th

    9th   9th
    6th   6th
8th   8th
    4th   1st   4th

lower

Teething

It is misleading to give a date when the first tooth will erupt as this can vary so much. Occasionally, babies are born with a tooth and yet it is quite normal to have no teeth at a year old. On the other hand, there are general rules about the order in which teeth erupt.
- ☐ The lower front teeth erupt first.
- ☐ The upper front teeth usually follow.
- ☐ Then the upper side teeth.
- ☐ Followed by the lower side teeth.
- ☐ The first upper molars then erupt.
- ☐ Followed by the first lower molar.
- ☐ Next the upper eye tooth on each side.
- ☐ And then the lower eye teeth.
- ☐ Next the second molars on the lower jaw.
- ☐ Then the second molars in the upper jaw.

A baby's first tooth usually becomes visible as a small pale bump for quite some time before it finally emerges with a sharp, hard edge. Teething should never be blamed for your baby being ill and it can never cause loss of appetite, vomiting, diarrhoea, fever or convulsions. If your baby seems ill while he is cutting a tooth, do not neglect a real illness in the belief that it is caused by teething: call your doctor immediately.

The only signs that you can consider normal with teething are if a baby is slightly more fretful than usual and dribbling, in which case you should comfort him a lot, keep him physically close to you and gently wipe away the dribbles from his chin. If he appears to want to bite a lot, give him a teething ring or a rusk to chew on. If you're still sterilizing bottles, keep the teething ring in the sterilizer, otherwise keep it household clean.

As soon as your baby has several teeth you can encourage him to start looking after them early by making a game of tooth brushing. Let him watch you brushing your teeth, then offer him a toothbrush to play with. You will find that he is soon trying to perform the same movements as you and will be putting the brush into his mouth. By extending this playful game you can encourage toothcleaning as a regular daily habit without force or making it a chore.

The milk (primary) teeth are well worth looking after. Primary teeth which are lost through decay can be the cause of permanent teeth growing in crookedly. You can start looking after your baby's teeth from the time they appear by making sure that his diet does not contain sugary foods e.g. chocolates, sweets, cakes, biscuits and foods to which sugar has been added. Drinks are also especially dangerous and blackcurrant juice and rosehip syrup are no exception. Do not allow your baby to continue to suck a bottle, dummy or dinky feeder, as newly developing teeth may be bathed in sugary liquids which encourage tooth decay.

A young child cannot clean his teeth effectively for himself, he will need your help with this, just as he needs help with having his hair washed, but do allow him to join in the activity. It is easiest for you to stand/sit behind the child and support his head against your body. Then steady his chin with one hand and brush the teeth making sure that you reach all surfaces using a special baby brush with a small head. Make this a daily activity. Use a fluoride toothpaste but watch the amount, a piece the size of a pea should be enough.

The British Dental Association recommends that children can take fluoride drops or tablets daily, but check first whether your local water supply already has enough fluoride. If not, the daily dose for a baby under 2 is ¼mg, for 2-4 years old ½mg and for older children 1mg per day. The tablet should be sucked or chewed so that the fluoride coats the teeth as well as being absorbed into the body when swallowed.

The sick child

It is almost impossible for any child to run the obstacle race of growing up without becoming ill. Modern medicine is so effective that all but a few children with very serious conditions can be nursed at home. Your doctor will visit your sick child at home as often as he thinks necessary to check on progress and in between times the district nurse can be called in if special nursing is required. This is rarely necessary. Mothers are first rate nurses, as they put the health of their child before anything else.

Confinement to bed

Over the past decade or so, the attitude of doctors has changed towards keeping a child in bed if he is ill. We no longer believe that a child with a high temperature should stay in bed since a temperature is not always a good guide to a child's state of health. There is no need to keep a sick child in bed. At home and in an even temperature, he can be allowed to do what he wants to do and be where he wants to be. You will probably not have to make the decision to put a very sick child in bed, as he will almost certainly take to his bed without you suggesting it. On the other hand, if your child wants to get out of bed, then he is almost certainly well enough to do so. As with many aspects of child care, your child knows as well as anyone what is best for him and you should follow his lead.

Don't make the mistake of bundling your child up in lots of warm clothes and keeping him in a very warm room. This will only increase his overheating. Light, warm, clothing is all that is necessary and it is much more important to keep the temperature of his room constant, i.e. the one at which the rest of the house is (68-70°F), rather than hot. Be flexible about where your child rests. If he wants to lie down he will be much happier and more comfortable lying on a couch downstairs in the living room where he can be near to you and other members of the family. As a guide to the temperature of the room, if it feels comfortable for the rest of the family, then it is suitable for your sick child. If your sick child is getting tired, and most sick children tire easily, put him to bed. He will probably welcome this, especially if someone will stay with him in his room and read and play with him for a while to keep him company.

If your sick child has spent a few days in bed, the time for him to get up is when he asks to. He will be tired and weak so make the period downstairs with you and the family fairly short at first and not too exciting. It will make a lot of difference to his speed of recovery if you let him move into another room simply to change his surroundings and make life more interesting. Once on the road to recovery, a sick child probably becomes bored and will use his energy to be naughty or get into mischief. This is another reason why it is best not to keep him in bed if you are not prepared to entertain him.

Should you isolate your child?

The old fashioned rules about isolating a child who is sick or has an infectious fever (see page 132) involving isolation from the rest of the family and sterilization of plates, cups, dishes and utensils and separate laundry, have now been abandoned. We now realise that all the precautions have little point as most infections are passed on during the first 48 hours that they are carried. In this time, the symptoms are not very clear so by the time your child has developed an illness, the other members of the family have almost certainly come in contact with the condition and will be carrying the germ themselves.

Your sick child's diet

There are very few illnesses that necessitate a special diet for your child. Let her eat whatever and whenever she wants and let her drink as much as she wants. Most sick children eat small meals quite often. Never force your child to eat as this will only add to her distress. Fever, especially if accompanied by vomiting and diarrhoea, quickly leads to dehydration so you should make absolutely sure that your child takes plenty of fluid and you should encourage her to drink often. It does not matter at all what she drinks. It is water that she requires and as long as she gets fluid she will be all right. Children quickly make up any lost nutrients when they get well and their appetite returns, so you need not make a fuss about your child having especially nutritious drinks or those which are specially formulated for sick people. If necessary, spoil her for a short while and let her have a favourite drink, which you normally restrict to a treat. The important thing is to keep her drinking and keep her happy.

However, if you can, it makes good sense to give your sick child nourishing drinks. Fruit juices are especially good because they contain many vitamins, not just vitamin C, and if they are sweet as well, they will provide sugar for energy. If your child will take it, milk of course is the best food because it contains vitamins, sugar, minerals and protein. Many sick children however, find plain milk unpalatable when they are ill, so make it more pleasant for your child by adding a fruit flavour or making a milk shake.

Giving medicine

Taking medicine is made easy for children because there are specially formulated medicines
which are fruit flavoured and pleasant to taste.
Most children therefore are quite happy to take
medicine off a spoon as long as you don't make a
fuss about it being a medicine or the need to take
it. If your child is unwilling to take medicine from
a spoon, try showing her that you are prepared
to take a little of it yourself and this may persuade
her to swallow it satisfactorily.

However, dentists are concerned that very
sweet medicines, if they need to be taken for a
long period of time, say weeks or even months,
may damage the newly developing teeth. If your
child needs medicines over a long period of
time ask your doctor if he can prescribe tablets,
or else make sure that when possible the medicines are taken at mealtimes and not between
meals.

If your child has to take tablets help her by
crushing the tablet between two spoons and
perhaps disguising them in some other food. If
your child is taking a course of antibiotics, it is
essential that she has her medicine at regular
intervals for the period prescribed by your
doctor, so do whatever you have to do to get her
to take her medicine without a struggle.

Taking a temperature

A mother can usually tell whether her child has a
temperature or not. A cool mother's hand on the
forehead is often as good an index as any in the
diagnosis of a fever. But again, remember that a
fever is not a very good indication of your child's
condition, so you should not rely on the presence of a fever to confirm that your child is ill.
There are many other more important signs
such as loss of appetite, lethargy and lack of
brightness. If you do have to take your child's
temperature and wish to be exact, use a clinical
thermometer which can be bought from any
chemist.

Most thermometers, whether they are cali-
brated on the Fahrenheit or Centigrade scale,
will have the normal temperature marked with a
small arrow. On the Fahrenheit scale this will be
at 98.4 degrees and on the Centigrade scale at
36.6 degrees.

Body temperature can be taken by placing
the thermometer in the mouth, under the arm or
in the rectum. It is never advisable to put a
mercury thermometer in your young child's
mouth, so use either of the other two methods
(see page 87). When you buy a thermometer,
make sure that you get one which only has to be
placed in position for half a minute to give an
accurate reading. Anything longer is a strain on
a child. They are not readily available, but if you
go to a large and reliable chemists they should
be able to supply you with one. As your child
grows older and can be trusted, a thermometer
can be placed under her tongue in her mouth.
Be careful that you do not take a child's temperature immediately after a hot or cold drink as this
will affect body temperature.

How to treat a temperature

If your child develops a fever, do a quick check
to make sure that she is not bundled up too
tightly in heavy blankets and that there is sufficient fresh air in the room.

One of the best ways of bringing your child's
temperature down is to use tepid sponging as
described below. When your child has a high
temperature she becomes distressed and you
can reduce her fever most effectively by this
method, without waiting for instruction from
your doctor. You should check your child's
temperature while you are using this technique
of cooling and stop when it falls below 102 degrees Fahrenheit, or 38.5 degrees Centigrade.

Do not feel that you have to reach for the
sponge and water every time your child gets a
temperature. You must make a common sense
judgement depending on how ill, how feverish
and how distressed your child is. As a general
rule you should not apply tepid sponging unless
your child's temperature rises to 103 degrees
Fahrenheit or 39.4 degrees Centigrade.

To treat your child with tepid sponging, undress her and lay her on a waterproof sheet
covered by a towel. Using a sponge or soft
flannel dipped in tepid water, cool, first her face,
then her trunk and limbs by gently rubbing it all
over the skin. Never use cold water because this
will result in contraction of the blood vessels of
the skin and therefore heat loss is diminished.
Water from which the chill has been taken does
not make the blood vessels contract down, they
remain dilated and there is a substantial cooling
effect when water evaporates from the surface
of your skin. If you have one, an electric fan will
also help to keep her cool.

If you want to increase cooling even further,
then wrap your child's neck and groins in damp
flannels. Make sure that you take your child's
temperature every 10 minutes and stop the
tepid sponging when it falls below 102 degrees
Fahrenheit (38.5 degrees Centigrade). Then do
not dress her in pyjamas, only cover her with a
light sheet. If her temperature rises again, you
can repeat the tepid sponging.

(Above) Although the
strip thermometer is not
a strictly accurate
device for finding if your
child has a temperature,
it is very easy to use and
is better than nothing, if
you are not confident
about the other methods
of taking a temperature
(page 87).

Keeping your child amused

Most young children need a lot of amusing when they are sick and at home. Young babies become very 'mummyish' and will probably want to be in close physical contact with you a lot of the time. Illness makes every child unhappy, so do whatever you have to do to keep your child in the best possible spirits. He will need extra special loving care and attention, so leave everything else and devote yourself to nursing your sick child and making him as comfortable and as happy as possible.

Relax all your rules and allow your child to do whatever he wants. Put a polythene sheet over the bedclothes so that he can paint and allow him to play with toys which are normally forbidden such as those of the older children. He will need a lot of diversion and if it does not cause too great an inconvenience, move the television set temporarily into his bedroom. This will keep him occupied and interested and do a great deal to improve his spirits.

For a sick child there is no substitute for your company, so do make an effort to play with him, read to him, help him to cut out pictures from old magazines, just sit and chat, sing songs or nurse him. Other members of the family can take their turn too. While your child is ill, turn a blind eye to an untidy bedroom.

When your child is recovering and is not in danger of infecting anyone else, it is a great treat for him to have a visitor. Try to arrange for a neighbouring child to call. As soon as your child is fit enough to be running around the house, he is fit enough to go outside.

Helping your doctor

A mother's observations are always very helpful to a doctor. Even if you cannot describe specific symptoms, your anxiety about your child's general condition is very often the only warning sign that a doctor needs. This does not mean that you should be overprotective and run to your doctor with each snuffle but if you are seriously worried, consult him even though you feel the complaint may be trivial.

Remember that your doctor is working on a busy schedule and give him fair warning that all is not well. If you want him to visit your home, most surgeries require that you make a call before 9.30 in the morning so that your name can be placed on the visiting list before your doctor leaves the surgery.

If you discover that your baby is sick during the morning and becomes worse after lunch, then it is only right that you should inform your doctor straight away rather than waiting until the evening and possibly having to get your doctor out of bed to make a call.

When your doctor arrives, try to explain as concisely as possible what you have noted. If your baby has been sick or has had diarrhoea, keep a specimen for your doctor to see. If there are small things that you notice and are afraid of forgetting, then jot them down on a pad before he arrives.

The infectious fevers

The infectious fevers of childhood are measles, German measles, chicken pox, mumps, whooping cough, scarlet fever. The first four are caused by viruses, the last two by bacterial infections. Scarlet fever is now very rare. Diphtheria used to be a common infectious fever but it has been almost completely eradicated by the widespread use of immunization.

The infectious fevers are so-called because they are highly contagious, usually passed from one child to another and because all of the illnesses are always accompanied by a high temperature. They are commonest when a child starts to mix with other children but babies from the age of six months are in danger of contracting the infectious fevers.

The first attack of an infectious fever confers active immunity on the child. In other words, the presence of the virus or bacteria in your child's body stimulates the production of antibodies to that germ. A second infection is therefore very unusual and casts doubt on the first diagnosis.

Although it is no longer thought necessary to isolate your child and observe the rules of quarantine, there are some precautions you can take against spreading the infection. If you suspect an infectious fever do not take your child to the doctor's surgery where the infection might be passed on. Warn visitors to the house (especially women, if your baby has German measles, see below) about the infectious fever, so that they can keep their own children or small babies away. As it is to the advantage of most children to have had the infectious diseases before they start school, do not be obsessive about taking precautions to protect healthy children. Even the best efforts may be thwarted because the most infectious time is the beginning of the illness when it is very difficult to make a definite diagnosis.

Many of the infectious diseases tend to come in epidemics. These outbreaks tend to build up the pool of antibodies in the community and it is usually a couple of years before an epidemic breaks out again. Other than catching the disease, the only way you can give your child active and long term immunity against one of the infectious fevers is a programme of immunization, see page 113.

The time between catching the disease and developing signs of it is called the incubation period. Quarantine was the length of time that a child should be isolated from other people until he became non-infectious. Quarantine regulations, however, are now more relaxed.

Most of the infectious fevers have a tell-tale rash which by its character and distribution will implicate one of them. The main symptoms are summarized in the ready reference chart at the top of page 135. If the appearance of a rash raises your suspicions do not take your child to the doctor's surgery but telephone your doctor and ask for advice. Your description over the telephone may well enable your doctor to diagnose your baby's illness and he will tell you how to nurse your child.

decide whether or not specific treatment with antibiotic cream is necessary. If your baby is young, ask your doctor if you can have a cream or an ointment to put in his eyes rather than drops. Drops always upset small babies. If your child's mouth becomes very dry and his lips cracked and sore, encourage him to rinse his mouth out with boiled water and use a lip salve. The only essential with diet is to give your child plenty to drink. Let him choose whether he wants to stay in bed or not.

The commonest complications of measles are bronchitis, infection of the middle ear (otitis media) and inflammation of the brain (encephalitis). This latter condition is very rare. If your child does not begin to recover once the rash has faded, or develops a cough or complains of ear ache or has a convulsion, contact your doctor immediately.

German Measles (Rubella)

Contrary to what the name imples, this condition has no connection with measles. It is a different germ, it is less infectious and the illness is much less severe. In addition, it tends to affect older children.

You may notice that your child is slightly unwell for a few days before the rash appears. The diagnostic sign is enlarged glands at the back of the neck just at the hairline which will remain throughout the illness and for several weeks afterwards. The rash of German measles is fleeting. It may last only one or two days and like measles, it starts behind the ears then spreads to the forehead and then the rest of the body. The spots themselves are different from measles, being flat, pink irregular blotches which merge with one another so that the body looks pink all over. The temperature rarely reaches high levels and side effects are rare.

The accurate diagnosis of German measles is very important so that you can take the appropriate action with regard to pregnant mothers. In the early months of pregnancy, women must be kept away from contact with German measles at all costs. If your child develops German measles you must tell all women visitors to the house about the illness. If a woman has contact with a case of German measles and later finds herself to be pregnant, she should consult her doctor who may consider giving her tests to see if protection with an injection of gamma globulin is appropriate.

Except in epidemics it can be extremely difficult to be sure of the diagnosis. If it is essential to know, antibody tests can be done. Accurate diagnosis is particularly important in girls as they need to know if they have had German measles before they become pregnant.

Chicken pox

This mainly affects children under 10 and is one of the most infectious of the fevers. The virus is spread through two routes: through droplets of moisture which are exhaled by the infected

Measles

Measles should always be taken seriously because the side effects of the disease may be severe. Measles is one of the most infectious fevers and unless a child is immunized against it he will probably catch it at his first contact. Children are most susceptible to catching measles between the ages of one and six years. The younger the child, the more serious the illness will be and it is nearly always serious in a child who is less than three years old.

The first symptoms of measles are similar to those of a bad cold, with a running nose, cough and inflamed eyes. Your child will probably have a fever and he may vomit and have diarrhoea. At this stage before the rash appears, your doctor can confirm the diagnosis of measles by looking in your child's mouth. If there are small white spots called 'Koplik's' spots on the inside of his cheeks, then that clinches the diagnosis. The rash usually appears on the third to fifth day of the illness but may be later. It usually begins behind the ears, then spreads to the face and then to the rest of the body. At the beginning, the spots are small and dark red but later they enlarge and become red blotches. The illness is at its height while the rash is developing and your child may have a high temperature, even delirium.

If you have a very young baby who has been exposed to measles, consult your doctor about the use of gamma globulin. This is the fraction of the blood which contains antibodies. The gamma globulin for measles has been taken from people who have had measles infections and whose antibody level against the virus is high.

If your child is bothered by the light (quite a common symptom with measles) then darken the room, otherwise there is no need to. If his eyes become crusted, bathe them with boiled water or a glass of water in which you have dissolved a teaspoon of salt. Use cotton wool swabs, a separate one for each eye. If your child has a severe conjunctivitis, your doctor will person and also from the spots which are infectious until they are covered by scabs. The infectious period therefore is from 24 hours before the spots appear until all the spots are covered by scabs. The virus which causes chicken pox is the same one which causes shingles (herpes zoster). This is why it is possible for an adult with shingles to give a child chicken pox.

Your child will probably be unwell for a day or two prior to the appearance of the rash. The spots come out in groups for a few days so there will be spots in all stages of development in your child's skin. They start as dark red, slightly raised spots. Within a few hours, small blisters appear at the centre of the spot which are very fragile and easily broken.

The blisters dry into scabs which usually drop off between 10 and 14 days later and may leave shallow scars which generally disappear. The illness is usually mild and the number of spots is very variable. While some children only have one or two, others are covered in them, with spots in the mouth, ears, nose and scalp. The peripheral parts of the body are affected least and very often the skin of the arms and hands, legs and feet will be completely free.

The spots are itchy so keep your child's nails short so that they do not tear the skin and with young babies it may be necessary to bind the fingers so that they cannot damage themselves. Relieve the itching by dabbing on a cooling lotion such as calamine and if it looks as though the spots are going to become infected, ask your doctor for a specific antiseptic. If your child is still in nappies, try to leave the nappies off as often as you can so that the skin can be exposed to the air and dry out. Also ask your doctor for a special cream to apply to the nappy area to prevent secondary skin infections.

Mumps

Mumps rarely occurs in children under the age of five and is usually a mild illness. It is not as highly infectious as the other fevers and may also attack adults. The virus usually settles in the salivary glands particularly the parotid gland which is just in front of the ear.

Your child may be slightly unwell before any swelling appears and the first diagnostic sign is swelling and soreness over one of the parotid glands which can swell up quite a lot. The other gland may follow suit a day or two later and the salivary glands in the floor of the mouth may also be affected. Quite often swallowing is difficult and painful and the lack of saliva will make the inside of your child's mouth dry.

You can keep your child comfortable with a mild analgesic such as paracetamol to relieve the pain in the glands and the throat, rinsing the mouth out periodically with boiled water and using an invalid's feeding cup to take food which should be puréed.

Complications are rare but occasionally a meningitis may develop about 10 days after the illness begins. The symptoms are headache, stiff neck, dislike of light (photophobia), high fever and possibly delirium. Mumps is not too severe an illness and rarely leaves hearing problems. If you suspect that your child's hearing has deteriorated after an attack of mumps, ask your doctor to examine the hearing.

Whooping cough

This is probably the most serious of all the infectious fevers, especially in a baby under a year old. If you decide to immunize your baby it is important to do it as early as possible, because no baby receives passive immunity to whooping cough from the mother. Be sure and keep your baby away from any person who is suspected of having whooping cough.

A child is infectious for four weeks after the onset of symptoms which are usually a cough and a running nose. There is nothing unusual about the character of the cough when it first starts. After about ten days it becomes more distressing and your child will cough several times on each breath. The cough comes without any warning, so that your child will become short of air while she is coughing and a whoop is the sound of the air as it rushes through the unopened larynx as she gasps for air. Whooping cough is sometimes difficult to diagnose in young babies because they never learn the trick of whooping and because of this it can be a very distressing disorder, particularly as a spasm may terminate with vomiting. You should consider any severe paroxysmal cough that goes on for longer that a week and distresses your baby to the point of vomiting as whooping cough until your doctor has diagnosed something different. Children who have been immunized against whooping cough sometimes still catch the disease but it is nearly always in a milder, attenuated form.

The two commonest complications are middle ear infections and bronchitis which may go on to pneumonia. For this reason it is essential that your baby has treatment early in the disease. Antibiotics can kill the bacterium which causes whooping cough if given early enough so you should take your child along to your doctor if there is whooping cough in the area and he develops a severe persistent cough. Cough mixtures have no effect on the condition at all so do not give them. If your child is vomiting you may find feeding difficult. One of the best times to feed your baby is immediately after he has vomited. Make sure that meals are small and frequent and give lots to drink.

Scarlet fever

Scarlet fever is rare nowadays. It is really just a sore throat (caused by a particular strain of streptococcus) and a rash. The illness usually starts without any warning. The child will suddenly go off her food, will develop a high fever and may vomit. Swollen glands are a common feature of the condition and may account for the abdominal pain which is a common complaint if the abdominal glands are swollen. It is possible

Disease	Symptoms in order of appearance
MEASLES	Runny nose, cough, inflamed eyes, fever, vomiting, diarrhoea, white (Koplik's) spots, rash behind ears, then on face, then on body.
GERMAN MEASLES (RUBELLA)	Slight temperature, enlarged glands at back of neck, rash behind ears, then on forehead, then on rest of body.
CHICKEN POX	Dark red, irritating, groups of spots.
MUMPS	Swelling and soreness of glands at sides of face, in front of ears, painful swallowing, dry mouth.
WHOOPING COUGH	Slight temperature, runny nose, slight cough, then convulsive cough followed by whooping breath.
SCARLET FEVER	Lack of appetite, fever, vomiting, swollen glands, tiny red spots.

(Left) This chart summarizes the main symptoms of the infectious diseases which a young child may catch.

to confuse this condition with tonsillitis, but is easily distinguished on the second day when the rash appears, starting around the neck and the front of the chest and then spreading over the whole body. The skin appears pink and flushed all over and is superimposed with tiny red spots. A particularly striking feature of scarlet fever is that the area around the lips is usually quite pale and this sign can be diagnostic. About a week after the rash has appeared, the skin over each spot begins to peel. The doctor will usually treat this condition with antibiotics.

Safe medicines

While I would never agree with an overstocked medicine cabinet or the keeping of old medicines that are only half used, there are a few simple medicines which are safe and effective and can be used without consulting a doctor. You should use your own good judgement and common sense. Do not use any medicine frequently or regularly, that is more than once a twice a week without consulting your doctor.

Paracetamol: a mild analgesic and anti-pyretic (lowers the temperature) substance. It is safer than aspirin in that it does not irritate the stomach and has fewer side effects. It is formulated into a special low dose paediatric syrup which is pleasant for babies and children to take and as long as you conform to the manufacturers' instructions on the packet, your child should come to no harm. It is available as paracetamol elixir from most chemists.

Even though paracetamol is quite a safe medicine, do not give it for longer than 12 hours without consulting your doctor. Any condition in a baby or child which lasts longer than 12 hours and requires an analgesic or anti-pyretic also requires expert medical attention.

Calamine lotion: an excellent, simple, soothing and cooling lotion to apply to a baby's skin if it is hot and irritable, especially after too much sun. Soak a cotton wool swab in calamine lotion and gently smooth it on to your baby's skin every two or three hours if necessary.

Cetrimide antiseptic cream: Cetrimide is the antiseptic used in hospitals and can be bought from any chemist. It is an all purpose antiseptic application, very safe and very effective. Keep a large tube by you for cuts, abrasions, minor burns, etc. The cream will not only keep all minor injuries clean but the base is soothing and takes away stinging.

Gripe water: is still extensively used but is of doubtful value.

Warnings about medicines

Never resort to a baby aspirin as a cure for all your baby's ills or give it lightly. Aspirin is most useful for bringing down your baby's temperature and for soothing a definite pain. Always follow the manufacturers' instructions and never give your baby aspirin for more than two doses without consulting your doctor. As adults we use aspirin so often and carelessly we tend not to think of it as a drug at all. But it is very potent though also very useful if used properly. Do not give aspirin to a baby under one year old.

Avoid the use of any creams or ointments which contain local anaesthetics. Many of the teething gels contain such substances but they should be avoided because they may cause allergies and your child may be in trouble the next time he needs a dental injection of a local anaesthetic. In the list of ingredients on a tube of teething gel any word ending in 'caine' will indicate an anaesthetic.

Never, never, use up old medicines, like eye ointments, liquid antibiotic, medicines, antiseptic creams that you have kept in the medicine cabinet in the hope that one day they will be useful again. The probability is that the active ingredient has deteriorated and the medicine is no longer active. If you use it for your baby you may be doing him a great deal of harm. It is best to throw away any leftover medicine, once the course of treatment is finished.

Do not use proprietary medicinal products except for very simple conditions like nappy rash. It is possible that your baby needs a specific medicine and this is only available from your doctor, so consult him.

Encouragement and praise

A small child thrives on the satisfaction from praise and the more he gets, the better it is.

As well as encouraging him through praise, you should also be aware of his day-to-day need to share in your activities. At this age he will be fascinated even by routine housework and will want to watch and join in whatever is going on. In order to satisfy this curiosity he will want to be with you all the time and will be happiest if you can take every opportunity to explain what you are doing and help him to 'help' you.

Critical phases of learning

We know that a baby may start learning very soon after he is born and we also know that his rate of learning is not constant. There are 'learning peaks' when he seems to be able to develop new skills with great ease. He reacts to new information very quickly and, if possible, will put his new experience to immediate use.

The learning peaks occur at different times in individual children. It is much better to respond to the signs your own child displays than to check his progress against development charts. Learning peaks last a variable length of time and each one may be different in your own child, sometimes lasting a few weeks and sometimes a few months. During these peaks your child may take extraordinary leaps forward. It is vital that you are alert to the appearance of these spurts and that you are especially helpful to your child when they occur (see below). Devote to them all the time and attention you can spare and remember that one or two hours of concentrated work or play with your child is more valuable to him than a whole day of half-hearted tolerance of his demands.

Besides these critical phases of learning, there are almost certainly periods when parts of the brain associated with special skills mature. It is probable that unless the special skill is introduced at the time when the part of the brain associated with it is maturing, the receptive phase passes and the skill can then never be properly learned. This has been proved to be the case with some birds and animals. Baby birds reared in complete silence up to the age of eight weeks never learn to sing, even though they are exposed to bird song later. Kittens kept in darkness for more than six weeks stay blind, even though the rest of their days are spent in daylight. It is unlikely that human babies develop on the same time scale but the evidence for short aptitude peaks is substantial.

The importance of this finding is that the development of centres in the brain associated with learning occurs in the first years of life and the development is completed in the first five years. Many of the learning processes such as the development of memory, the ability to judge and make decisions, the capability for problem solving and for planning ahead, being methodical, giving attention to detail, developing the powers of concentration, are established in the first five years for the rest of life.

So we must conclude that it is the parents' responsibility to provide the necessary stimuli for their children to encourage and develop emerging skills. Otherwise, your child may never have a second chance to develop them. As most of these skills emerge before school age, it is the job of parents and not teachers to give a child a flying start in life.

This does not mean that you should force your child to read and write against his will.

There's no magic formula for giving your help in a learning spurt. Nor can you find out or even anticipate when a critical learning phase will come. But any observant parent will know when it does. Your child's horizon suddenly expands, his ambition soars, his interest in everything comes into sharp focus. Skills are mastered quickly and he is avid for new experiences. All you have to do is watch, wait for your cue then feed the hunger in whatever way your common sense tells you. If your child picks up a pencil and scribbles give him coloured chalks and a blackboard. Try finger paints. Show him shapes. Suggest he copies. Name the things you are using. Repeat the names of colours and shapes. If you draw a circle show him that a ball is round and it rolls. In fact all round things roll even cotton reels on their sides. It's endless and as much fun for you as your child.

Talking

About the eleventh or twelfth month your baby will comprehend the use of a particular word with a particular object but it may be a few months before she matches the right word to that object. There are several practical ways in which you can help your baby to talk and listen.
☐ Talk to your baby about the things which are there for her to see. If you are in the garden talk about the flowers and show her them. If you are playing with the ball, talk about the ball, name it and roll it so that she learns the characteristics of the ball. If you are stroking the dog, talk about the dog and then name some of his characteristics, such as ears, paws and tail.

You will help your baby to build up speech patterns if they are based on visual images, actions and functions.
☐ Talk about things which are of immediate interest to your baby. Something which every baby loves is to be told a story about herself with herself as the central character. It is all the more exciting if you relate it to an incident which occurred during the day and then make it into her favourite fantasy.
☐ Always try to look at your baby while talking to her, and if possible, look into her eyes. This is one way of concentrating her attention and helping her to pick up specific sounds from the blur of noise that is going on around her.
☐ Never correct her baby words or her own jargon. It may become boring and repetitive for her. Worse it may make her feel ashamed and this may put a brake on speech development. With recurrent use and recurrent hearing of the correct use of that particular word, your baby

(Below) A good parent supports with encouragement when it's needed and then pursues a policy of non-interference. A child playing alone with shapes and water and soil is learning many things, not the least to remain absorbed in a project until it's finished. Don't curtail the adventure by meddling.

(Left and below) The local park is a fruitful store of entertainments. There are interesting seats to study and climb on, as well as challenging climbing frames to swing on, whilst you help to push.

will make the transition to adult pronunciation in her own good time but never when forced by you. Some baby words are so delightful that I could not help using them myself because I did not wish my baby to stop using them. They seem to lose them all too fast.

☐ It follows on that you should try very hard to understand her new words, even if they are mispronounced. This will encourage your baby to make new sounds. Make the most of any clues she gives you like pointing or turning round and if you share with her the discovery of the object and name it for her clearly when you hand it to her, her joy will be doubled.

☐ Make sure that you use specific words and say them clearly when you talk to your baby. Try to discard substitute words like 'that', 'it', and 'them', talk about 'door', 'bottle' and 'shoes'.

☐ Follow the instinct to overact and exaggerate emotions when you are talking to your baby. The information you are sending her will reach her as clear, strong messages. You will find your baby is soon imitating your inflections of solace: 'Oh, never mind then', or delight: 'pretty flower'.

(Below) There are many opportunities outdoors for developing your child's senses. He will learn new words and sensations with you to show him the way.

Discipline

As your child's understanding increases, you will start introducing her to the very early stages of discipline. Over-discipline and under-discipline can be equally bad for children as both lead to insecurity. It is important that you take a rational view of discipline. Every time you are tempted to discipline your child, decide whether your disciplining action is for your convenience, or whether it is for the child's good. Only go ahead with it if it helps your baby.

Introducing your baby to discipline should be a gradual process. It should be done in a gentle, loving way. You should remain calm and you should not raise your voice. Small children who are used to hearing their mother's voice only in tones of gentleness and reassurance may be very frightened the first time she raises her voice in anger. Many cry because they feel insecure at the prospect of your love being withdrawn from them. Disciplining your small child should never have this overtone. She will learn the lessons much more easily if you are gentle and firm and your voice is not shrill.

Offering your child no guidance at all really serves her badly. You are only making life harder for her than it need be. When she comes to play with other children, they will be unwilling to tolerate an ill-mannered, selfish child. Adults will be even less likely to welcome her. There have to be a few rules in the home just as there are in any organized group, if only for the sake of safety, justice and efficiency. Sensible, loving parents, however, keep their rules to a minimum and retain only those which are reasonable.

Children can understand, indeed they are interested in, your reasons for doing things much earlier than you imagine. Like adults, they are much more likely to comply with your requests if they understand why you make them. An example is when should your child go to bed? There are two ways of dealing with this. If you spend most days at home with your baby, you will probably want to establish a fairly inflexible bedtime. This will involve a firm attitude to all your child's delaying tactics and crying at bedtime. Most children will accept this routine in time even if they are difficult initially.

On the other hand, if you leave your child regularly for a large part of the day, for instance if you work, and if there is no good reason why your child should go to bed, other than the fact that you would find it more convenient, then she is likely to resist. If she is not sleepy, she will be very unhappy at being left alone in her bedroom imagining the activities going on downstairs. And it would be very sad if she got into the habit of crying herself to sleep. It is far better if you give up a little more of your time so that she can play downstairs until she falls asleep. This way your child is assured of your love and attention, which makes discipline easier, not more difficult. There is plenty of time when your child is older to explain to her that you enjoy time on your own just as much as she does, then she will readily accept the idea of playing alone in her bedroom even though she is not sleepy.

(Above) A sleeveless, quilted jacket provides extra warmth when needed and is light to carry around if it gets too hot.

Clothing

Your main concern in dressing a one year old should be his comfort. Do not try to force your taste on him as you may be surprised at how clearly developed his own taste is at this early age. For your baby's sake, choose clothes that are warm, dry and protective. They should never restrict movement, so avoid stiff, heavy material. For your own sake, choose clothes that need minimum care with washing and ironing and do not spend a lot of money on them. Your baby is growing so fast that they will be in one piece when he grows out of them, no matter how cheap they were.

Stretch materials like stretch terry towelling, or lycra for heavier garments are ideal for your child and easy for you to look after. Though you may want to dress your child in pastel or bright colours, you will have less washing to do if you choose dark or muddy colours that do not show up the dirt.

Regardless of sex, your crawling baby will be best protected in a garment which has long trousers. Choose one which is all in one with the top and avoid restrictive waist bands. When it is cold, avoid thick hairy knitwear next to the skin, as it is irritating and curtails movement. It is preferable that you put several lightweight layers of clothes on your child to keep him warm.

You do not need to spend a lot of money on a winter coat. It will only last your baby one winter. It will also need to be dry-cleaned and will restrict easy movement. It is easier for you and better for your baby to have a lightweight quilted showerproof anorak with a hood. This is a comfortable piece of clothing, which can be washed and dried overnight.

As a general rule you should avoid manmade fibres as they prevent free evaporation of sweat from the skin. There is no need to wear conventional underclothes at all. A T-shirt and a pair of stretch towelling pants can double up as under-clothes and as play clothes when the weather gets warmer. There is no need for your child to wear socks until he wears shoes and no need for him to wear shoes until he is walking outdoors.

Everyday care

Even if you feel anything but, try to be as cheery as possible when you get your one year old out of his cot. He may have been awake for some time and will be craving your company and attention. He may be a bit irritable and impatient while you take off his overnight nappy which is soaking wet. He might tolerate the removal of a nappy which is causing him discomfort but his early morning mood may make it difficult for you to wash and dry him as thoroughly as you would wish. Whatever you do, do not start off the day with a tussle. Make it easy for the two of you. Give him a toy or a mirror to look into to distract him while you clean his bottom and wash his face and hands.

By the time your baby is one year old, he will be helping you with dressing and undressing movements. Go with him, not against him. It is easier if you dress the top half and the lower half separately. Dress the top half first because it is usually easier and quicker and if you have any difficulties, make it into a game so that you both end up laughing instead of being angry with each other. At this age, babies start to be very playful. Even when you are putting his nappy on he may tease you by trying to roll away or make your job more difficult by hanging on to his feet. You could cut these tricks short by keeping a toy handy that you can give him if his games become too boisterous. Make sure that it is a favourite toy that is certain to distract him. Never start putting on a nappy without having anything near you. While you are searching for a pin he will have wriggled away again.

Once your baby is confident in the large bath, you can let him play around happily in the bath water. If he is feeling rebellious don't go at him like a sergeant major with a flannel and soap. It is much easier on you (because you will not have a dirty bath to clean) and on him, simply to put a specially-prepared soap liquid into the water and he will cleanse himself as he is splashing about. Put lots of colourful floating toys in the bath to amuse him and make bath time fun. Even if your child can sit up quite confidently never leave the room while he is in the bath. A one year old can pull himself up to a standing position by hanging on to the edge of the bath and then fall quite suddenly when he loses his grasp on the slippery edge. Put a towel or a rubber bath mat at the bottom of the bath to stop his feet slipping.

Naps

By now your child will be sleeping much less and will probably be awake for most of the day other than during her one daily nap. It does not matter whether she takes her nap in the morning or in the afternoon but for your baby's sake, it is a good thing to encourage a nap immediately after lunch. If your baby sleeps from 11.30 am to 1 pm there will be five hours to go before the usual bath and feed at 6 pm and after five hours your baby may be scratchy, irritable and difficult. Do not let your baby's nap go on for too long otherwise she will not be sleepy when it comes to bedtime and you will have a playful, wide-awake child to cope with later in the evening. If a baby sleeps too long in the morning, she may miss out on her midday meal and this will throw the rest of your day out of routine. However, if you are going to wake your baby out of her nap you must do it with care and gentleness.

Sleep requirements

Sleep requirements are variable. Some children of a year still need 12 hours, some only need six. One thing is certain: *you* can't decide how much your child sleeps. You can put her to bed or in her cot but if she doesn't need to sleep from 6 pm to 6 am she will play alone for a couple of hours until she drops off. This may suit you. It doesn't happen to suit me. I'd rather my baby played with or beside or in the same room as me. You will also find that your child sleeps the same number of hours and goes to sleep at the same time whether you have a set bedtime or not. That is why I never did with any of my four children. Just as I favour demand feeding so I favour demand bedtimes. And for that matter demand naps – as long as they weren't too late in the day. But then, if a child goes to sleep which reasonable mother will wake her? Not I.

Equipment
The baby bouncer

Your child will have a lot of energy and will need all the physical play you can give. One of the best forms of play and exercise is a baby bouncer. If well positioned, your baby can see you as you move about the house and so she never feels lonely. It also gives her a magnificent view of the outside world, especially if the weather is warm and you can fit the baby bouncer over an outside door. It is also very good for strengthening the legs and helps your baby to learn co-ordination of her upright body. You can use it from the time that your baby takes pleasure in taking her weight on her feet, until she learns to walk. The length of the elastic strings should be just sufficient for your baby to get her whole foot on the ground when she sinks down on it but short enough to allow her to rest completely and take the weight off her legs if she bends her knees. A baby bouncer is good for you too because it keeps your baby happy and occupied and out of mischief while you get on with other chores but at the same time you can keep an eye on her.

Play pen

I am in favour of play pens only if they are used properly and do not become an easy way out for the parents and a trap for the baby. The purpose of a play pen is to stop your child from getting into mischief. This implies two things: your child is mobile and adventurous and you do not have the time to keep an eye on him. It is not good for him to be penned up when he wants to explore the world, nor is it good for you to ignore him. The fascination of being in a play pen is exhausted within half an hour. Try not to rely on them for longer than this.

Toys

By the time your child is one year old, he will be physically adventurous and intellectually sophisticated, so his toys should reflect this. At this stage when he is pulling himself up to a standing position, make sure that toys which help walking are sturdy and safe.

Especially useful toys at this age are:
Toys that fit together
To help your child develop the use of his hands, he will need a few toys which will exercise his hands and his imagination sitting down. Make sure that the pieces of the toy are large so that your baby can handle them easily. Some are –
☐ Any set of toys which is hollow and increases in size and can be fitted inside one another. These come in cubes, beakers, etc.
☐ The hammer and peg toy which has a wooden frame with holes through which pegs are banged with a mallet. Your child then turns the frame over and they can be banged back again.
☐ Rods on a stand. This is often the toy on which a child learns to count and learns his colours. The stand has rods of different lengths which take different numbers of coloured balls. The coloured balls are pierced with a hole so that they slide easily on and off the rods.
☐ Any toys which are easy to put together and simple to take apart. These toys would include plastic people whose accessories can be collected and interchanged and simple cars and trains that have detachable parts.

A baby who is crawling will enjoy any toy that can move along the ground, especially if there is a string attached so that he can pull it towards him. Balls, especially large, light multicoloured ones, are a perennial favourite. To protect your baby and your furniture, provide toys that can be thrown without damage like balloons, small bags, bean bags, etc. He will still have a delight in banging things, which may be heightened if you introduce him to musical instruments such as a xylophone, a drum or a tambourine.

Your baby will enjoy his toys more and they will last longer if you organize them for him. Keep most of his everyday toys in an open basket in a special part of the room which becomes 'his'. He will quickly learn where they are and crawl to his corner to find them. Even at an early age you can encourage him to put toys back when he has finished with them by making a game of tidying up with you leading the way and lots of exhortations to your baby to follow suit. Keep a few special toys out of your baby's reach which you can bring out for him to play with on special occasions only.

Swimming

Many children coming up to one year of age have a special delight and aptitude for swimming. If both you and your child are brave enough you might try taking a six-month old baby to special swimming classes. Up to the age of one year most children retain the ability to make almost reflexive swimming movements. Though it may sound cruel, many people experienced with teaching youngsters to swim state that children of this age who are thrown into a swimming pool will come to no harm. As long as you are standing there to grab them when they surface, they enjoy it and come to no harm.

I am not suggesting that you should follow this routine with your child but it is a good idea to get your child used to a swimming bath and to swimming at a very early age.

(Above) Many local swimming pools have special sessions for parents with young babies. The children usually have great fun and if you are lucky and persistent with swimming tuition, you may have a baby who can keep his head above water and even propel himself along by the time he is one year old. Make sure that your child always wears some type of water wings.

Safety procedures

Now that your toddler is really mobile it is important to scan the house constantly to try to remove hazards and protect your child from accidents. It is well known that some of the worst accidents to children and babies take place in their own homes. One of the best ways to protect your child from accidents is to take her around the house with you. Never leave her alone in a room. If you have to dash to the phone, or answer the front door bell, pick your child up and sling her on your hip. Some basic precautions that you can take are as follows:

1. Fit bars to first floor windows and rooms that your child frequents.

2. Never leave first floor windows open more than a few inches. Make sure that they have a special fastening to stop them being open for more than a few inches.

3. Make sure that your garden is safe by cutting off any access to a drive or the road.

4. Make sure that all of the utensils she uses daily are made of unbreakable materials.

5. Always keep medicines out of a child's reach and in a locked cupboard.

6. If you have a fire, be it open or electric in rooms that your baby has access to, always use a fire guard.

7. Even though your baby is quite good at going up and downstairs, there may be a time when she trips and falls. If she is toddling about upstairs, keep a removable gate handy and fix it across the top of the stairs as a reflex as you and your baby reach the top.

8. Make sure that your baby is always wearing a harness in the high chair, pram or car.

9. If you have an open fire make sure that all your child's clothes are non-inflammable.

10. Nothing which is hot, like a kettle or a paraffin heater, should be left in any room that your child may wander into unguarded.

11. Have pan guards fitted to your cooker. These safety rings drop down over the burners putting them out and hold the pans so that they cannot be tipped over.

12. Always turn the handles of your pans inwards and use the back burners of the cooker whenever possible.

13. Never ever leave anything cooking if you leave the kitchen when your child is in it.

14. Always put a hot object well out of reach of your child as it may retain its heat for some time after it has been used.

15. If you are a smoker, make sure that your lighter and matches are never left lying around. Also make sure that your ash tray is out of your child's reach as a cigarette end can give a nasty burn.

16. Never allow a child to touch anything electrical.

17. Never give a child an electric blanket.

18. Always make sure that your household electrical appliances are earthed.

19. Make sure that all your electric plugs are child proof. You can buy plastic safety discs which fit on to unswitched sockets very inexpensively from most hardware stores.

20. Always switch off switched sockets.

21. Use flex holders to stop trailing wires.

22. Keep all cleaning materials in a cupboard out of your child's reach.

23. Garages, garden sheds and workshops should be kept locked.

24. Keep all house equipment like knives, scissors and screwdrivers, cutlery, sewing materials, pencils and fountain pens well out of the way of your child.

25. Never leave your child alone with food or a bottle or in the bath.

26. Never let your child play with anything which is small enough to be swallowed, pushed up his nostrils or pushed into his ears. N.B. Beware of peanuts, which can be pushed into any orifice and may make him choke (see page 155).

27. Keep polythene bags well out of the way.

28. Laurel and laburnum are poisonous plants, so keep your child away from them.

29. If you have a pond in the garden, make sure that it is safe or that your child is always supervised when he is near it.

Learning to walk

Learning to walk is one of your baby's greatest achievements. There is a wide variation in the age at which your baby learns to walk and there are several phases which she must go through.

First phase

Once your baby has learned to stand up with support she will then start to 'cruise'. In this movement she slides her hands to one side or another of her support until she is almost off balance and then she brings her feet along the floor to come under her hands by sliding them one at a time. This brings her body straight again. During cruising you will notice that she always hangs on to her support with two hands. She is never prepared to trust her weight to her feet and one hand alone. You will also notice that her feet are some distance from the support and she leans forward so that quite a lot of her weight is taken on her hands.

Second phase

Your baby is now standing with her feet closer to the support and she is leaning a little further backwards so that most of her weight is taken on her feet. Very little weight is taken on her hands and she is using them only for balance which is now much steadier. She has the courage to move her hands over one another instead of sliding them along. As her confidence grows she begins to move her hands and feet together so that for a second she is taking all her weight on one foot and relying on only one hand for support.

Third phase

Her balance is now steadier and her co-ordination improved. She is prepared to venture across small gaps between one support and another. Try to arrange the furniture in a way that helps her so that she can make runs down one side, across the end of the room and up the other. Leave gaps between the furniture which are about the width of her arms.

Fourth phase

Your child will now take her first unsupported step. Her confidence has grown to the extent that she will try to negotiate a gap which is just wider than her arm span. She does this by moving her feet out into the centre of the gap, while holding on to the first support with one hand. When she is balanced, she will take one ungainly step towards the new support and grab it with the other hand. At about the same time, she is able to stand alone unsupported. In the standing position, her legs are splayed out so that she is standing on a wide base. It is easier to balance on a wide base than a narrow one. To help her balance she holds her arms away from the sides of her body so that her elbows are held up and her hands are about the level of her neck.

(Right) Your child learns to walk in well defined stages. She can't stand until she's learned to pull herself to her feet. She won't take a step until she's learned to stand quite steadily. And when she does take her first steps she'll hold her arms up and out to help keep her balance. But it shows that she is gaining confidence when she is prepared to hold a toy in both hands, rather than keeping one free to grasp hold of the nearest support.

Fifth phase

After the first single step, it is a very short time before your toddler will take two or three steps between supports. Again you can help her with this phase by arranging the furniture in such a way that she can cruise for a few feet and then have to negotiate a slightly wider gap that requires one step, cruise a little more and then make her way across a gap which necessitates a few steps. She will improve all the more rapidly with lots of encouragement and praise.

Sixth phase

Your child starts to walk unsupported and confidently. This does not mean that she will be able to walk any distance, she may only walk across the room and then require support for a rest. The main change is that her gait is no longer unsteady and she no longer topples to one side and sits down with a thump in the middle of the room. When she sets off to cross a room she does so in a straight line and gets to the other side without needing support.

This description of how your child learns to walk has only taken a few minutes to read, but of course it is not all smooth. She may make rapid progress for a few weeks, and then appear to make none at all. There may be setbacks, due to illness or distress.

Don't forget that your baby is learning about a lot of other things at the same time as walking. She has only a certain amount of concentration to devote to each, and on one day she may give more of her attention to learning about a new

(Right) Reins need not restrain – if you're a good follower. They needn't restrict freedom, they can give it to you and your child. Personally, I don't see any other way of giving your child the freedom of a busy pavement and the chance to explore places where a hazard may lurk around the next corner.

(Below) These charts continue the record of weight and height development for small, medium and large 1 to 1½ year olds.

way of using her fingers than to walking. Skills do not develop uniformly across all fronts. They develop in a piecemeal fashion and some go ahead of others.

Encourage the progress of walking by helping your baby. She will prefer your support to any other. You can greatly boost her confidence about standing upright, maintaining her balance and co-ordinating her movements if you are the support around which she cruises and if you provide your hands as the grips for hers when she takes her first independent step.

You can also help with toys that aid the development of walking. The best one is the spe-

cially designed baby walker. This is an almost indispensable toy for the toddler because it helps all stages of walking. Remember at this stage that she is not strong enough to go for any long distance without a rest, so every now and then you should pick her up to give her a rest.

Once your baby is walking confidently and no longer wants to hold on to your hand, it is important to use a set of reins with a harness and straps so that your baby can make forays but never get far away from you. They have been criticized because they are thought to restrict a toddler's independence but I cannot think of any other way in which you can give a toddler any freedom at all and still be sure that she is safe.

You should look out for the time when your child is ready to go without reins. She must be quite steady on her feet, she should have good control over her legs and her body so that she can stop and start easily from any pace and she should be able to control the direction in which her body moves so that she can safely negotiate obstacles without crashing into them. Your child will probably be able to do this by the time she is two to two and a half years old. This is the time to forsake your reins.

Increasing manual dexterity

By the time your child is 18 months old his manual dexterity has improved to the extent that he can build a tower of two or three bricks and he can manipulate his food with a spoon and turn over the pages of a book though only two or three at a time. If you show him how it is done he may try to open and close a zip fastener.

At two years your baby will have just about learned to open a door by turning the door knob and possibly to unscrew the lid which you have loosened for him. He will try very hard to put on his shoes and socks and he probably quite enjoys washing and drying his hands.

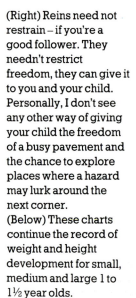

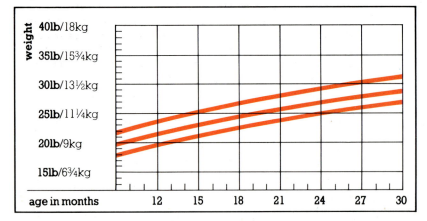

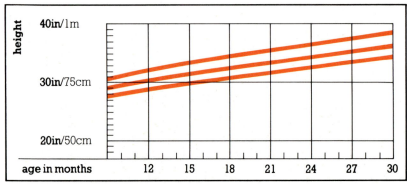

Feeding

After your child's first birthday, his weight gain will slow down and will probably be no more than one to two ounces (30 – 60 g) a week. You will also notice that your child's proportions are becoming quite different. Your child's head will still seem large in proportion to the rest of the body and he may appear to have no neck at all. His shoulders and chest may be thin, his stomach may stick out and his legs may seem bowed. His feet will appear flat. Over the next 12 months however, be assured that all this will change. By the time he is two years old, his proportions will become more adult. He will probably have lost his pot belly, his legs will be straight, his head will be smaller in relation to the rest of his body and his neck will become more obvious. His legs will have probably got thinner and his body will have elongated.

As a child grows up and acquires new skills and independence, he develops his own individuality. One manifestation of this is that he likes to choose for himself, and most of the time he should be allowed to make a personal choice. One of the ways in which you can ensure a happy relationship with your baby is to be very flexible in allowing him to make up his own mind. He will start to find meal times disturbing if he finds that his loyalties are pulled in two directions.

In the first place, he has a tremendous desire to please you. You are the centre of his world and your approbation and love count above all else. He may be longing to eat the food you have prepared because he knows that will please you but at the same time there is an instinct drawing him in another direction. He feels a very strong desire to choose for himself and please himself. A young child confronted by this situation does not have the ability to resolve his difficulties and make a choice. His only reaction is to become irritable, sulk and misbehave. In the process, his food remains uneaten.

Your first reaction may be that he is doing it on purpose or doing it to spite you. Nothing could be further from the truth. You are faced with a child who cannot solve a problem. If you take a defensive attitude or try to force the issue, you will find that the difficulties recur at the next meal and possibly again and again. Before you know it mealtimes will have become terrible stumbling blocks which disturb the whole family. This is a state of affairs you should avoid at all costs. Encourage your toddler's independence at meal times, let him stop eating whenever he indicates he is satisfied and never use food as a reward or a punishment. Also, vary his food and include a few 'treats' like chocolate and ice cream as part of his normal diet. Otherwise you may encourage furtiveness about food. If you introduce them as treats, you remain in control. Remember that no one food is indispensable. There is always another equally good food.

Food fads

Children quite commonly go through phases of an especially strong liking for a particular food, or of liking only a few foods. The only time food fads become dangerous and therefore the only time when you should try and change them is when they exclude essential foods. If your child has too many sugar-containing carbohydrates, such as biscuits, sweet drinks, sweets and chocolates this may prevent him eating more nourishing foods, it will also be bad for his teeth and may make him overweight. But just because your baby prefers some foods does not necessarily mean they are 'inferior'. The fact that he prefers sausages to minced beef should cause you no anxiety at all. Provided he eats enough, sausages will give him exactly the same first class protein that minced beef would (see page 127). Though fish fingers are not quite as nutritious as the same number of ounces of pure fish, they do contain first class animal protein and will do your baby a great deal of good. It is much better for your baby to eat a good helping of something he likes such as baked beans,

(Below) As your child's manual dexterity increases you can find games that will encourage it even more. Games such as this letter cut-out. It teaches the alphabet, too, without your child even being aware of it.

sweet corn or peanut butter on bread, than to eat very little of an egg or cheese. Always remember that your toddler can get almost all the protein, vitamin and minerals he needs for one day from a pint of milk, which he is probably drinking in addition to his other diet anyway. Conversely, if your baby hates milk, don't worry. As long as he's eating a balanced diet milk isn't essential and other dairy products, such as yogurt, are good substitutes. Your child's chosen diet will probably be much more nutritious than you think.

The way to handle food fads is to play them down. Even better, serve your child his favourite foods as often as you both like. Food fads pass very quickly and the more often you serve a child one food, the more quickly he will tire of it and go on to something else. If on the other hand you make a lot of food fads, then your child will also quickly realise that they are a weapon which he can wield three or four times day.

Meal times are part of the learning process, and you should allow him to experiment at his own pace and in his own way.

Though it will not do him much good, it does not matter at all if he puts his plate of food on his head and lets his dinner run down his face. Wipe up the mess and start again, and if you can, have a good laugh with your baby about it. Next time you serve a meal, use a rubber suction cup on the bottom of the plate so that he cannot lift it off the table.

It is part of your baby's physical development to learn to let go of things and while he is going through this stage he will drop anything out of his pram or high chair, including food. Don't make a fuss, simply cover the floor with newspapers before you start so that you can clear up the mess quickly when the meal is over.

A further stage of your baby's development is to start to throw things. When he is going through this phase he will almost certainly start throwing his food. This should not bother you either. Simply make sure that your baby has a clear enough space around his high chair while he is feeding, so that any food which is thrown does not reach something which is precious. Some time after 18 months old you can start discouraging your baby from using his food as play material. Some babies are quite fastidious from an early age, others never learn to stop being messy eaters. If you have a messy eater, you will have to be more flexible in your attitude towards table manners. Most children up to the age of 10 have to have some clearing up done for them when a meal is finished.

Never make the mistake of calling a fat baby a bonny baby. A fat baby is almost certainly a sick baby. Fat babies have been shown to pick up infections, especially respiratory ones, more easily than a baby who is not overweight. A fat baby is nearly always fat because he is overeating and the person to blame for that is his mother. You should make sure that your baby's diet does not contain too many carbohydrates, starches and sweet, sickly foods, nor should you allow him to eat excess fat.

Bowel and bladder control

It is quite wrong to train a child to have bowel and bladder control. We have been used to talking about potty training but it is a dangerous concept, as children need to reach a particular mental and physical maturity before they can learn the necessary *control*. This stage is reached at different ages by different children. Bladder control is a very complex physiological mechanism which involves not just the muscles and nerves of the bladder and bowel but the brain as well. The brain has to give three commands. Firstly, it must reverse the full bladder's natural instinct to empty itself. Then when the time is right, the brain cancels the first order to 'hold on', simultaneously signalling 'let go'. The bowel mechanism is similarly complicated.

Many babies empty their bowel and bladder during a meal or just after a meal as early as two or three months old. If you are lucky enough to have one of these babies, do not assume she is beginning to learn control, it is merely a reflex. Voluntary control rarely begins before 15 to 18 months and often later. Girls are usually earlier than boys. You will know when your child is reaching a level of development when bladder control is possible, because she will tell you very clearly that voluntary control is beginning. You should never expect, nor should you try to enforce any kind of bladder or bowel control on your baby until she has given you a sign.

This sign may be given when your baby is about 15 months old but may not be before she is two years old: she will show you, by pointing, that she has noticed the fact that she is passing urine. This awareness gradually develops so that she can tell you whether or not she wishes to use the potty if you ask her. Subsequently, she will actually tell you before she is going to pass water, although this will probably only be a few moments before the event. Later she will learn to control this urgency at least long enough for you to be able to take her clothes down and sit her on the potty. Of course, the transition to this stage will be gradual and so accidents will happen. It is best to treat these as lightly as possible to avoid causing anxiety. At this point you could show your child how to use the lavatory. To start with, you can fit a smaller seat and provide a special stool in front of the lavatory, see page 177. This will make it easier for her when she wishes to go independently of you. You can help by encouraging each stage of development and by praising all achievements. The remarkable progess from initial awareness, through control of the instinct to self-reliance takes place over relatively few months.

Bowel control normally comes before bladder control and bladder control at night comes last of all, since a two and a half year old cannot hold urine for much longer than four to five hours and often less.

The results of a study showed that at two and a half 90% of girls and 75% of boys have complete daytime control. Whereas 50% of all children still needed nappies at night though they were dry during the day.

before two and a half years and is much more likely to be three.

The timing and frequency of bowel control differs from child to child as it does with adults. And your idea of bowel regularity may not be right for your child. Children do not necessarily empty their bowels every day and are not harmed by missing a day. You can, however, help your child by encouraging her to respond to the call to stool. This will usually happen after a full meal and quite often after breakfast. If you are going to go out after breakfast, do leave your child enough time on the potty. However, don't force her to stay there until she has performed satisfactorily, or bribe her to keep still with sweets and toys. This will on the one hand teach her to dislike the potty and on the other to learn to use the potty only as a means of getting your attention. Try to treat the whole thing naturally and never ridicule, punish or threaten her. When your child is going through this rather difficult part of growing up you and your husband should remain placid at all costs and avoid causing any sort of pain, emotional as well as physical.

If she feels uncomfortable about using the potty to empty her bowels, she may hold back the stool. When this happens the rectum and the lower bowel dilate and become loaded with hard faeces. After a while the rectum becomes insensitive to being stretched and therefore the normal warning signs are not given. In addition, the hard faeces irritate the lining of the bowel, thus stimulating the production of mucus. This may appear as a watery diarrhoea, so the unlikely combination of constipation with diarrhoea occurs. True constipation, that is a lazy bowel, rarely occurs provided that your child is being given the right things to eat. She needs plenty of roughage i.e. brown bread, green vegetables and fruit. But if constipation does develop, do consult your doctor, who may recommend special treatment.

Sleep disturbances

With their widening experience, toddlers quite often wake in the night after a bad dream. Quite often it may be enough to answer his cry, turn him over, tuck him in, pat him reassuringly on the back and sing him a song until he goes off to sleep. On the other hand, your child may need the reassurance of your company for a little while. So if your child does wake up in the night, make sure of the following things:

1. That he does not go to sleep feeling cold. Go back to his room 15 minutes after you have put him to bed to see that he has not gone to sleep on top of his bedclothes. If he has, lift the clothes gently over him, or just put a spare blanket over him. If he does not mind you might try putting him to bed in a sleeping bag.
2. That he is not hungry or thirsty during the night. If your toddler has missed a nap or is so tired in the evening that he cannot eat his supper, the probability is that he will wake up hungry. If this becomes a pattern, try giving your

(Above) This session on the potty is quite the opposite of the archaic Victorian idea of potty training.

When he has to sit on the potty for any length of time, give your child a toy such as this to while away the time. Keep potty-times pleasant, unfussy and (like food) only on demand.

Try not to take off your child's nappies too soon. Wait until she is able to tell you whether or not she wants to pass urine and can control this desire long enough for you to get her to the potty or lavatory. I would not recommend the use of trainer pants. They suggest a training programme, which I firmly disagree with. They are also an unnecessary in-between stage. If your child can anticipate when she needs to go to the lavatory, she will not need them but if she cannot control this desire then she still needs a nappy.

The first stage to night-time dryness is to try leaving off the nappy for the daytime sleep. Encourage your child to pass urine before she goes to bed. Then if she is still dry when she wakes give her lots of praise but never accuse her if she hasn't.

The next stage is to put your child on the potty last thing at night before you go to bed. She will probably not even wake up when you do this and you certainly should not make an effort to awaken her. This would disturb the pattern of her sleep and make the idea of being potted an unpleasant one. Replace the nappy. If she is dry in the morning, then you can try leaving off the nappy for the night. This stage is rarely reached

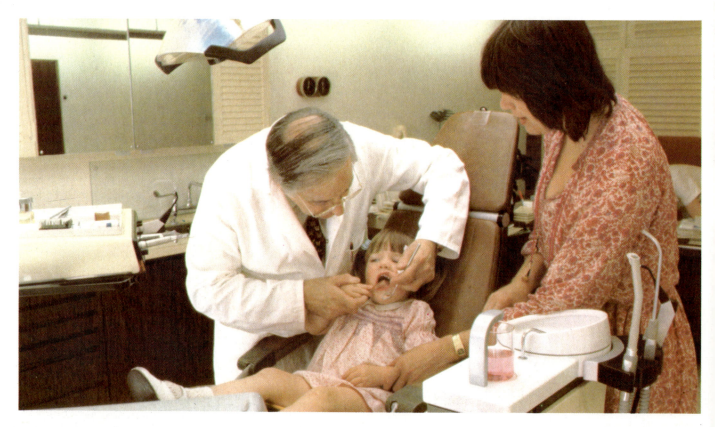

(Above) In nearly every district there's a dentist who takes a special interest in children's teeth. Find him. He'll be gentle and slow and take pains to gain your child's confidence. He'll also keep you up to date on the latest dental theories about healthy teeth.

child a substantial tea with only his milk in the evening. To get over thirst, let your child drink as much as he wants before going to bed.

3. That you are not disturbing your child by going into his room unnecessarily.

4. That he has his dummy or his favourite blanket by him to grasp on waking. Before you go to bed, make sure that they are firmly attached to the cot side or tucked beside him.

5. That he is not afraid of the dark. If he is, put a small nightlight in his bedroom.

6. That he is not being disturbed by noises inside or outside the house. You may have to double glaze the window of his room to cut down outside noise and half close the bedroom door to prevent loud household noises reaching him.

If your baby wakes up afraid in the middle of the night, there is only one thing to do. You must give him your reassurance, love and physical contact. Never let your child feel abandoned. Stay in the room with him and don't hesitate to take him downstairs. This latter is my personal view, though not accepted by everyone. Or take him into your bed with you. Don't be put off by statements that this will set bad habits – it won't if you don't want it to. And even if it does, your child **will** grow out of it. In the light of this you should put comfort and security first. As soon as your toddler is safely asleep again, put him back into his own bed.

Teething and dental care

For most of his second year your toddler will be teething and while this is likely to cause much less discomfort than in the first year, he may have problems cutting his molars. The first are cut between 12 and 15 months and the second molars between 20 and 24 months. You may

notice that your toddler develops a bright red warm spot on the affected cheek when cutting a tooth. You can soothe him by letting him have something to suck or chew, like a teething ring. There are a few other things that you can do to help your baby. Avoid taking your child out in a cold wind. If you have to go out in the winter, make sure he wears a very snug warm hat or hood that covers most of the face. Apply something cool to the gums like a teething ring that can be put in your refrigerator and will stay cold for an hour or so. You will be very proud to see your baby's new white teeth coming through. There is every reason why these teeth should remain healthy and your child need never have a filling. Good daily habits at home are most important. Remember the following points:

☐ Decay is caused by sugar, and sugar-containing foods and drinks. If your child has any sweet foods these should be kept to mealtimes. Choose unsweetened or savoury foods such as cheese, small sandwiches, pieces of fresh fruit or vegetables for snacks between meals.
☐ Be especially careful for babies not to use sweetened comforters containing sweet substances or fruit juices after the age of twelve months (see page 126).
☐ Get your baby used to daily tooth-cleaning and help him.

In addition to these you may also use a small amount of fluoride toothpaste (see page 129).

Your child should see a dentist for the first time by the time he is two years old. Before the visit make a game of looking at each other's teeth to get your child used to the idea. If possible, have the dentist examine your mouth first.

Nursing your child in hospital

Never keep hospital secret from your child. If you have the opportunity, introduce her to the idea that sick people occasionally have to go to a special building where they are tended by doctors and nurses to make them well again.

Another way to get your child used to the idea of hospital is to play games. Most children love dressing up as doctors and nurses and tending to their dolls once you have introduced them to the idea of what sickness means. An excellent time to do this is when your child has been ill herself and she will remember that she had to stay in bed, that you took her temperature, that you gave her medicine and you were especially kind to her.

Alternatively, have a look in the local library for hospital stories, so that children can follow the adventures of a fictional character and learn about hospital stays. It is wise to do this quite early on in a child's life so that if she has to be admitted to a hospital as an emergency, she will not be going to an entirely strange place. Hopefully, she will have smelled that hospital smell before and will not be frightened by it.

One of your child's natural fears is that she will be separated from you if she has to go in to hospital. Up to the age of two years old there is absolutely no reason why you should leave her. In most children's wards there are facilities for mothers and you can stay overnight with your child. More important, you can do all the fetching and carrying for her as well as feed her, bath her and nurse her. Up to the age of one year, many children do not seem to suffer at all if they are separated from their mother. But after this, most children can be seriously affected by a period of separation and they may be affected for quite a long time, so do not let this happen with your child. Most children's departments will allow a mother to sleep in an armchair next to the child's cot if a bed is not available.

If it is absolutely impossible for you to have a bed on the children's ward, you can do much to alleviate your child's sense of being abandoned in a strange and rather frightening world if unrestricted visiting is allowed. Unrestricted visiting means that you can go on to the ward as early as you like and stay as long as you like until lights out. Your child is bound to be happier if you can be with her for most of the day and simulate the sort of routine that you have at home. This makes it easier for your child to adjust both to hospital and to her own home

(Below) Many hospital wards are like playschools with beds. If you can, take your child along to see the children's ward before he's admitted. Meet sister and ask about ward routine. It's usually flexible and sister or staff-nurse will explain how you can help and what procedures are followed. If your own child is sleeping, make a fuss of another child who has no visitors.

when she returns. However, if you have other chidren, try to make sure they do not feel deprived, because you need to spend more time with the sick child.

If you have to leave your child overnight, do not be surprised if she is rather withdrawn and sulky when you first visit her. This is just her way of showing you how sad she feels because you are not there all the time. So it is very important for you to visit her as often as you can. And do not get upset if your child has a good cry when you come to leave. This is a very natural reaction and infinitely preferable to the child who is silent and seems stunned.

If your child has to have an operation the doctors may decide that it is best for you not to be with her until she is well round from the anaesthetic. At a different hospital you may find that the doctors are quite happy for you to accompany your child to the anaesthetic room and to stay with her until she starts to go to sleep. They will also suggest that you are waiting for your child when she comes back from the operating theatre and regains consciousness.

The atmosphere on most children's wards is relaxed, friendly and bright. Do not be concerned if the ward is in need of a lick of paint, or if the building seems somewhat old-fashioned. Far more important is the friendly attitude of the staff and their ability to see what happens on a ward through a child's eyes and to make it as homely as possible. Always feel you can ask questions and ask for help if you have a problem. The staff will be only too pleased to help you because they know that it will make you and your baby happier.

Do not be concerned if your child suffers a few temporary setbacks as a result of a stay in hospital. There may be an interruption in weight gain and you may find that she loses some of the skills that she had before she went into hospital. It is to be expected that walking skills and the ability to feed herself might regress a little as the result of a stay in hospital but do not worry as your child will quickly catch up. Be patient with her and go over all the old ground again. You should be able to do it better a second time as you have covered it once already.

Some common illnesses

Below are descriptions of the symptoms and treatment of illnesses which commonly affect young children.

Skin disorders

Cold sores

Cold sores have little to do with colds. They are caused by a virus (herpes simplex) which lives permanently in the skin. These viruses are inactive most of the time but if for any reason the body is heated up, then the virus is activated and a cold sore will result. A high fever or even sitting out in strong sunlight is sufficient to bring out a cold sore. They normally occur round the lips and cheeks and are very often transmitted from mother to child by kissing. A tingling sensation is felt over the skin where a cold sore is beginning and if you treat it immediately it may be possible to stop it developing. There are several preparations on the market which can alleviate the symptoms but those which will actually prevent a cold sore from appearing are only available on prescription. If you do not start treating a cold sore when the symptoms first appear it will take 10 to 14 days to go from spot to blister, to scab, to normal skin, no matter what you do.

Warts

Warts are also caused by a virus and have a natural history of about two years. It takes the body that long to build up sufficient antibodies to kill the virus and the wart. Warts are unsightly on the hands and painful on the feet (verucae). Proprietary wart cures are largely ineffective. There are many now available on prescription which can be used quite safely in the home and are often successful. Recalcitrant warts and verrucae will need special treatment in a dermatology department at a hospital.

Ringworm

Ringworm is caused by a fungus which may affect the skin or the scalp, causing the typical red circular patches in the skin, or bald spots on the scalp where the hair has split off. It is quite easy for a doctor to diagnose ringworm as the hairs which are affected with the fungus will fluoresce a greeny yellow colour if placed in ultraviolet light. Treatment for ringworm is simple, effective and free of discomfort but it must be obtained from your doctor.

Nettlerash (hives, or urticaria)

Children have a tendency to develop hives which is lost as they grow older. Nettlerash is the only skin condition which disappears completely within minutes and is fairly easy to diagnose. It is very itchy when it lasts but you can do quite a lot to relieve the itch by cooling the skin with the application of calamine lotion.

It can be caused by foods, bacteria, viruses and by medicines. One of the commonest offending agents is aspirin which can give rise not only to nettlerash but to swelling of the face, eyelids and mouth. Unless attacks of nettlerash are persistent, there is no need for any specific treatment but they should be investigated to try to find a cause. A particular form of urticaria called Papula Urticaria is caused by flea bites, usually from fleas on the family cat. If a child becomes allergic to flea bites, he may develop spots all over the body which resemble nettlerash, but which persist. The cure is to get rid of the fleas on the cat.

Sunburn

By far the best cure is prevention. On the first day in strong sunlight keep all but the toughest parts of your baby's skin covered by a light T-shirt and pants. Make sure that he is wearing a hat with a brim so that his neck is protected and apply an ultraviolet sun cream to the face, arms and legs, paying particular attention to the back of the legs and the thighs. If the sun is very strong, do not expose any part of your baby's skin for longer than 5 to 10 minutes on the first day. On the

second day you can increase the length of exposure by a few minutes. Never fall into the trap of thinking that your child's skin has become acclimatized to the sunshine before it has. Toddlers really do not mind running around in a light cotton top and a pair of pants with a hat, as long as they can play freely. The trouble is that you will never know the moment at which your child's skin starts to burn and you may only find out at bedtime when you have a very sore, red and possibly even ill child to put to bed. It is better to err on the side of caution. If it is very hot indeed keep your child indoors. Protective clothing and sun screens will help prevent sunburn but they will not stop your child from getting overheated and he can be very ill with heat stroke.

If your child does get sunburn, calamine lotion is the best thing to apply to his skin to cool it down and some paracetamol elixir will help relieve soreness and any fever. Severe sunburn and heatstroke require a doctor's attention.

Minor skin infections

An infection in the skin may be anything from folliculitis (infection around a hair shaft) to impetigo, (severe infection of the skin with characteristic bright yellow scabs, often affecting the area around the mouth). Skin infections will be less likely if you are careful about hygiene and you can stop it spreading to other parts of her skin and to other members of the family by seeking prompt advice from your doctor.

Here are a few guidelines which might help you if your child does develop a skin infection:

☐ Use a special flannel and towel and soap for your baby and wash them separately.
☐ After bathing, make sure that the skin is well dried, particularly in the skin creases in the neck, groins and under the arms.
☐ Never squeeze a septic spot.
☐ If your child develops a boil, do not use proprietary antiseptic creams, consult your doctor.
☐ For minor skin infections, a cream containing cetrimide, an antiseptic agent which is used in hospitals, is a good standby, so keep a tube in your medicine cabinet.
☐ If your child develops a septic spot which is swollen and red, do not apply a sticking plaster. Removing it will be painful for your child and difficult for you. It is much better to apply a large dressing and secure it with sticky tape well away from the sore area.

Croup

This is an inflammation of the vocal chords, as a result of which the windpipe becomes constricted. Once it has appeared it tends to recur. The air being drawn through the obstructed windpipe makes the typical croup sound and may result in laboured breathing and a rasping cough. If you see that your child is having difficulty with breathing, you should call the doctor whatever the time of day or night. Whilst waiting for him, you can do the following things to help

☐ stay by her side to reassure her.
☐ try not to communicate any worry you are feeling to her as this will only make it even more difficult for her to breathe.
☐ prop her up in a sitting position with pillows to make her comfortable and help her to breathe.
☐ if her bedroom is centrally heated, open the window a little to cool the air.
☐ a humidified atmosphere also aids breathing difficulties. To achieve this, keep a kettle on the boil in a far corner of the room (but never leave the room while it is boiling).

Ask your doctor to give you instructions on how to deal with possible future attacks.

Asthma

Most small babies wheeze if they have an attack of bronchitis or bronchiolitis, see page 112. This is not because they are asthmatic and it would be wrong to label them so.

Asthma quite often accompanies infantile eczema. This means that your child has a sensitive skin and chest. In a person suffering from asthma, the lining of the air passages in the lungs is very sensitive and responds to infection, allergy and emotional disturbance by going into spasm and secreting large amounts of mucus. The lining of the nose is equally sensitive, sometimes showing as hay fever.

If asthma persists, your doctor will almost certainly test your child as she gets older to see if there is an allergic background to her asthma and it is a simple precaution for you to get rid of any bedding which contains feathers, down or hair, as these commonly cause allergies. The commonest cause of allergic asthma, however, is the house mite which lives in house dust. If you notice that your child's asthma is worse after you have been dusting or shaking the mat, then this may be the cause. Mites flourish in damp houses so there is now a scientific rationale for the observation that a child's asthma is nearly always worse when she lives in a damp house.

In addition to the allergic aspect of asthma, there is nearly always an emotional aspect. Asthmatic children tend to be very bright, intelligent, highly sensitive individuals. They need a lot of care but they will reward you one hundred times with their happiness and friendliness. If emotional factors play a part in your child's asthma, then it is up to you and your family doctor to work out the best way of minimizing the stress in your child's life. A child with asthma is worrying but the parents of asthmatic children tend to be worriers and over-obsessive. As part of your child's treatment, you will have to take yourself in hand too, so do not be surprised if your doctor suggests this.

One of the most important aspects of treating asthma is that you and the whole family should view it simply as a minor nuisance and not as an illness. In other respects of course, your child is absolutely normal. If you minimize the condition, it will cause the least stress to the child and the least upheaval in the family. Treatment of attacks is with special medicines prescribed by your doctor. Make sure that you find out from him exactly how you should go about treating an attack and at what point you should call your doctor for assistance. If you are in doubt, never wait, call the doctor immediately.

Worms

Infection with worms is much rarer than it used to be. The only kind of worm that is found with any frequency in children in non-tropical countries is thread worm.

Thread worms usually produce only one symptom – itching around the anus. This is caused by the female worm when she comes up the rectum to lay her eggs, usually at night. Some times bed wetting can result from this irritation. The itching may half wake your child in the night and he will scratch almost subconsciously. The infection is spread when the eggs become caught under the fingernails of the child who has scratched himself and he either re-infects himself by putting his fingers in his mouth or passes them on to another host.

Signs of a thread worm infection are small white, fine threads in your child's motion, or even worms around his anus. If you see these, consult your doctor immediately. He can prescribe a treatment which will eradicate the worms and eggs with a single dose. Your whole family should be involved in the treatment and everyone must take a second dose two weeks later, as an extra precaution.

You can help your child by dressing him in a small pair of elasticated towelling trunks at night so he will not be able to get his fingers at the skin and cause irritation. Make sure that your child's nails are cut short and be punctilious about hand washing after using the lavatory.

Bones and joints

Bow legs
When children first stand upright, their legs tend to be bowed. This is partly due to the way they are standing which accentuates any bowing and partly because their bones are still quite soft and they tend to bend a little when your child starts to take his full weight on them. Bowing may also be due to the deposition of fat on the outer side of the leg. This normal bowing of the legs is sometimes quite obvious for the first two years of

life but eventually the bone will grow and strengthen along the line where the stress is greatest. So it follows that your child's bones will straighten out as they gradually grow around the vertical line down which body weight is transmitted. There is therefore no treatment for this kind of bow leg. The only disease which causes bow legs is rickets and this is due to vitamin D deficiency. This is a very rare condition in western countries as all baby foods contain sufficient vitamin D supplements to guard against it. When your baby first starts to walk, try not to use bulky nappies as this will only increase any tendency to bowing by keeping the legs wide apart.

Knock knees
Knock knees are a normal part of bone and joint development which usually occur between the ages of three and seven. The commonest cause is overweight and if you can help your child to lose weight the knock knees will probably disappear. Ninety five per cent of children with knock knees find that the condition has cured itself by the time they are seven.

Flat feet
Flat feet in babies are normal and need no treatment. The flatness is caused by a pad of fat on the inner side of the sole which disappears as your child grows older. When a baby first starts to walk, he often turns his feet outwards and this tends to exaggerate the appearance of flat feet. It is much more important to look at the foot when it is in action than when it is still. Ask your child to stand on his toes and you will see that his arch is high. Remedial exercises can very rarely change the shape of the child's feet.

First aid
Electric shock
If your child gets an electric shock, switch off the power source as soon as you can. If you cannot, pull your child away from the electric wire or the electric socket with any material which does not conduct electricity, e.g. a piece of wood such as broom handle, plastic tubing, such as that on the vacuum cleaner. Make sure that it is dry before you put it anywhere near your child. Do not touch the child directly as the electric current will be transmitted to you.

If your child is in a state of *medical* shock, e.g. pale face, cold, clammy skin, sweating, can't see properly, dizzy, breathing rapidly, take her straight to the nearest hospital casualty department. For minor shocks when your child is obviously only shaken and frightened, reassure her, lie her down with her feet on a cushion and stay with her until she's composed. Offer her a sweet drink, e.g. fruit juice.

Choking
Hold your child firmly around her waist, bend your right knee, tip her over it head first so that her head is about the level of your knees, then give her a sharp pat on the shoulders. Repeat this movement until your child coughs the object

(Top right) Don't rush in and reach for your child if she's had an electric shock. Grab the nearest length of non-metallic material (wood or plastic is best) and gently pull your child away from the power source.

(Bottom right) If no bones are broken, raise the part that is bleeding, take any piece of clean material, a handkerchief or wad of tissues will do, and press it firmly over the bleeding point for several minutes.

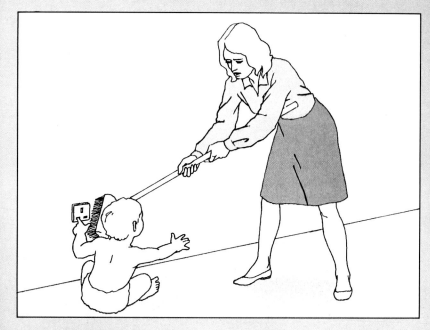

(Middle right) You'll have to be cruel to be kind to remove a piece of food blocking your child's airway. Hold your child firmly over your knee and slap her fairly hard between the shoulder blades.

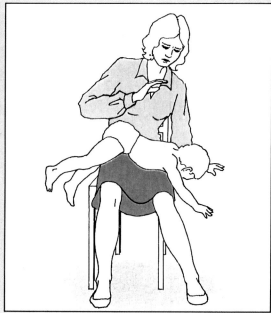

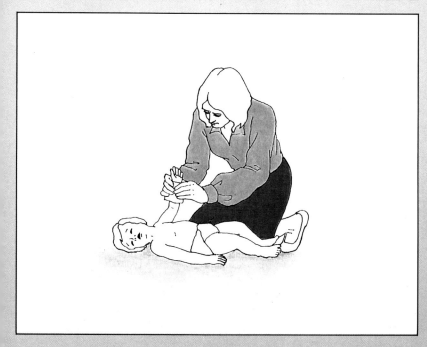

out. If the object reaches her mouth and she is still gasping and struggling, hold her head steady with your left arm holding her chin steady with your left hand and hook out the object with the forefinger of your right hand.

Burns

For a minor burn, don't apply butter or anything oily, soap, creams or ointments and do not burst a blister. Simply cover the area with a piece of clean dry linen or cotton and consult your doctor if you're worried.

Stings

If possible, remove the sting with a pair of tweezers or, if you can get a friend to hold your child, with the point of a needle. Don't, whatever you do, squeeze a sting or more of the irritating substance will get deep in the skin. Don't use antihistamine creams (see page 135). Use a piece of cotton wool or a handkerchief soaked in a solution of bicarbonate of soda strapped over the skin. If the sting is in the mouth and is swelling try to get your child to swill out his mouth with bicarbonate of soda solution and call your doctor immediately. If there is a hospital near give him a piece of ice or an iced lolly to suck. Lie him down in the back of the car with an adult next to him and take him to hospital.

Unconsciousness

1. Decide if your child is breathing. If not perform the kiss of life.
2. As soon as possible feel for a pulse, the carotid in the angle of the lower jaw is easiest to feel. If there is none try a short sharp punch on the lower end of the breast bone then rhythmic hard sharp pushes downwards over the left nipple.
3. Call an ambulance immediately.
4. If your child's breathing and has a pulse lay her down on her stomach, head face to the right, right hand and knee bent up, left hand and knee bent down. Call an ambulance.

Fire

Lay your child down with the part which is on fire uppermost. Cover the flames with any large cloth which is available, a towel, a blanket or a coat. The flames will be smothered and go out because of lack of oxygen. If there is no cloth near to hand, smother the flames with your own body by lying on top of your child.

Arterial bleeding

Apply strong pressure directly on to the bleeding point with a clean piece of cloth if you have it. Raise the injured limb above the level of the child's body and this will reduce the flow of blood to it. If it is difficult for you to get your hand on to or around the wound, lie your child down and compress the bleeding vessel between your fist and the underlying bone.

Learning and understanding

You may well find that your child is well ahead of these milestones, so hurra for him. On the other hand, a working guide is as follows.

18 months

By this age your child will point to pictures like 'dog' and 'duck'. He will recognize and say 'duck'. He will appreciate that while the picture of a dog and a real dog are quite different, they are still dogs. He knows parts of his body like foot and nose and he can distinguish between his nose and Mummy's nose. He will bring things to you if you ask.

21 months

He will take you to show you things. He loves scribbling with a pencil. He understands and obeys a variety of requests.

Two years

He is able to play quite creatively on his own. He may try to make up and down strokes if you give him a pencil and paper.

Two and a quarter years

He will try to build cars or trains with bricks. He is becoming increasingly negative. He uses the word 'no' more and more often. He disagrees with you, sometimes defies you.

Two and a half years

He will draw horizontal and vertical lines and can name three or more objects. He loves helping and will put things away for you. He is beginning to notice his and others' sex organs.

Learning to speak

At two years old he is learning the names of familiar objects and he may repeat words said to him. He can make very simple requests. He distinguishes in speech between himself, 'I' and others 'you'. He is becoming a chatterbox. He can say his first name.

During the first six months of your child's second year, many newly acquired skills seem to come together which make him want to explore and make learning easier. Also, he needs less sleep and is much more wakeful and alert. He wants to find out about everything that is going on around him. Because he has the capacity to reach an interesting object by walking to it, picking it up and examining it, he is never bored and is on a constant journey of exploration. His actions may seem purposeless. He picks up an object, simply because it is in front of him. But he is absorbing information faster than any computer. When your baby is at this age, give him as much time as he wants and plenty of things to explore.

After this phase of finding out, your toddler starts to put his ideas to the test. He starts to do things to find out what will happen. He will tip a beaker of water to see the water pour out and tip a bucket of sand to see the sand fall out and he will note the difference. At the same time he will also note that water wets him and his clothing if he spills it over himself, whereas sand does not. You can help your child with his experiments by giving him the freedom of the sink for as long as he wants. Let him splash about in the water and provide different size utensils for him to practise measuring up. You could also give him rice, split peas, dried peas inside sealed containers to shake about. Make sure they are sealed in so that he can't put them in his mouth or up his nose. This also applies to nuts.

Instead of just dropping or throwing objects he will now be more purposeful about letting things go and will realise that when a ball is dropped it bounces but when a stone is dropped it does not. Though he does not know it, he will begin to learn about gravity. Your child will also start to classify things, even though on the face of it they do not appear to resemble one another very much. He is very astute. Even though he has lots of books of different shapes and sizes, he knows that one book resembles another book more than it does several sheets of paper that are not joined together. Even though he eats lots of different foods, he knows that a piece of brown bread is closer to a biscuit than it is to cardboard. While he may have a fluffy toy dog, he knows very well that your own dog is not a toy.

Once your child has noticed the differences and similarities in things, he is in a position to

(Below) Water is one of the best and cheapest playthings. Most children are happy for a long time tipping and pouring water from one container to another. Water is an educational toy. Liquids run, liquids have no shape of their own, you can't get a quart into a pint pot.

make a considerable intellectual leap in thinking. He is well on his way to forming complex concepts of what constitutes the intrinsic nature of something. For instance, what is 'dogginess'? In his animal book there is a page of lots of dogs of different shapes and sizes and colours. He has his toy dog beside him and on his other side your real live pet dog. As part of your teaching about dogs, you have taught him that dogs say 'bow-wow'. You will have also taught him that cows moo. He will have grasped the concept of dogginess when he points to the dog in the picture and says 'doggy, bow-wow', 'cow – moo'. At this stage you will find that your toddler is delighted to spend endless hours sorting out and classifying information. This is the best kind of play which is true learning.

Just after his second birthday, your toddler will start to express abstract ideas. While your child may have been saying 'more, more' when his appetite was still unsatisfied, he did not necessarily understand the word's true meaning. It simply meant that he had learned by saying 'more' the pleasant experience of eating food was repeated. Even fairly simple abstract ideas like food are very difficult for your child to understand. This is exemplified by children who name all food with the word for their favourite food, or the food which they first remember eating with relish. All food can be named 'nana' (banana). Your child is beginning to think abstractly when, for instance, he asks for a toy which is not actually there. This means he has an idea and a picture of that toy in his head. The other characteristic of abstract thinking is that your child will start to plan ahead. It is very thrilling to hear your toddler say for the first time, 'tomorrow go shops', or find that he has put a piece of fruit to one side for later on.

By about two and a half, your toddler will have built up a vocabulary of several single words. He then starts to put them together. One of the first ways that he connects words is to use adjectives. He will say 'petty fower' (pretty flower) or 'big horsey'. You can help him with these word associations. Whereas before you only named new objects for him, now you should start describing them. Sometimes he will start to put two words together in a very primitive way but nonetheless in a way that communicates with you very efficiently and he uses all of his body to get his meaning over to you.

Here are some of the ways you can help your child to understand and use language.

☐ Always talk directly to him and look at his face. If you do this you are helping your child to focus on specific things being said in a room which may be a blur of conversation to him.

☐ Interpret difficult statements for him. If he obviously does not understand something you are saying to him, break it down into simple words with emphasis and intonation and gestures so that he understands what you mean.

☐ Show him what you mean if you can. Name the object as you hold it out to him.

☐ Help him to understand things by letting him see your gestures and expressions.

☐ Encourage him to learn that talking to someone is one of the most important ways of communicating. This means that you should not speak to him without looking at him and if he starts to talk to you, you should turn and give him your attention. It also means that you must not devalue talking by leaving the radio or the television set twittering gratuitously in the background. Your child may well show annoyance when the radio is on for this reason.

☐ Help him to understand something quite complicated by giving him lots of extra clues. You can say 'Let's go upstairs now to have our bath', then you take your child upstairs, start running the taps, get out all the plastic toys and let him throw each one into the bath. You get the towel, his pyjamas and his clean nappy ready, you start to undress him and you say 'First your trousers' and you take off his trousers, 'Then your shoes' and you take off his shoes, and finally when he is undressed you say 'Now it is time for your bath'. He will understand immediately but if you had said the same words downstairs without all the clues, your child probably would not have had any idea what you were saying.

(Above) Sometimes other children are the best teachers. It's not so long since they learned and they remember very clearly their lessons and how their minds worked.

Beware of an older sibling making your child lazy by translating baby language and obviating the necessity for your baby to learn words and how to use them clearly for himself.

Fears

A child who is anxious, or harbouring a fear, will behave in a certain way. You will probably notice that he seems more clinging than usual, that he does not want to let you out of his sight, that he goes off his food, that he does not like strangers or new places, that he is having difficulty in going off to sleep, he may even be less naughty than usual.

When your child is behaving in this way, he is asking for your help. Try to discover what frightens him and how he expresses his fear. He cannot verbalize his fears very clearly and so you must be observant. Once you have nailed the problem down, you must take a very friendly, understanding and sympathetic attitude towards him.

If he shows a specific fear, accept that it is real to him, even if it is not to you. Do not minimize it and do not scoff him for it. You can reassure your child that there is nothing to fear in thunder but do not tell him not to be afraid. The only way he will learn not to be afraid of thunder is when he experiences it several times and realises that nothing nasty happens to him. If he is frightened of thunder, tell him that he will come to no harm but also say 'I can see and understand why you are frightened, so come close to Mummy, sit on my lap and I'll give you a cuddle so that we are both safe together'.

Play

Your baby's concentration is really beginning to flower, so encourage this with new toys, skills and activities. She may be dying to do a puzzle but she does not really know how to fit the pieces together, so spend a little time showing her how. Help her to do the puzzle to its completion. She may want to read a new book but quickly becomes bored because she turns over two pages at a time and therefore the pictures have no continuity, so sit her on your lap and go through the book slowly with her page by page.

One of the most important things that you can help her to do at this stage is to start playing happily with other children. This is one of the first of your child's social acts and it is not easy for her. It will help if you give each child a separate toy to play with, or a different activity to get involved in. However, it's very tempting for your child to see the other activity as more interesting than her own. Be ready to act as judge, jury and peace-maker. One of the best ways to get over the envy your child may feel for another child's toy is to try to find one which is very similar. You will have triumphed if the two children start playing with their toys together.

The importance of play

Whilst the pre-school activities of a child may all be grouped under the title of play, they do in fact contain many of the aspects which will later be developed by 'work' at school, i.e. she is learning physical, intellectual and social skills.

Physical
☐ she will explore her strengths and weakness through energetic play.
☐ she will improve her muscular and eye co-ordination, through skipping, climbing, running and jumping.
☐ doing a jigsaw and building structures with interlocking bricks will help her to make her hands work as tools, a useful preliminary to later creative work with handicrafts or woodwork.

Intellectual
☐ she will develop her own ideas and grasp of language through games of make-believe.
☐ certain types of toy will stimulate analytical thought. To begin with these will be simple shapes which have to be fitted into appropriate holes but later on a chemistry set or a chess set will serve the same purpose.
☐ she will develop a planning sense through playing with railway sets or with construction sets where things have to be done in a certain order.
☐ she will learn to sort out problems and overcome frustrations through her attempts to play

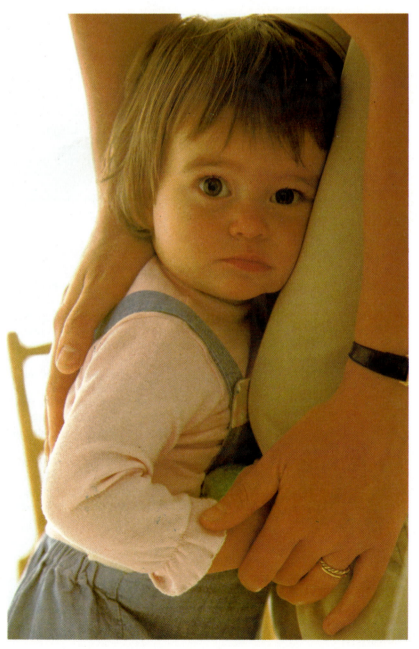

(Below) It's hard to understand a child's fears. Like ours they're often irrational and it's impossible to reason with a child who's less than three years old. So don't try.

Be a reliable, reassuring presence and offer endless love and affection. Never say your child is stupid for being afraid. It doesn't help and may make her feel stupid.

She's braver than you think, all she needs is some encouragement from you.

with mechanical toys or intricate games, provided that you are there to help her through some of the difficulties.

Social

□ playing with dolls (including the 'Action Man' type) helps her to rehearse various emotions from protectiveness to aggressiveness and thus learn to control them.

□ dressing-up clothes (e.g. nurses' uniforms or cowboy outfits) foster an interest in other people and the work they do.

□ sets of toys such as a garage with pumps, attendants and cars or a farm with various animals help to introduce her to aspects of life which she might not normally come across or which she would find difficult to assimilate except when reduced to a miniature scale.

□ toys are possibly the first things which a child is aware of owning and through which she will first learn about sharing.

□ playing with other children eases the way to forming friendships.

Temper tantrums

From two to four years of age temper tantrums must be considered as 'normal' behaviour. During these years children have developed a strong will without the necessary logic to match it. Therefore, attempts by parents to alter their chosen course of action for whatever reason will result in a clash of wills and a display of temper on the part of the child.

There are certain ways of dealing with a tantrum:

□ Try to stay calm, he may catch your mood.

□ Ignore him and leave him on his own. A tantrum may lose most of its point if there is no audience but do not shut the door on him or go far away. Let him see where you are so that he does not feel deserted and this leaves him the option of making it up with you.

□ Try not to punish him which will only aggravate the situation and do make the first overture of friendship once your child has finished with the tantrum.

Breath holding attacks

Breath holding attacks are really just extensions of temper tantrums. They often occur with bright children who are stronger-willed than average and have a similarly stronger reaction when frustrated. Usually it is a particular incident, more frustrating than normal, which will trigger off an attack. It rarely occurs without an audience (the favourite one being the parents). The signal for the start of an attack is a sharp intake of breath as though your child were going to cry but then he holds his breath. His face goes red, then blue and he may clench his teeth. An attack is best dealt with by laying your child face down on your knee, then very gently placing a finger over the back of his tongue and hooking it forward. This makes him involuntarily breathe in. Once you have dealt successfully with an attack you are calmer the next time and your

(Left) Temper tantrums are part of growing up, of testing your standards, of setting limits, of pitting her authority against yours.

You can't avoid them. You'll make them worse by getting worked up when they occur.

Most temper tantrums end if there's no audience. So clear a space and ignore them.

child is less likely to repeat the performance.

The theory is simpler than the practice and it is easy to criticize other parents' handling of a tantrum but quite another matter to deal with one of your own children in public. I found that I preferred to take my children off somewhere quiet or where we could be alone, so that we could both work out the situation without feeling the pressures of an audience, however well-intentioned.

Punishment

As your child gets older, there are certain to be misdemeanours which quite rightly should be punished, which raises the question of what form the punishment should take. I feel that, provided that your normal relationship with your child is kind and loving, a quick smack at the time of the trouble, when you are still angry, will do little harm. This will have a more immediate effect than lengthy explanation and the whole thing can then be quickly dismissed.

If, on the other hand, a child does not enjoy an affectionate relationship with her parents, she will interpret every smack as proof of their lovelessness. Also if the smacking is delayed, it becomes a cold calculated act, which will always be seen as such by a child.

However, it is best to restrict the number of times you smack your child to the more extreme offences so that this remains an effective form of punishment.

Just as continual smacking ceases to have an effect, a bad-tempered shout from a habitual shouter goes unheeded. Try to forget the incident as soon as it has been dealt with and do not bear a grudge.

Useful toys

From a very early age all of my sons have found the following natural materials and simple toys great fun to play with:

Water

They've all enjoyed being given the freedom of the kitchen sink and sometimes they would play happily there for a couple of hours or more. Most children are the same. Turn on the taps, show your toddler how to use the plug, give her lots of unbreakable kitchen utensils which she can use in a variety of ways. If it's mess you are concerned about, spread some old towels over the kitchen floor and do a great mopping up job when the games are finished. As they grew older and more adventurous, all my children were just as delighted with a small plastic paddling pool.

Sand and earth

Sand and earth are equally popular with most children. The silver sand used in sandpits is clean and so there is the joy of getting down into the sand without getting into a mess. Soil has the advantage, as far as children are concerned, of becoming mud when it is wet. Most children adore playing with mud and occasionally you should let them. Once they start to get dirty you may as well let them really get dirty and dump them all in the bath they are finished.

Shells and stones

Most children are collectors and hoarders and if you point out the beauty of pebbles your child can spend many a happy hour searching for pebbles which take his eye in your own garden. When you are on holiday, point out how lovely different kinds of shells are. Collecting them can occupy your child for quite a long time especially if you share the joy of discovery with him. Washing them and placing them on his bedside table is an added thrill.

Miniature toys

Children love any toy which brings the world down to their scale: small cars, small buses, small train sets, small tanks, small boats, farmyards with animals, cowboys and Indians, especially on horses, toy airports, toy garages, dolls houses, play people, etc.

Toys which lock together

The type of construction toy made of small units which lock together is endlessly fascinating for many years.

Dressing up clothes

All children go through a phase of loving to dress up, both in imitation of you and as a part of acting. Keep a box or a basket to one side in which you can keep old and interesting shoes, hats and clothes which will fulfil your child's desire to dress up.

Any form of cooking

Most children love mixing and making things, especially if they can eat them afterwards. Baking is an especial pleasure for your child, so always give him his own little dish to mix ingredients in or his own bit of pastry to make a currant man. Be sure to put it in the oven with the rest of your cooking so that he can see the results of his work when the baking is done.

Physical toys

Climbing frames, swings, rope ladders, are not only enjoyed by most children, they help to give them physical confidence and improve their muscular co-ordination, so if you can afford them, do buy them as they will last for years.

Paints, coloured felt tips, crayons

There is hardly a child who does not enjoy colouring and drawing. Make sure that you have as great a variety of these toys as you can afford.

Musical toys

Most children have a musical bent and you can encourage this from an early age with a toy like the xylophone, graduating later to gramophone records, not just playing nursery rhymes but light classical music too so that your child is exposed to a wide variety of music.

(Right) A party hat apiece will soon have your children clowning about. It's worth hanging on to a few pieces of clothing or accessories once you've finished with them. They are always useful for cheering up a rainy day. (Below left) Musical instruments will bring lots of pleasure to the player and may reveal a talent for music at an early age.

(Below) Outdoor games are sometimes the best of all. Wrap your child up in warm clothing, put on gum boots and denim dungarees and let him rally around on his truck – even if it means watching out for the flower-beds.

(Inset below) Games with grandad can be great fun because many grandparents have an especially loving and understanding way with children. Grandads are exciting, glamorous and of course can always be relied on for special treats.

Equipment
The push chair

Many an outing is made very miserable for a child if he has to walk home. The chances are you will be just as tired as he is and you will not want to carry him all the way home. Your child will probably not be content to hold your hand and walk with you. He will probably be slow and will jerk away from you. He may wander in the opposite direction and then sit down. You will go back to him, stand him on his feet and then walk slightly ahead of him. Unfortunately, your toddler may not know how to follow you, you will go back again and your child will put his arms up begging to be lifted. If you do not lift him, your journey home will be extremely long and very wearing to both of you. Your child will be crying and you will be angry. Make it easier for you both by never leaving the house without a foldable pushchair. Try to remember not to leave it in the boot of the car when you get to your destination and decide to go for a walk.

Unless your child is very strong, he will probably be five years old before he can attempt a walk of any distance.

Clothing

Your child will only need shoes and socks when she starts to walk outside. Indoors, bare feet are safer as she needs to feel the texture of the floor directly on the skin of her feet to help her keep her balance.

When your child starts to wear shoes, make sure that they are properly fitted and regularly checked as she cannot tell you if the shoes are pinching. The bones of her feet are so soft that they can be squashed without causing any discomfort at all. The damage however is being done, so you should go to a shoe shop which specializes in fitting children's shoes and have them checked every two to three months. Make sure that the shop uses proper measuring and fitting techniques.

Your child will grow out of her shoes quite quickly, so there is no need to spend a lot of money on them, so don't insist on leather, and there is no need for them to give your child's feet good support. The best support for your child's feet are well-developed muscles. Light shoes like sandals and canvas beach shoes are quite suitable.

Your child will need socks once she starts wearing firm shoes. The same rules that apply to shoes apply to socks. They should give your child's feet good length and width and should not restrict the foot in any way. Never use a pair of socks once they have shrunk in the wash, or your child has grown out of them.

Your toddler will be playing outside quite a lot and will need Wellington boots to splash around when it is raining or to play on muddy ground. Wellington boots should also be checked every two to three months to see that there is plenty of room in them. During wet weather, the best outdoor clothing for your child to wear is a light waterproof 'all in one' jump suit.

(Below) There's some wonderful wet weather (or wet games) clothing around for children.

These all-in-one waterproof suits are a good example – few fastenings, loose for easy movement, hood to cut out draughts.

They come in all sizes so you can look grown-up like your sister and they're smart with a racing stripe down the side.

Stair climbing

Many accidents will be avoided on the stairs if you teach your baby to go up and down stairs as soon as he can crawl. As soon as any of my babies could crawl to the stairs, I spent several hours over a period of about a week teaching them to go up and down safely.

Most accidents occur because a baby comes downstairs head first instead of backwards, which is the safest way. When my baby approached the top of the stairs, I would swing his bottom round so that it faced downstairs and my baby's head faced upstairs. Then I would say firmly to him 'backwards'. Whilst repeating the word 'backwards' I would gently pull one of his legs down over the top step to the second step, then holding him well balanced I would pull down the other leg. This action, plus the repetition of the word 'backwards' over a period of a few days whenever the stairs had to be negotiated, usually resulted in him learning the lesson. Once he had mastered coming downstairs, going upstairs was easy, except that we had to teach him to resist the temptation to stop, turn round and try to come downstairs head first. We would follow him upstairs until he stopped and then if he attempted to swing round and come down, we would point him back up the stairs, move one leg backwards and downwards and say 'backwards'. This system worked with all my children. We did not wait for accidents, we tried to pre-empt them.

(Above) Although your child may not want to sit in the pushchair for the whole trip, it usually comes in useful for the homeward journey. It can also serve as a walking aid and will speed up the normal pace.

(Left) All parents are scared of tumbles down the stairs. The best prevention is training. Train your child to come down backwards. Every time he crawls to the stairs and tries to come down head first, turn him around, pull his legs down over the top step and say 'Backwards!' He'll soon learn and avoid accidents.

Growth and development

During the pre-school years there is a further slowing down in the rate of growth. In your child's third year he will probably gain about five pounds (2.3kg) and three and a half inches (8.5cm). As your child changes from a rather chubby two year old to a straight and slim five year old, he may appear thin. Most children pass through this phase and it is quite normal. But it is not until the child is somewhat older that plumpness is replaced by muscle.

It is pointless to weigh and measure your child frequently during these years. Every six months

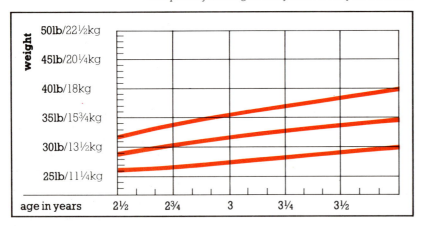

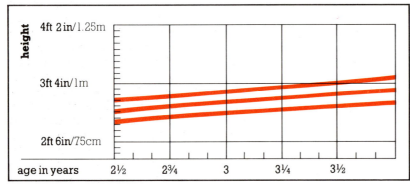

(Above) These charts record the increasing weight and height of small, medium and large children aged from 2½ to 3½ years.

is often enough. Using the chart above and plotting his weight and height you will know that growth is proceeding normally. If on the other hand, weight rises much faster than height, you will know that your child is getting overweight. If your child's height does not increase during six months, check that you have measured his height correctly and if there is no change, take your child and your chart along to the doctor.

Most children like being measured and like to see a record of their height. It is not a bad idea for you to have your child's height recorded on a wall or a door in a place he can run off to see and compare. To measure your child's height, you should stand him up against a wall or a door with his heels flat on the floor and touching the wall. His head should be straight so that he is looking directly in front of him. Put something flat, such as a ruler or book, on top of his head, touching the wall, then make a pencil mark on the wall. Measure from the floor to the mark on the wall for your child's height, write it on and put the date next to it. Next time you measure, you and your child will be able to see the amount he has grown in six months.

Food

Pre-school children are usually very hungry. They are constantly active and so use up a lot of energy and usually have large appetites. Your job is to make sure that the food you give your child is well-balanced (see page 126) and contains proteins, carbohydrates (particularly whole grains), minerals and vitamins. The food which your child chooses to eat from this diet will be well balanced for her own needs. If a valuable food is refused, just supply an alternative that your child likes. There is no need to be concerned because as a general rule, a child who eats freely from the ordinary family diet, is having a pint of milk and, if you're really anxious, the right dose of multivitamins for her age each day, will not go short of anything.

If you accept this fact, there is no need for you to be forceful about certain foods nor is there any need for you to restrict foods. Encourage your child to be adventurous about her food and give her anything which you serve to the rest of the family – spaghetti Bolognese, curry, kedgeree, risotto. Most children do not overeat and will stop when they are satisfied even though on occasions they may be a bit greedy.

Your child will now be starting to eat at the table on a chair like the rest of the family, so it becomes more important for her to eat sociably and you can help her quite a lot in learning how to do this. She will feel more like one of you and therefore more likely to behave like you, if she sits at the table alongside you with her own chair, her own place and her own knives and forks. You should give her the same utensils and the same plate, cups and glasses as everyone else. Whereas plastic is unbreakable, she has to learn that plates and crockery are.

Table manners are best taught by example, so make sure yours are exemplary when your child is sitting at the table.

You can also make mealtimes seem special if you give them a sense of occasion. In this way she will see how people behave under more formal circumstances. You can do this by asking your child to help you arrange a few flowers to put in the centre of the table. Or you could use coloured napkins and show her how to fold them so that they look attractive by each plate. A meal is always more exciting when there is a special drink and you and your child can concoct one between you. You can use serving dishes instead of serving straight from the pan as you may do if the meals are rushed. If you show her how a knife and fork is held properly, or tell her to put her knife and fork down between mouthfuls during one of these special mealtimes, she will probably cooperate. But if you nag her to do it during a scratch meal in the kitchen, she is less likely to see you are trying to be helpful.

During the pre-school years, your child should be getting used to foods which the rest of the family eat, so get her used to very quick but nutritious meals such as:

☐ Bread; cheese; orange
☐ Potato crisps; ham; ice cream
☐ Biscuits; cheese; apple

thing on her plate when you are the person who has decided how much should be put on the plate. If your child is particular about this, let her decide how much she wants and if she is hungry at the end of it, she will ask for more;

☐ you make your child eat when she says she is not hungry. Her appetitie varies just like yours and loss of appetite may be a symptom of her sickening for something.

Your child is being unreasonable if

☐ she demands food which is different from the family menu which she normally likes;

☐ she demands all of the best part of a certain dish. She may like the skin off the rice pudding but she can only have the skin off the part which would have been her portion, not the skin off the whole dish, so that no other member of the family can have skin at all.

With a pre-school child you have to be understanding and flexible about eating between meals. A child of this age is using up a lot of energy fast and needs to replenish stores at fairly frequent intervals. If a child runs in red-cheeked from the garden and asks for her 'elevenses', then she is ready for them. She is feeling hungry and she knows instinctively that she needs food as fuel. Do not grumble and do not say sharply that she will be spoiling her lunch. (At this age her appetite is so great that practically nothing can spoil her lunch.) Join her in her elevenses, even make it a treat by having a cup of energizing hot chocolate and couple of biscuits at the kitchen table with her. But don't stop and make your child something special. You can do a great deal to prevent dental decay by making sure that any foods or drinks taken between meals do not contain sugar. You could let your child know that, say, bread and peanut butter or crisps are always available for the asking, as are tomatoes and fruit. Your child will get to know that every time she feels she is hungry, these foods are hers for the asking when she cannot wait until the next meal.

If your child has a tendency to be overweight, try the following tips.

☐ Consult the weight chart on page 166, overweight means more than 7 lb (3 kg) over the desirable weight.

☐ Grill foods when you can and if you do fry, use a non-stick pan using very little or no fat.

☐ Discourage the use of butter with spreads that do not need it, e.g. cream cheese, sandwich spread, peanut butter.

☐ Do not keep very sweet fizzy drinks in the house for general purpose use, reserve them for special occasions only. Very often it is the fizz which children like. All my children have been quite happy with soda water or fizzy mineral water, lime juice and ice cubes.

☐ Use food in miniature whenever you can, e.g. marmite fingers instead of sandwiches, very small cakes, tiny sweets, miniature bars of chocolate. Very often what is important to a child is that she has three sweets or one cake, not how big it is.

(Above) Don't be too firm about table manners until your child is of school age. It's more important that she eats the apple and reads her book than that she does neither.

☐ Cold meat; fresh tomato; biscuit

These meals are well balanced and contain all the essential foodstuffs that your child requires at one meal. They only take 30 seconds to prepare and need not even interrupt your day if your child feels hungry. Also, you can get at least one of them at any roadside café, so feeding your child out of doors should not present a problem.

As your child's taste develops she will be very definite about her likes and dislikes. As I have said before, in general, you should accommodate them. If your child becomes faddy about her food, then you should be flexible (see page 147) but there is a point where she may become unreasonable. From your child's point of view, you may seem unreasonable sometimes too.

You are probably being unreasonable if

☐ you get upset if your child won't eat a particular food which she has refused in the past. Try to serve your child something you know she likes, even if it means substituting one of the dishes in the family meal. If you force a child to eat something she does not like you may put her off that food for the rest of her life.

☐ you insist that your child finishes up every-

Bowel and bladder control

By the time your child is three, lifting him up just before you go to bed and encouraging him to pass urine will help him to be dry in the morning. This should never be done if it distresses your child and accidents must be forgiven light-heartedly. Many children, especially boys, still occasionally wet the bed when they are over the age of four. A change of surrounding or routine, an illness or unhappiness, may cause bed wetting to recur, see page 175. So what should you do? If you remember that helpfulness and sympathy are the key words and try to get rid of the idea that you are training your child, it is mainly common sense.

□ Dress him in clothes that he can take down easily and quickly so that accidents due to his urgency can be avoided.
□ When he is older, build his self-reliance by showing him how to take down his own clothes, how to use the lavatory and how to reach with a stool if it's high.
□ Always praise success and he will probably become very proud of his new skills and take pride in staying clean and dry.

Once your child can stay dry at night, try taking off his nappy and helping him by putting a potty by his bed. Encourage him to manage on his own and to be self-reliant. When your child is ready to do this, it is important to help him. It is quite a big step for him to stop relying on you and take the responsibility for himself. Accidents will of course still occur, so you could minimize your work, and his anxiety, by keeping a small rubber sheet on top of his ordinary bedclothes and then put a half sheet over that. This small top sheet can be easily whipped off and washed.

Physical activities

The pre-school child uses his extraordinary level of activity to test his limits. He wants to see how strong he is. He wants to find out how good his sense of balance is, he wants to know how far he can run and whether he can run faster than you or his friend. Many of his activities are to see how far, how fast, how clever, how skilled, how strong he is.

Very often your child is setting his own internal standards and really is competing against himself. Later, of course, he starts to compare his own performance with others. In either case, what he is trying to do is to find out what his body can and cannot do and then try to master those things which he finds are beyond his ability.

Pre-school children involve their bodies in almost everything they do and for this reason they are rewarding participants in games, outings and entertainment. They are also very openly emotional. It is as though your child has taken up ham acting. Every emotional response seems exaggerated. This is quite natural and you should not try to curb it because it is teaching him to come to terms with his own emotion.

Body language

Because your child is so aware of her own body, she becomes aware of the bodies of other people and the language that they speak. It is about this time that your child will come up to you and put a hand on your shoulder and say 'are you all right Mummy?'. This is because she has noticed that you are sitting with your shoulders hunched and your head in your hands at the kitchen table. She instinctively knows that you are in a body posture that means all is not well.

Freedom to explore

To help your pre-school child develop her full physical, intellectual and emotional capabilities, you must give her freedom and that means trusting her. Your child needs to explore the garden herself, not by being taken round holding your hand. Try not to be easily scared and over-protective. If you discover your child on top of a high wall, it is best if you don't tell her sharply to get down. If she gets down in a hurry to please you, she may fall. If she gets down in her own good time, she almost certainly will not.

If you say, 'hold my hand or else you will fall' every time you come to an obstacle, you will be getting between your child and her body and prevent her learning about what she can and cannot do. You must try to take a philosophical attitude towards giving your child freedom. The only way you could prevent all accidents would be to imprison your child in an empty room.

A child sets her own limits which are within her own capabilities when she is on her own so you should trust her to play alone. But when she is with a group, watch out for feats of daring, when she may go beyond her limits if teased. If you leave your child in the charge of older children, make sure that they are old and sensible enough to stop your child doing things which are easy for them but dangerous for her. If there are machines about, be cautious. Poking a stick through the spokes of a bicycle is all right when it is stationary but it may break her wrist if the wheel is moving. Never ever let your child play near to traffic. If a ball rolls out on to a road she will not think before she retrieves it.

Bedroom space

By the time your child is pre-school age she will be wanting a place of her own. Her bedroom or her part of the bedroom very often becomes the centrepiece of her life. So encourage her sense of pride by making it as nice for her as possible. Allow her to say where the furniture goes, what should go on the walls, where she should keep her clothes, etc. Make her feel like a real person by involving her in all the decisions which affect her place before you actually do or buy anything. Take her shopping to help choose items.

If you help to make her bedroom pleasant in a way she wants it, you will be indirectly avoiding problems with sleeping. She will like her bedroom and will feel happy and relaxed to be in bed when it is time to go to sleep.

(Above) Climbing frames are good for testing strength and daring.

Nightmares

The life of your pre-school child is so full of new events and first-ever experiences that unpleasant thoughts and frightening things are easily imagined, so that she may have the occasional nightmare. Nightmares are a sign of anxiety but a normal one. Quite often they come in phases and your child may have a nightmare for several nights in a row and then none for quite a few months. The most important thing you can do if your child has a nightmare is to get to her quickly. When you reach her she will probably be unaware of what has frightened her. Your presence and closeness will usually be reassuring and you will be able to calm your child down. Once she is calm, put her back into her bed, tuck her up soundly, sing a little song while you rub her back, kiss her goodnight, assure her that you are just outside and leave.

Sleepwalking

If you find your child sleepwalking but calm, just take him gently back to bed and tuck him in securely. If he is upset follow the routine for night terrors (below). Your child may appear to be wide awake while sleepwalking and may speak normally and be very rude. Before you do anything ask a question to see if he is awake or sleepwalking. If he is sleepwalking, he will not answer. If you can, be gentle with a child who sleepwalks, even if your patience is tried.

Night terrors

More frightening to a parent are 'night terrors', which should not frighten you, unless habitual. They are a normal part of growing up and will probably stop around 6-8 years old. Your child will wake with a scream but when you reach him you will find he is neither awake nor asleep, but in a sort of delirium state. He may be imagining all sorts of horrors in his room and he may incorporate you into them when you appear. He may not recognize you as his Mummy, nor even as a friend and tell you to go away or appear frightened of you. Despite this, don't go away, he needs you. In night terrors all emotions are exaggerated. You will feel helpless because you cannot break through the delirium and reach your child to give comfort.

The only thing to do is to stay with him until the disturbance is over. You should put on all the lights so that you can see what you are both doing. As your child is not awake he is not open to reasonable persuasion, so do not argue with him, just keep repeating 'don't worry, Mummy is here'. Take absolutely no notice of any of the upsetting things he says or if he's afraid of you, he does not know what he is saying. Do not do anything to wake your child up. It is better that he goes through this rather disturbed state while semi-conscious. In that way he will not remember anything about it in the morning. I have found that my sons wanted to go to the lavatory and if led to the bathroom they would pass urine and, still asleep, go quietly off to bed.

Emotional illnesses

It has been known for many centuries that the mind can have a great effect on the body. Many physical illnesses are connected with emotional disturbances. As we have already seen, your pre-school child wears his emotions on his sleeve. He is a jumble of rather wild emotions which he has not yet managed to bring under control. So it is not surprising that his reaction to pain and illness is affected by his state of mind, in addition to whatever discomfort the illness may bring. Every person has an inbuilt threshold of pain. Those people with a high threshold feel less pain from, say, a hard knock than people with a lower threshold, so the fact that your child cries whenever he is hurt does not necessarily mean that he is lacking in stoicism or is a cry baby. It may simply mean that he has a low pain threshold. An extrovert is more likely to complain of pain than is the introverted, quieter child.

A person's pain threshold can be altered by circumstances. If you are depressed, even a minor cold can make you feel really miserable but if you are in a really good mood you may ignore the cold. It is also probable that we have a higher resistance to infection when we are in a good spirits than when we are low. It has been reported that the children of anxious parents get more colds than the children of more happy-go-lucky parents. When your child complains of pain or discomfort, try to take a constructive attitude to his complaint and find out what is wrong with him. In this way you will be able to give sympathy when it is needed and pay little attention to complaints when it is not.

There is very often a link between body temperature and recurrent aches and pains that children complain of quite commonly. Such recurrent conditions would include abdominal pain, headache and limb pain.

If you find your child is suffering from recurring illness of emotional origin, then the first thing that you should do is to look to yourself and your family. Quite often you will find that you or other members of the family react in a similar way to emotional disturbances and may even suffer recurring nervous symptoms, such as acid indigestion, tension headaches, insomnia.

You should take your child along to the doctor so that he can be examined and investigated if necessary. It is important to make sure there is no physical (organic) cause for your child's symptoms. If your doctor says there is no organic cause, stop worrying and do not pursue it. Prolonged investigations can only make your child more sensitive to his health and to his body.

The best way to help a child who reacts physically to stress, is to try to minimize the stressful situation when it occurs. Then you can gradually expose your child to the situation which causes his stress while supporting and helping him to get through any unpleasant experiences. For instance, your child may not like to go visiting. He prefers the familiarity and security of his own home but don't let his fear stop you from going. Help him, however, by making very little preparation for the outing. Don't demand that he washes, brushes his hair or changes his clothes but quite casually just before your leave, wipe his hands and face with a flannel, run a comb through his hair and allow him to come with you in his play clothes.

Emotionally induced pain is no less real than physical pain. To your child it is real and he does feel it and it does hurt. You will find that as your child grows up and is better able to cope with the stresses of everyday life, his emotional reaction to them will settle down and his symptoms will gradually diminish and then disappear. If you feel that your child is continually using illness or pain as a weapon, talk to your doctor about it who may suggest specialist help.

Abdominal pain

Abdominal pain of an emotional origin usually occurs without any other symptoms. This usually allows you to distinguish it from serious causes of abdominal pain that need your doctor's immediate attention (see page 110). If your child is highly strung then it is very important that you do not do anything which draws his attention to his abdomen and his 'inside'. You should avoid being fussy about meals and eating, or rigid about bladder control and obsessive about bowel movements. All these things may trigger off a child's awareness of what is going on inside his body.

Even though your child's pain is of emotional origin, he will nonetheless be frightened by it. Your pre-school child is usually old enough to understand if you explain that there is nothing wrong with him inside. He will find the pain easier to deal with once he knows that there is nothing seriously wrong with him.

Abdominal pain of the recurrent type can nearly always be related to a clearly stressful situation such as going to the dentist, Mummy going away for a few days, Grandma coming to visit, or going to a party. In this case, you can help your child best by playing down the event and treating it in a perfectly normal, rather offhand way. Once you have decided there is nothing seriously wrong with your child, however, try to give him enough self-confidence to face the situation and go through with it.

If he complains of stomach ache on the morning you are due to take him to the dentist, suggest that you go and tell the dentist about the stomach pain. A good dentist will be very understanding and will distract your child enough to get a proper look inside his mouth. Before you know it you and your child will be surprised to find yourselves outside the surgery door with the visit over. Then you can praise your child and make him glow with a sense of achievement. He will find the next dentist's visit much easier, but don't expect him to be unafraid.

With an older baby, a pain in the tummy is often used as a general term to describe that he is not feeling very well. Even in older children, abdominal pain can be a symptom of general illness such as a cold, tonsillitis, or middle ear infection. As with younger babies, abdominal pain is a serious symptom if it is accompanied by fever, vomiting or diarrhoea and in these circumstances you should consult your doctor. Never try to treat abdominal pain yourself and never ever use laxatives in this condition as they very often make it worse. If your child has severe abdominal pain, call the doctor no matter what hour of day or night. On the other hand, if your child seems fairly well and happy and particularly if his appetite is good and he has eaten recently, then there is probably nothing for you to worry about, so wait to see if the pain goes away. Only if it persists for several hours should you consult your doctor.

Recurrent headache

There are a few old wives' reasons for children having headaches such as eyestrain and bad teeth. By all means have your child's teeth and eyes checked but neither of these things causes headaches. Recurrent headaches are nearly always of an emotional rather than a physical origin. The treatment is the same as for abdominal pain.

Limb pains (Growing pains)

A child may have pain in her limbs for many reasons while she is growing but growing is not one of them. Growth is painless. You can usually tell if a pain in the limb has any serious cause by observing your child.

If she rushes in from the garden to say that her leg hurts, it is quite probable that she has knocked it. Examine it to make sure that there is no deformity or bruising, rub it gently, apply some of your mother's 'magic' cream (i.e. something like vaseline or baby cream) and see what happens. If your child sits for a moment and then dashes out again, there is obviously nothing seriously wrong. The same would apply to a pain which wakes your child at night. If she is comforted by your presence and turns over and goes back to sleep, there is probably nothing seriously the matter.

As her mother, you will know instinctively if there is something seriously wrong when your child complains of limb pain. You will notice other symptoms of illness, your child's loss of appetite, general listlessness, loss of enthusiasm, tiredness and you will know as soon as she develops a fever. If any of these things happen, contact your doctor as soon as possible.

Incidentally, you can be certain that your child has broken no bones if she can move the part that has been injured without any help. A child with a broken bone will not move the limb in which the bone is broken.

Even when you know that your child has got nothing organically wrong with her, never tell her that she has no pain. As far as she is concerned, she does have pain and it does hurt. She will come to you for help and you will seem less than a comforting friend if you try to tell her that it is imaginary.

The eyes
Defective sight

Your child should have a routine eye test somewhere around her third birthday so that any defect in vision can be picked up and corrected early. Thereafter, she should have eye tests at yearly intervals. If you suspect that your child's eyesight is defective at any other time, go along to your doctor and have the eyes tested whenever you are worried. The commonest visual defect in children is short sightedness for which glasses are needed.

Colour blindness

About 8 out of every 100 boys but only 4 out of every 1000 girls suffer from colour blindness. If your child is colour blind to any degree, it will usually show up before he goes to school because you will have noticed that he persistently makes mistakes about the naming of colours, especially red and green. If you have your child's eyes checked at the age of three, colour blindness will show in the tests.

Stye

A stye looks like a small boil on the eyelid. It is in fact folliculitis and occurs when the hair follicle of an eyelash becomes infected. If you are very worried about a stye, consult your doctor for specific treatment. However there are certain things that you can do at home. If the eyelash is loose and your child is co-operative, pull it out with a pair of tweezers and this will allow the pus to drain. If the stye has not already reached a head, you can encourage it to do so by dipping a cottonwool bud into warm salt water and bathing the stye with it. Never use proprietary antiseptic creams on styes, only use a specially formulated eye ointment which has been prescribed by your doctor.

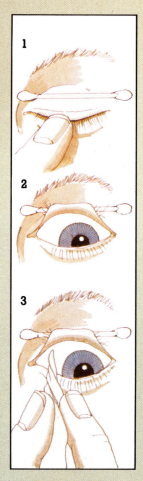

(Above) To remove a foreign body from your child's eye:
(1) hold a matchstick on top of the eyelid
(2) bend back the eyelid over the matchstick
(3) quickly remove the object with the corner of a clean handkerchief.

Foreign body in the eye

If your child gets something in his eye, the best way of removing it is described below. However, this is best attempted only if you feel confident. Don't do it if you feel nervous or shaky.

☐ Take a matchstick and twist some cotton-wool around the end so that the sharp sides of the wood are padded.
☐ With your child's co-operation, lay the matchstick on the middle of his upper eyelid.
☐ Take hold of the eyelashes of the upper eyelid and bend it back over the matchstick.

You will find that the lid 'pops' back over the matchstick revealing its undersurface and the upper half of the eyeball. If the foreign body is visible, remove it with a quick but accurate flick with the corner of a clean linen handkerchief. If the foreign body is not visible, ask your child to swivel the eye around in different directions until you can see it, then remove it. If your child objects, get someone to hold him still. Lay him on a table and if necessary get an adult to lie on top of him. You have to be cruel to be kind.

The only alternative is to bathe the eye with a piece of cotton wool or a handkerchief which has been soaked (so that it is wringing wet) in a glass of warm water containing a teaspoon of salt. For this procedure, you should ask your child to keep his eye open. If either method doesn't work, take him to the casualty department of the hospital. A child should not be allowed to suffer for longer than one hour.

Bloodshot eyes (conjunctivitis)

If your child develops a 'red eye' examine it to see if there is a foreign body (see above). If you can find none and the eye is sore and your child tries to keep the eyelid closed, then this could be an infection of the conjunctivae which may need local antibiotic treatment and you should take your child along to see your doctor.

The ears
Wax

The skin of the outer ear contains glands which produce a reddish brown wax which tends to collect. This wax is produced for lubrication, for protection and to increase resistance to infection as it has anti-bacterial properties. It also stops the canal from becoming wet and soggy. There is no time when you should make strenuous efforts to remove it. If you see a small lump lying loosely on the skin, then by all means blow it off but never poke anything down your child's external auditory canal to try to get the wax out. You may impact the wax further down, or worse, you may rupture your child's ear drum. If your child is complaining of deafness and you can see wax, then take her along to the doctor who may decide' to remove the wax with a syringe.

Otitis media

This is an infection of the middle ear and is a common side effect of some of the infectious fevers. (See page 132.) The major symptoms are earache and occasionally pus in the external auditory canal which can be seen running out of the ear. This is a serious condition because if allowed to become chronic it may result in permanent deafness. It is therefore essential not only for the child's comfort but for her future health that she receives medical treatment as soon as possible, so contact your doctor if ever the symptoms occur. It is especially important that otitis media does not become chronic and if it is associated with recurrent tonsillitis, it may become necessary to have the tonsils (and possibly the adenoids) removed.

Diabetes

Only 1 in 20 diabetics in the UK is a child. Diabetes, however, can appear very suddenly in a child. The main symptoms are usually intense thirst and the output of a greatly increased amount of pale urine. If this occurs at night it may give rise to bedwetting. Some children complain of abdominal pain and vomit and this may lead a parent to mistake the illness for an abdominal upset. Diabetes may show up in some children as drowsiness which eventually leads to loss of consciousness. Your doctor will confirm the diagnosis by testing a specimen of urine and finding sugar in it. Diabetes is caused by failure on the part of the pancreas to produce insulin which helps to keep the blood sugar down. Children who develop diabetes therefore require insulin.

A type of insulin will be chosen which suits your child best and you will be shown how to test his urine for sugar and when and how to give the insulin. You may have to inject it and you may have to show your child how to give the injections himself. Many children can manage this with complete equanimity when very young. This helps them to feel self-reliant and independent which is an important aspect in treating diabetes in children. As the tendency nowadays is to give a child as much freedom as possible with their diet, you may find that your doctor does not prescribe dietary restrictions. Diabetes cannot be cured. The probability is that your child can lead a completely normal life while taking insulin. Do not become distressed or depressed over your child, this will only make him feel different from his family and his peers. Try to make him feel absolutely normal. In all the important aspects of life he is. It is a good idea to join the British Diabetics Association for helpful advice and support (see page 184).

Pre-school immunization

Before your child starts nursery school visit your doctor and discuss immunization. Many doctors feel it's the time to give immunization against measles and boosters of the protection your child was given during her first year.

Language and speech

Use words freely in your conversation. Your child does not understand all of them but gradually she will come to grasp the place of the word and how it is used. Do not self-consciously use very complex words. On the other hand, do not try to simplify your conversation down to a child's level. If your child is interested in a word and does not understand it she will almost certainly ask you what it means, in which case you can translate it into terms that she can understand. You will find in a very short time that she is starting to use it, perhaps not correctly in the first instance but that does not matter. She is experimenting with language and this takes her forward. Once she has started to use the word, she will very quickly learn to use it properly.

When your child tackles new words, she will probably mispronounce many of them. Try not to correct her or you will stifle her spirit of adventure with language and it will become boring for her. Also, you may dampen her sense of pride in having acquired a new word. Some children's pronunciations are so quaint and pretty that you won't want to correct them. They will correct these pronunciations of their own accord when they hear the word used several times, as their ears are acutely aware of complex words. If you want to, you can help them by using the word a second time in a new sentence.

In her early years, your child will regard you as omniscient and will naturally turn to you for advice on all subjects. If you remain approachable and welcome questions, she will grow up feeling she can talk to you about anything, see page 178. Discouraging a child when she is young and uninhibited will do little to lessen her inhibitions as she grows older. If you are determined that you will always remain the ready confidante of your children, it is worth keeping the channels of communication open no matter what it costs you.

You may think that your child is acquiring speech more slowly than she should. If you are really worried, take your child to your doctor but before you do so, check that there is not an obvious reason for the development of speech having slowed down.

Boys tend to speak later and more slowly than girls, so you should not make comparisons between boys and girls. If you have several children in your family, the older ones may interpret what your child is saying or what she wants on her behalf and this may mean that the younger child is never presented with a need to communicate properly. Children do not necessarily teach each other to speak and may make a baby lazy by acting as translator. If there are several children in the family, your private conversations with your child become even more important because in these circumstances you will be her only 'formal' teacher.

If the person who looks after her most of the time is not of the same mother tongue as the

(Below) Having a special girl friend and sharing a secret makes words and sentences valuable and perhaps for the first time thrilling. Your child's speech may take a leap forward when she starts to mix and play with other children.

(Above) Many children have their own special way of comforting themselves. Thumb-sucking and a security blanket are so common as to be normal. Don't ever tease or scold. Your child will give them up in her own good time. There are few thumb-sucking adults about!

child, then the child is bound to learn slowly. If you have a foreign au pair in your house you must make a special effort to make sure that your child has the maximum amount of language practice with you. If you are French and your husband is English, then she will take considerably longer to pick up two languages than she will learning one but much later on, of course, she will find the second language useful.

If she is learning a new skill which is taking a lot of her concentration, then again you would expect the development of speech to slow down dramatically or halt altogether.

You may notice that your pre-school child develops a minor stutter which appears when she is excited or uneasy. This is usually just a temporary hiccup in speech development and very rarely turns into a real stutter that lasts into school years.

Behaviour problems
Comfort habits

From an early age a child gets pleasure from sucking his thumb and so will continue to seek this form of pleasure as a counter to outside experiences, for example when he is bored, tired or afraid. Do not worry about it. After all, adults occupy themselves at similar times with similar distractions. He'll stop anyway when it becomes embarrassing in front of his friends. Sucking habits early in life may sometimes interfere with the way that the teeth grow. However, once the habit is stopped the teeth will normally come into place quite naturally. However, do

make sure that any comforters, such as dummies, do not contain sweet substances.

Nail biting does not usually begin until a child starts school. However, it is quite common among schoolchildren. It is an unconscious nervous habit which should not be forcibly prevented. It is better to encourage your child to take a pride in his appearance, which will, in any case, happen naturally later on.

The need for a comfort rag is not a sign of insecurity or lovelessness. Comfort rags are carried by children from all sorts of backgrounds, both happy and unhappy. Let your child take his rag everywhere and remember to pack it if you are going away for a night. Eventually he may leave it behind in the daytime but still need it at bedtime. If you wish to wash it make sure you have an identical replacement.

Aggression/destructiveness

These disturbing types of behaviour are essentially a cry for help, resulting from some unhappy circumstance in a child's life. It may be that he is neglected by his parents or that they are too strict or that they are often arguing with each other but it may also happen with loving, compassionate parents. So, although his behaviour is bad, it is not really his fault. Curing him of his behaviour and his distrust of adults may take years, not months. This work is often carried out with infinite patience by teachers, psychologists or social workers in the absence of helpful parents. Nasty little boys and girls are nearly always responding to someone else's nasty treatment of them and they need help.

Lying and stealing

Lying and stealing are also a reaction to some unpleasant external circumstance. This does not apply to the odd fib which nearly every child will tell at some point, because he finds fantasizing or fooling another child fun. These fibs are not disastrous but if a child habitually tells lies, you should investigate the cause, which may be neglect or loneliness, and try to correct it.

If the lies are always told when your child is trying to avoid blame it is because she is frightened of telling the truth. This means that she has previously been too severely punished or is being subjected to painful threats. In this case the lying will not stop until the child learns that telling the truth is more comfortable than telling a lie. It is easy to understand how a child will find an escape from a painful punishment by telling a lie. So the best way to stop the lies is to make telling the truth a more attractive proposition.

Bedwetting

There is nothing abnormal about bedwetting and it does not mean that your child is physically backward. Boys tend to be slower than girls at achieving total bladder control and one in ten boys still wet the bed at the age of five. Total control of the bladder is a gradual process which begins with knowing when to use the lavatory but progresses to being able to hold urine for longer and longer but it may take some children a very long time to develop the capability to last out the 10 or so hours through the night. While he is still in the process of gaining total control of his bladder a child should not be labelled a bedwetter. There are some things you can do to help a child before his bladder has reached its full capacity.

☐ You can discourage him from having a drink after 6 p.m.
☐ You can make certain that he empties his bladder before going to bed.
☐ Then you can put him on the potty again before you go to bed, see page 168.
☐ You can give him a potty so that he doesn't have to go far in the night.

The potty is quicker, easier and safer than a journey to the lavatory in the dark.

An emotional upset may cause a child to lose control of his bladder.

Starting nursery school, moving to a new house or the absence of parents could all stimulate the same pattern of behaviour. If none of these things has happened, the possibility of infection should be investigated by your doctor.

There is no doubt that some perfectly normal children acquire bladder control later than others and may give their parents a few problems. Often there is a history in the family of lateness in acquiring control. Most doctors believe however that there is no need for a full investigation before a child is three years old if he is wet during the day and five years old if he is still wet at night, though your general practitioner may ask you to take along a specimen of urine so that he can examine it. Medicines rarely help unless an infection is present and assiduous efforts by parents only make matters worse. When your child is young, the best you can do is to be especially kind and take things slowly.

As the process of acquiring control can be delayed through the child's anxiety, it seems illogical and even unkind to add your worry to that of your child's. You should only take steps to deal with bedwetting if your child specifically asks you for your help. Dragging an unhappy and embarrassed child from doctor to doctor will only make his emotional problem worse. The bells and buzzers which are designed to wake a child when he first starts to pass urine will also heighten his anxiety. The most suitable treatment for your child should be chosen by a consultant paediatrician to whom your doctor will refer you.

However, I strongly believe that the problem of bedwetting should be minimized and accepted by the household as normal. You can help yourself to make less of it if you are not too exhausted by dealing with the consequences. You can help your child by never, ever scolding him about his bedwetting. No matter how tiresome it becomes, try to make light of it and change the subject. Although it is not much help in the short term, comfort yourself with the fact that most bedwetters have disappeared by the age of ten, often despite treatment.

A new baby

The coming of a new baby into your house upsets all your children, no matter how well adjusted they are, or how good your relationship is with them. You should accept this and be sensitive to it. Try to do all you can to make it easy for your pre-school child to deal with this rather difficult, and, for her, unpleasant situation. The following are a few suggestions.

Do make sure to tell her about the new baby before someone else lets it out in front of her. She should get to know from you, not from a stranger.

Tell your child where the baby is and how it is growing. Let her feel your swelling abdomen and your baby kicking. Try to give the baby a personality before it arrives by discussing whether it will be a boy or a girl and what names you would like. You might also try showing her some photographs of herself when she was a tiny baby. In this way you will also prepare her for the small size of the new baby, and therefore she will not be expecting an instant playmate.

Try to make sure that she doesn't start on any new activity like going to school just about the time when the baby arrives. This will increase any feelings of exclusion she may have and also give her two difficult hurdles to cope with simultaneously. Make sure that she has lots of friends of her own that she can visit and that come to visit her. In other words, try to encourage her to be as independent as possible before the new baby arrives on the scene.

Try to plan ahead to what is going to happen when you are going into hospital to have the baby. If your child is going to have to stay with someone, make sure that she spends the odd night with them so that she will be on familiar ground when you leave her.

A couple of weeks before your baby is due to arrive, explain to your child in some detail what the arrangements are. Include her in making the arrangements. For instance, she could help you pack your hospital case. She could also help you to arrange the new baby's clothes, get the cot and nappies, etc. ready.

Before you go to hospital, make sure that you say goodbye to your child even if you have to wake her up in the middle of the night, should your labour start then.

If the hospital will allow it, make sure that your child sees the new baby before you come home.

When you bring the baby home, make sure

that someone else is carrying it so that your outstretched arms are for your child and make quite a fuss of her before you turn to the baby. To make the meeting more pleasant, bring with you a gift from the new baby for your child.

In the early days you can avoid much jealousy by not breast feeding the baby in front of her.

As far as you can, do as many of the things that you did with your child before the baby arrived. If you had a special time of day with her, then still reserve it for her. Make sure that your new baby does not make her feel second best.

With the arrival of a new baby, an older child often regresses to baby behaviour. She feels that being like a baby is something that you love and so she wants to be more of a baby than she really is. You can help her by offering her a chance to behave in a babyish way now and then. You can pat her and sing to her the way you do with the baby, or allow her to play now and then with the baby's fluffy toys.

Let your older child feel that there are some advantages and privileges in being the older child. For instance, you can point out that she can stay up later in the evening than the new baby, or she can watch television, or she can go to the cinema, or have some chocolate.

Do everything you can to convince her that the baby really likes her. As soon as your new baby starts to react to people and smiles at them, you can say to your older child 'Oh look, he is smiling at you'. And you can say to strangers 'Oh, he always stops crying when his elder sister pushes the pram'.

Having a generally understanding attitude to your children's jealousy about the new baby does not mean that you should overlook acts which are frankly wrong. You should deal with each incident the way you would if your new baby was not involved. As long as you are as affectionate with your children as you were before the new baby's arrival and you continually tell them that you love them in exactly the same way as you did, you should not be afraid to discipline as normal. Each incident should be dealt with quickly then forgotten.

In the early stages, never interpret small acts against the baby as being purposely malicious. They rarely are because a small child doesn't understand that complicated emotion. Such an act is nearly always a demand for attention and if you give it, you stand a better chance of stopping your child from behaving badly than by chastizing and punishing her.

Before you fly off the handle at some of the things your children may do to the new baby, find out if the act was meant as a kindly one rather than the way you angrily interpreted it. The pebbles which have been put in your new baby's cot may be meant as gifts. But be careful never to let your older child hurt the baby and in the early days watch very carefully how she behaves and what she does when she is with him. If you feel any sort of uneasiness with a toddler, a cat net may be sufficient to protect the baby. Tell your older child what it is and that it is to protect your new baby against cats.

(Below) Help your child to understand about new babies by letting her hear the baby's heart beat and feel the movements. It will also help her to prepare herself pyschologically to be no longer the centre of your world and to welcome the new baby.

(Above) Your child will get more fun out of games if you are there to help, especially with those things which she can't quite manage to do herself.

After the potty

Most children can use a potty reliably by the time they are three. Some have even graduated to using the lavatory for both passing urine and passing stool. If your child has got this far, you should start to show him how to manage the whole business of bowels and bladder under most circumstances.

The first thing that he will have to learn is to use the lavatory like any other member of the family. He will learn this most quickly if he watches other members of the family using the lavatory, so do let him, particularly Daddy. Most toddlers sit down to pass urine but make sure they are quite comfortable passing urine in the standing position before they join any sort of group activities such as play school. If you let your toddler see that other members of the family use a lavatory, you will probably have no difficulty in weaning him off his potty on to it. Similarly, of course, a girl will learn from Mummy.

However, make sure that it is easy for him by having a little chair or stool next to the lavatory so that he can climb on to it with ease and make sure that his clothes cause no problems. Trousers with elasticated tops are a must.

Once your child is used to your own lavatory, introduce him to lavatories in other places, like Granny's, or a friend's house and take him into public lavatories. Once he is confident and self reliant about using lavatories, you will find that he shuns going into the ladies' lavatory with you and will even prefer to go into the gentlemen's lavatory as long as he has someone older (and male) with him.

Even though your child has reached this stage, be ready for accidents. They continue to happen until your child is five or six. Quite a few three and four year olds have frequent accidents. It is a good idea to carry a change of clothes with you on any outings. Try to remember that your child's embarrassment at wetting or soiling his clothes is much greater than yours, so never make a fuss. Sympathize with your child, say it doesn't matter, change the pants quickly and carry on as though nothing had happened. Accidents happen more often when a child is nervous, so if your child is under any sort of emotional stess, be prepared to take him to the lavatory more frequently than usual.

You will also have to show your child how to manage outdoors. It is as well to introduce your child to the idea of stopping the car so that he can have a pee by the roadside as soon as possible, otherwise trips and outings may be spoiled for a long time. One of the easiest ways of getting a boy to accept being outside is to let Daddy take him to a quiet spot and let him see Daddy doing it. Girls find difficulty in squatting and up to the age of four, may like you to hold them. Children of both sexes may want to remove their pants as they find it difficult to keep them out of the way.

Activities

Your pre-school child has so much energy and curiosity that you will have to think how you can help fill her day with interesting activities. She has much time on her hands now because she no longer takes regular naps and it will need organizing so that she has complete changes of what she is doing and where she is doing it. She may be quite happy to play with her toys during the morning, while you are doing your chores but will get bored if she is left too long alone. Try punctuating her morning by taking your elevenses together in the kitchen and then go on to a fresh activity in a different place. You might take her to the shops or to visit a friend. After lunch she could have a fresh activity outside if the weather is fine, then tea and something new until bedtime. Youngsters like routine and they like their days to be predictable to a certain extent, but they also like new experiences.

Your child has very few close friends other than yourself. She relies on you for everything. She relies on you to organize her day and to provide her with ideas for play, she even relies on you to fetch the paint and paint brushes and organize the water and the easel if she wants to draw a picture. Because of this responsibility you have to think every day of new experiences to feed her. At this stage she can get them through nobody else.

You are the keystone in her life but you are by no means enough. It is essential that she meets as many people as possible of all ages. Include your child on as many outings as you can to visit friends and make sure that she is with you when friends visit the house, unless it is late at night. If at all possible, seek out neighbours who have friends of a similar age so that your children can play together. Invite one of your neighbour's children to tea and if your child is quite happy to go somewhere without you by all means let her go to tea at a friend's house.

Almost every day there will be some task which your child finds too difficult to complete herself. She will have disappointments and failures. Without your support and encouragement she would probably never find the determination and effort to finish her task or try again.

Try to punctuate the weeks, months and years

as well as each day with interesting events. Weekends will almost certainly be special because Daddy will probably be home but there are birthdays, Christmas, new moons to look at, the longest and shortest days of the year to note, the first bulbs coming through and the leaves turning brown.

Questions

Your pre-school child will be full of questions. The first ones will be mainly concerned with 'what', 'who' and 'where'. You should answer with simple and if possible, short replies. 'That is Daddy's coat, here is your ball'.

Later on questions turn into 'Why?'. Always try to answer your child's questions honestly, never dodge the issue. You will encourage your child to ask more questions and learn more. Studies have shown that children who are encouraged to question and who are given explanations, who are listened to, turn out to be happier children and grow up less authoritarian and bossy than those whose questions are ignored and who are not considered individuals with something valuable to say.

Telling your child about sex

Some questions may be embarrassing especially if they are asked in public but it is best if you do not avoid giving an answer altogether, even though you may defer it. Questions about sex are an obvious example of this. However, you do not have to go into all the details the first time the question is asked but show that you are willing to respond to your child's curiosity with a truthful answer. If he doesn't get the facts from you, he may get distorted, furtive ideas from his friends. A child's sex education is learnt through physical contact, beginning with the first cuddle and is reinforced by his parents' own loving relationship. As he gets older, he will be fascinated by his body, without being self-conscious about it. If a child is used to seeing his parents unclothed, he will continue to be unconcerned by it and his own nakedness, though he may become curious about his mother's breasts and his father's penis. This is best satisfied by a frank chat and a good look. However, if you do not feel comfortable about open nudity within your family your embarrassment will quickly be transmitted to your child, so it is best not to attempt it.

Babies become aware of their genital organs by the time they are twelve months old and may touch them as they might do any other part of their body. Eventually, however, they will notice that this brings a pleasurable sensation and therefore will choose to do it. This type of fondling is more like real masturbation. It is a normal occurrence and does not have any of the disastrous consequences predicted by old wives' tales, such as blinding or insanity. Do not worry unless you think it happens when your child is trying to escape reality. If it happens in public, the best thing to do is distract your child, at home it can be ignored. Never scold your child as this will make an issue of the whole thing, encourage him to do it in private and introduce an element of guilt. If it is a regular occurrence, it may be a warning sign that your child feels somehow deprived and so merits investigation.

Infrequent masturbation may be for a number of reasons, e.g. when a small boy is proud of his penis, if he has just had a frightening experience and needs comforting, if he needs reassurance about his own body after noticing that he is different from girls or if he has nothing else to do. Very occasionally, it may be because the skin around the penis or vagina or sometimes the urine is infected and this will need to be treated by your doctor.

To sum up, masturbation may be caused by the need for a pleasurable experience as a result of fright, feeling inadequate or boredom. Whichever is the case for your child, it is better to try to deal with the causes than to interfere with the masturbation, unless it is habitual.

Questions about death

Questions about death are more difficult because a child will find the truth difficult to take

and will not really be able to accept it before the age of eight. However, when a child asks why a pet has died or the bird in the garden is dead or what has happened to a member of your family who has died, it is best to be straightforward in your answer. If you talk about 'sleep' when explaining death your child may become frightened about going to sleep. Similarly if you talk about someone being taken the child will fear it will also happen to her. It is a part of life that a child will have to come to terms with, so do not try to protect her from it. If someone in your family dies, she may well want to know if that person will ever come back, tell her the truth, say 'no'. This often leads to fears that she, too, is going to die and again you will have to be realistic and say that it is not impossible but that it is so unlikely that she should not worry about it.

Reading

Once a child has started to read, it is best to provide as many materials from as wide a range as possible. From the very first picture book, reading should be fun. Your child will not look at books just because you like them. Get him the books he likes. Any books. The important thing is that he finds it an interesting and enjoyable activity.

While it is important to encourage reading because it can widen a child's world more than almost any other pastime, there is nothing especially worthy about reading. A child who is slow to take an interest in words and then slow to read but who loves to make things with his hands is not necessarily less intelligent than the fast reader. Never force books on your child.

Helping in the house

Being allowed to help in the house is an activity guaranteed to make a child feel useful and keen to expand his skills. He is even happier if his help is actively sought. He feels his contribution is important to you and the family. As soon as children start to toddle they will try to help with all sorts of household chores. If you encourage your child to 'help' he is more likely to grow up thoughtful and more co-operative, ready to do his share and eager to give a helping hand with any project. It encourages him to be independent and self-assured and grow up with the idea

(Below) Painting should be free and easy. Prepare your child with aprons and old clothes. Prepare yourself by spreading newspapers on the floor to catch spills. Don't stop your child from making a mess – after all he's creating.

that he is needed. This is a great boost to anyone's morale but is especially valuable to a child who in most respects is dependent on you.

As a child gets older, he should be encouraged to help with less pleasant tasks like clearing away his toys, eventually putting his clothes together and helping to set the table. As a result, he will probably take for granted that groups of people interact as a team.

Father's role

Not everyone can afford to pay for help and it is up to individual members of the family to help out too. If both parents are working, I think it is essential that the father does his share and this must be understood. Sharing cooking, washing up, cleaning, laundering, nappy changing and the countless other household tasks is surely part of a modern marriage.

Older children ought to help out too. In institutions, children are well able to set the table at four, make their own beds at five, serve a simple cold breakfast at six, be trusted to watch over youngsters for a while at seven, run errands at eight and help with anything at nine if supervized. Why not at home? If necessary, jobs should be allocated. Qualities of helpfulness, patience, consideration and thoughtfulness should not just be encouraged but accepted as the normal way of life from an early age.

Most children have an acute desire to help from the time they can walk and bring small things to you. They wish to be given responsibility. If his efforts are praised and rewarded, even the most truculent child can become a useful and pleasant member of the household. Participation in the day to day activities of the home encourage self-assurance, self-reliance and like all of us, children get a kick out of being part of a team, especially when it works well.

Starting nursery school

At a nursery school or a playgroup your child will probably have his first experience of being in the charge of an adult other than the fairly indulgent friends or relations he has been left with up till now. He will also be introduced to a group of strange children in unfamiliar surroundings. This is then a big change for your child and needs careful handling both in the matter of finding the right school or group and in the way you introduce your child to it.

By the time he is about three years old your child is ready for learning experiences outside his own home and will enjoy meeting other children but do not rush him into it. Try to make it a happy experience. This may mean staying with him for the whole morning to start with. Then after perhaps a week of this, he will let you go after you spent the first hour with him. Tell him what you are going to do while you're away and when you are coming back. Make it a short absence of about half an hour and be sure to come back when you promised, so that he can trust you. He will gradually become more absorbed in his new friends and activities and miss you less and less. Eventually he will run to join his friends as soon as he gets to school and say goodbye to you quite happily. Let your child become accustomed to this new situation in his own time. It may well not be a smooth process, so be prepared to revert to an earlier stage if necessary. If you push him against his will he will build up a resentment against you and against schooling which will be difficult to overcome later on.

Choosing the right nursery school or playgroup means visiting the various places with your child, talking to the teachers and observing the daily activities. Most teachers are happy for you to do this and will welcome rather than reject your interest.

(Below) Children love helping and enjoy making things grow. You can combine the two if your child can help Dad do the gardening. And it's a special time for just her and Dad.

Child minders

Whether you work or not, there are going to be times when you have to leave your child with a baby sitter or a child minder. The help you can give a baby sitter has already been mentioned on page 92.

If you are going to engage a child minder, there are two alternatives. Either she will look after your child in your own home or she will have a creche in hers. Your child will probably be happier with the former, as at least her surroundings will not be strange.

If she is to spend the day away from home, do make sure that you have seen the child minder's facilities and in either case try to find out whether or not she will look after your child properly. Try to get recommendations from friends or, if the person looks after other children as well, speak to their mothers to find out how it is working for them. Whilst many child minders are excellent, some do as little work as possible and in such care your child will suffer. Your local doctor or health department will supply you with a list of recommended child minders who are visited regularly by social workers or health visitors. People who mind children in their (the minders') own homes must be registered with the local authority.

Television

There are many homes in which television is banned for children, indeed, where there is no television at all. People who do this claim that watching television has a detrimental effect on children in that it excludes other forms of valuable entertainment such as books and music and 'amusing herself like I did as a child' and also because if watched alone, children may grow up thinking that television is the most important way of receiving information and worse, it can be received with no effort on their part. There is no two-way dialogue or input from the child.

My own feeling is that these people ignore the benefits of television and that used with discrimination and with some effort from a good parent, then it is a very valuable source of entertainment and education.

Here are a few of the rules that we have about television in our house:
☐ The television set is never left on in a room as a gratuitous background noise. As soon as a programme is over, or as soon as a child gets bored with what is on television and moves to another activity, the television set is turned off.
☐ There is no indiscriminate viewing. Every programme which is viewed is vetted by my husband or myself as being suitable for the

(Above) Always do careful research about your childminder and nursery school. Visit the premises, sit in on a session, talk to the person in charge. Never entrust your child to someone you don't have confidence in.

(Above) The best kind of television for your children is the kind you watch with them. Comment on the programme. Ask questions. Encourage them to grow up thinking it's only one of the ways of being entertained and getting information. Make sure T.V watching isn't seen as a silent self-contained activity for escaping.

children to see. One exception to this rule is children's programmes just after lunch and at tea time. If you give your children a good reason why a certain programme should not be viewed then they usually accept it happily, especially if you suggest an alternative pastime which they love and which you join in.

☐ Television can never be used as an excuse to stay up late. If a child is tired or his bedtime is due, then he must go to bed whether the programme is finished or not. We do have one exception to this rule, programmes which are of specific interest to the children.

☐ The children do not spend a long time watching television on their own. Whenever possible, my husband or myself join the children in the room so that the programme is not absorbed in silence. By asking questions and making comments you can teach your child to analyse and apply the information which she is receiving from the programme. Once you have started to comment on what is going on on television, then your child will also feel free to do so and will almost certainly ask you questions about what is

interesting or what she does not understand. In this way television can be a very powerful educational tool.

☐ A critical attitude towards television is always encouraged. If the programme appears moronic, then ask your child if she wants to go on watching it. If the answer is 'no' then you are in a very strong position to turn the programme off. After a while, your child will agree with you and may even get up and turn the television off when she is no longer interested.

☐ We encourage the children to watch programmes which introduce them to aspects of life, people, places or things, that would not ordinarily come within their sphere of experience. How else is it possible, for instance, for your child to know about the plants, insects and bird life in the Amazonian jungle?

Making things easy

One of the main aims is to make your pre-school child as independent as possible, to allow her to look after herself and make as many of her own decisions as she can. Each little bit of independence she learns makes it easier for her to cope with school and the demands that are made of her there. As far as you are concerned you have one less job to do. You will also be helping your child in that good habits started now will probably last her for the rest of her life.

One of the ways in which you can help your child to do things for herself is to make sure that it is possible for her to do them. She cannot go to the lavatory on her own if the handle on the lavatory door is too tight for her to turn or too high for her to reach. She cannot brush her own teeth if her arm cannot reach the tap to turn on the water (keep a little stool in the bathroom). As your child's independence grows, you should walk around the house and try to see it from her point of view. Imagine you are only her height with only her strength and her coordination and then imagine having to do all the tasks that you expect your child to do. You will see that very often a task is not done because it is impossible for your child to do it. She cannot dress herself because the sliding doors on her wardrobe do not slide. She cannot have a go at cleaning her own shoes because you have not told her where you keep the shoe cleaning box.

Making her own decisions is one of the most satisfying things for your growing child to do. You know very well that not all her decisions will be good ones, indeed, some of them will be actually harmful. The way you can help your child is to give her a range of options, not all of which are equally good but at least they are acceptable to you. Having told your child what the various choices are, then let her make up her own mind.

Your child will be developing quite a distinctive taste in clothes. Always bear her preferences in mind when buying and if you can, take her along with you when you choose her clothes, so that she can take an active part in deciding what she wears. When you come to dress her in the morning or when going out, try to let her exercise a choice over what she wears.

You will have fewer difficulties and complaints about clothes if you choose garments that are easy to put on and and take off, are comfortable to wear and do not restrict your child's movements. Try to find fastenings that are simple like 'Velcro', always have pants with elasticated tops for easy pulling up and down and avoid heavy stiff materials in any garment. If it is cold and you would like your child to wear gloves, make it easy for her by putting them on a tape through the sleeves. It will be some time before your child can manage to do up laces, so wherever possible, buy shoes that are slip on. For a boy, leave zip-fastened flys to the very last minute. They can sometimes cause nasty accidents if your child has to struggle to do up the zip and nips his skin.

Try to make boring chores as interesting as possible. One of the ways to make tooth brushing more appealing, is to make a competition of it. You and your child can compete to see who can clean their teeth the best. You can then show up how well the teeth have been cleaned by using a disclosing tablet in a glass of water. If you swill this around your mouth then spit out the solution, the plaque which has been left on your teeth will show up pink.

Hair washing can be made more pleasant by making a game of it too. Always use a non-sting shampoo and work up a good lather. Most children love to make their lathered hair all sorts of strange shapes and points. Let your child do this in front of the mirror and entertain herself for several minutes. If your girl has long hair, you can get round the problem of tangles when combing out her washed hair by using a conditioning cream or rinse.

Road safety

At three years old it's not too early to begin to teach the basic ground rules about road safety:

☐ never play near a road
☐ always close gates that lead on to a road
☐ never follow a ball on to a road
☐ cars are dangerous and cause accidents
☐ never ever cross a road alone
☐ never play beside parked cars
Repeat such rules whenever you can and add new ones and more advanced ones as your child can cope with them, until you're on to the greencross code by say 4 years old. Whenever you can, teach by example, e.g.:
☐ always heed traffic lights and point out the sequence
☐ always cross roads at zebra crossings
☐ always hold your child's hand as you cross
☐ never run across, walk carefully and steadily to avoid stumbling or falling
☐ always give a running commentary of why you're doing things and making decisions about the traffic
☐ show that you must use your eyes, ears, brain and body to be safe.

(Below) Children under five cannot cope with traffic on their own, but with you to show them how, they will learn to look and listen for traffic before crossing and, once it is safe, to go straight across without dawdling.

SPECIAL ORGANIZATIONS

Below are details of specialist organizations each providing information and advice on a specific aspect of birth and babycare. The addresses of the headquarters are given, but all have branches throughout the country and all publish information about themselves and their work.

BIRTH CENTRE
16, Simpson Street, London SW11
Aims: to promote preventive medicine and alternative forms of health care to ensure good health
to encourage natural labour where possible
Services: information on all aspects of birth
network of people throughout country to give support and help

BRITISH ASSOCIATION FOR EARLY CHILDHOOD EDUCATION
Montgomery Hall, Kennington Oval, London SE11 5SW
Aims: to promote the education and welfare of young people (birth – 9 years)
to provide sufficient nursery schools and classes so that all children have access to early educational opportunities
Services: courses and conferences
queries answered, information on all aspects of child development, welfare and education via headquarters (send s.a.e.)

BRITISH DIABETIC ASSOCIATION
10 Queen Anne St, London W1M 0BD
Aims: to give counsel and confidence to diabetics
to wipe out prejudice and ignorance about diabetes through information
Services: wide range of free advice on all aspects of diabetes
conferences and educational holidays for children aged 6 upwards
funds for individual and group research
takes up hardship cases with government
publications and visual aids

CHILD POVERTY ACTION GROUP
1 Macklin St, London WC2B 5NH
Aims: to work with and on behalf of poor families
to draw attention to the problems of poverty and campaign for change
Services: provides immediate practical assistance
free information, advisory and advocacy service through Citizens Rights Office
courses and teach-ins

FAMILY PLANNING ASSOCIATION
27/35 Mortimer St, London W1N 7RJ
Aims: to preserve and protect family health by preventing unwanted conception
to disseminate facts about procreation, contraception and health
to give medical advice and assistance with sexual problems
Services: national and local information and advice on all aspects of birth control, sexual relationships and population issues through clinics
sex education programmes
co-ordinating medical research and clinical trials of contraceptives
funds for family planning programmes

GINGERBREAD
35 Wellington St, London WC2
Aims: to provide support and advice for one parent families
Services: local groups within the community organize day-care projects, welfare advice and housing schemes
national headquarters with full-time staff to co-ordinate local groups
penfriend scheme and holiday schemes

LA LECHE LEAGUE
P.O. Box B.M. 3424, London WC1
Aims: to promote the advantages of and to provide advice on all aspects of breast-feeding
Services: mother-to-mother counselling by trained helpers
telephone contact for immediate help

NATIONAL ASSOCIATION FOR THE WELFARE OF CHILDREN IN HOSPITAL
Exton House, 7 Exton St, London SE1 8UE
Aims: to raise standards of care for all children in hospital
Services: practical help through play schemes, visiting, baby sitting and transport
meetings and discussions for parents and schools
information service

NATIONAL CHILDBIRTH TRUST
9 Queensborough Terrace, London W2 3TB
Aims: to improve women's knowledge about childbirth
to promote the teaching of relaxation and breathing for labour
Services: antenatal classes for expectant mothers and for couples with trained teachers throughout country
breastfeeding counselling and postnatal support
education in schools and through study events and conferences

NATIONAL COUNCIL FOR ONE PARENT FAMILIES
255 Kentish Town Rd, London NW5 2LX
Aims: to improve the position of one-parent families
Services: legal advice and welfare help through Advice Departments
promoting knowledge about the issues that affect one-parent families
campaigning for better services

NATIONAL COUNCIL OF VOLUNTARY CHILD CARE ORGANIZATIONS
Cheriton Barton, Cheriton Fitzpaine, Crediton, Devon EX17 4JB
Aims: to further and protect the common interest of children in the care of voluntary organizations
Services: acts as the voice for all voluntary childcare organizations
presents cases to government departments and national councils
social work with families in need

NATIONAL SOCIETY FOR THE PREVENTION OF CRUELTY TO CHILDREN
1 Riding House St, London W1P 8AA
Aims: to prevent child abuse in all forms
Services: a nationwide team of Inspectors providing a 24-hour service to children at risk
provides a number of special Treatment Units
provides a network of playgroups and day-care centres
provides a national advisory and consultancy service on child abuse

PRE-SCHOOL PLAYGROUPS ASSOCIATION
Alford House, Aveline St, London SE11 5DH
Aims: to help parents provide play opportunities and education experience for children under five
Services: individual playgroups with trained staff and voluntary workers throughout country
opportunity groups for handicapped children
support for childminders and encouragement of industrial day-care facilities
conferences, exhibitions

TWINS CLUBS ASSOCIATION
198 Woodham Lane, New Haw, Weybridge, Surrey
Aims: to give support to families with twins (or more) and to promote understanding of their problems
Services: clubs nationwide providing meetings, advice and support
campaigns for better facilities and discounts in local shops

INDEX

(Figures in *italics* refer to captions)

Abdomen: exercises for *14*
  stretch marks on 71
Abdominal pain: during
  pregnancy 29
  emotionally induced 170
  in young babies 110-11, 171
Aches, emotionally induced 170-1
Adenoids 112
Afterbirth *see* Placenta
After pains 84
Aggression in children 174
Air-travel: when pregnant 15
  with a baby 122
Alcohol 22
Allergies: to dust 153
  to flea bites 152
  to house mites 153
Allowances, maternity 34-5
Amenorrhoea 11
Ammonia dermatitis 86
Amniocentesis 27
Amniotic fluid 17, 18, 27
Amusement: of a baby 118
  of a sick child 132
Anaemia during pregnancy 21, 22, 25
Anaesthetic, general 53
Anaesthetic, local: creams and ointments
  containing 135
  during labour 52-3, *53*
  when pregnant 22
Analgesics during labour 51-2
Animals and babies 118, *119*
Ankles, swollen (during pregnancy) 15, 29, 71
Antenatal care, importance of 23, 45
Antenatal classes 25, 27
  to familiarize with hospital procedure *32*
  for husbands 25
  to learn about psychoprophylaxis 32
Antenatal clinics 23, *23*, 24-5
Antiseptic creams 135
Anxiety: during pregnancy 32
  in children 158, *158*
Appendicitis, acute 111
Appetite: increased during pregnancy 13
  of newborn 75
  lack of in newborn 79
  loss of 109: when to call the doctor 114
Arm control (baby) 106
Aspirin 135
Asthma: allergic 153
  emotional 153-4
Attention, crying for *96*, 97-8

'Babbling' 117
Babysitters 92
Backache during pregnancy 28, *29*
Back-strengthening exercises *14*
Banging head (of a baby) 119
Bath, baby 38
Bathing babies: newborn *80-1*
  transition to big bath 121-2
  one-year-olds 139
BCG (anti-tuberculosis) vaccination 113
Beakers, baby 120
  sterilizing 101
Bed: making child go to 138
  going to and television 182
  keeping sick child in 130
  wetting 168, 175
Bedrooms, children's 168
Bedwetting 168, 175
Benefits, NHS 34-5
Bibs 120
Birth *see* Childbirth
Birth marks: naevus (strawberry mark) 85

temporary 68, 84-5
Bladder control 148-9
  in a three-year-old 168
  see also Bedwetting
Bleeding: to stop *154*, 155
  nosebleeds 111
  nosebleeds during pregnancy 29
Blood: changes during pregnancy 21
  taking blood pressure 24, *24*
  low blood pressure 28
  tests 24-5
Boils, treatment of 153
Bones (of young children) 154
  broken 171
Boredom (in pre-school child) 177
Bottle feeding 77-9
  versus breast feeding 72-3
  equipment 77-8
  how much and how many 79
  when travelling 122
  constipation in bottle-fed newborn 70
  winding bottle-fed babies 78, 79
Bouncer, baby 140
Bowel control 148-9
  in a three-year-old 168
Bowel movements *see* Constipation, Stools
Bras: for pregnant women 15
  while breast feeding 70
Brain, the: how it matures 136
Braxton-Hicks contractions 18, 45
Breast feeding 72-6
  advantages of *72*, 72-3
  anxiety about 89
  in bed 99
  distaste of 89
  for the first time 75
  in hospital 59
  menstruation inhibited by 115
  the 'pill' and 116
  best position for 75, *75*
  when to stop 76
  twins 76, *77*
  versus bottle feeding 72-3
Breasts: and breast feeding 73
  care of during pregnancy 22
  changes during and after pregnancy
    11, 21, 71
  engorgement of 74, 75, 76
  enlarged (baby's) 85
  enlargement of (postnatal) 74
  leaking 74
  to prevent sagging 15
  stretch marks on 71
  see also Nipples
Breast shells 22
Breath, shortness of (during pregnancy) 21, 28
Breath-holding attacks 159
Breathing: difficulty in – when to call the
    doctor 114
  difficulty during pregnancy 21, 28
  of newborn 67-8
Breathing exercises *27*
Breech delivery 54
Breech presentation 44, *44*, 54
Bronchitis 112, 134
  from measles 133
Bruising (of newborn) 68, 85
Burns, treatment of 155

Caesarian section 56-7
Calamine lotion 135
Calcium: needs during pregnancy 12
  requirements of one-year-old 126-7
  supplements 22
Canned food *see* Tinned food
'Cap' (contraceptive) 115
Car journeys: when pregnant 15
  with a baby 122
Carriers, baby 92, *92*, 93
Carry cots 38, 39
Castor oil 43

Cephalic presentation 44, *44*
Cervix, dilatation of 46
Cetrimide antiseptic cream 135
'C-film' (spermicide) 116
Chairs, baby 123
  high 120, *121*
  push 162
Chewing 101-2
Chicken pox 133-4
  symptoms 135
Childbirth: Leboyer's methods 43
  natural 42
  suggestion in 51
Child minders 122, 181, *181*
Chill 111
Chloasma 21, 71
Choking 154-5, *155*
Cigarettes, distaste for 11, 22
Circumcision 87
Climbing frames 160, *169*
Clinics: antenatal 23, *23*, 24-5
  post-partum 115
  Well Baby 114
Clothes, baby 37-8
  for crawling babies 139
  for toddlers 162
  for wet weather 162
  dressing-up 160
  letting child choose 182-3
Clothing for pregnant women 14-15
'Coil', the (contraceptive) 115-16
Colds 111
Cold sores 152
Colic 97
Colostrum 22
  to express 22, *22*
Colour blindness 171
Comforters and comfort habits 119, 174
Confinement, home 60
  equipment for 60-1
Confinement case 39, *39*
Conjunctivitis 133, 172
Constipation: of babies 110
  of bottle-fed babies 70
  after a fever 110
  when potty-training 149
  during pregnancy 12, 28, 84
Contact lenses 30
Contraception and contraceptives:
  'cap' 115
  chemical methods 116
  'coil' 115-16
  comparative efficiency of
    contraceptives 116
  diaphragm 115
  hormonal methods 116
  intra-uterine device 71, 115-16
  'loop' 115-16
  oral methods 115, 116
  'pill' 116
  rhythm method 116
  'safe' period 115
  sheath 116
  spermicides 115, 116
Contractions: Braxton-Hicks 18, 45
  after delivery 71
  causing foetal distress 56
  during labour 45, (abnormal) 55
  during pregnancy 18
Convulsions 111
Co-ordination of movements 118
  see also Manual dexterity
Corset, supporting 28
Cots 38
  carry cots 38, 39
  decorating *121*
  sheets for 38
Coughs 111-12
  see also Whooping cough
Cradle cap 86
Cramps, muscular 22
Cravings, food 11

Crawl, learning to 127-8
Crawling babies: clothes for 139
  toys for 140
Croup 153
Crying: for attention *96*, 97-8
  when hungry 97
  when hurt 170
  when insecure 138
  at night 96
  when tired 97
  due to wind 97
Cups, baby 120
Cycling during pregnancy 15

Dancing during pregnancy 15
Day nurseries 122
Deafness 112, 172
Death, children's questions about 178-9
Dehydration 130
  after diarrhoea 110
  after vomiting 109
Delivery date *see* Expected date of
  delivery
Dental care in pregnancy 14
  free 34
  for women with heart disease 30
Dental complaints during pregnancy 14
Dentists: fear of 170
  visits to 150, *150*
Depression: during pregnancy 33
  post-natal 89-90
Destructiveness in children 174
Diabetes mellitus: in children 172
  during pregnancy 30
Diaphragm (contraceptive) 115
Diarrhoea 109-10
  dehydration from 110
  when to call the doctor 114
  when potty-training 149
Diet: during pregnancy 12-13
  to cure constipation 12, 28
  for fat babies 148
  for one-year-olds 126-7
  for pre-school children 166
  for sick children 130
  see also Food
Diphtheria, immunization against 113
Discharge, vaginal: during pregnancy 21,
  28
  post-natal 72
  in newborn 85
Discipline 138
  see also Punishment
Diseases, infectious 132-5
Dishes, baby 120
'Disproportion' 56, 57-8
Distress: foetal 56
  maternal 56
Doctor, when to call the 114
Drawing (of children) 160
Dressing and undressing a baby 139
Driving when pregnant 15
Drugs: to be avoided when pregnant 22
  used during labour 51-2
Dummies 97

Earache 112
Early morning sickness 11, 28
Ears, wax in 172
Ectopic pregnancy 116
Eczema, infantile 113
EDD *see* Expected date of delivery
Educational toys 108, 118
  water as *156*
'Effacement' 46, *46*
Egg (ovum): fertilization of 10, *11*
  implantation of 10, *11*
'Elderly primigravida' 45
Electric shock, treatment for 154, *154*
Embryo, definition of 10
  see Foetus
Emergencies: when to call the doctor 114

Emotionally induced illnesses 170-1
Encouragement, giving: to babies 118
  to children 136
'Engagement' *21*
Engorgement 74, 75, 76
Epidural anaesthesia 53, *53*
Epilepsy 111
Episiotomy 47, 53, 54
  soreness after 71, 84
Epithelial pearls 87
Examinations: internal 12, 24, 51
  of newborn 58, *58*
  post-natal 115
Exercises: for the abdomen *14*
  back-strengthening *14*
  breathing *27*
  for early pregnancy 14, *14*
  for the feet 29
  hip-strengthening *14*
  for the pelvic muscles 71-2
  post-natal 70, *71*, 71-2
Expected date of delivery 10
  to calculate 10-11
  chart 10
Expenses of having a baby 39
Expression: of colostrum 22, *22*
  of milk, manually 74, 75
Eye contact (with newborn) 67
Eyes: bloodshot 172
  colour (of newborn) 69
  colour blindness 171
  conjunctivitis 133, 172
  foreign body in 172, *172*
  'lazy eye' 113
  'red eye' 172
  spots before (during pregnancy) 30
  'sticky eye' 86
  see also Sight
Eye tests 171

Face, swollen (during pregnancy) 29
Faddiness about food 147-8, 167
Fainting (during pregnancy) 28
Falling (during pregnancy) 30
Fat babies 100, 148
Fathers: role of 88, 118, 180, *180*
  see also Husbands
Fear, children's 158, *158*
  of dentist 170
Fears in pregnancy 32
Feeding: as a game 93
  difficulties with 76
  finishing a feed 76, *76*
  frequency of feeds 75
  at night 75-6
  pre-term babies 84
  restless babies 79
  routine for newborn 75
  routine in hospital 62
  schedules for six-month-old 103
  shedule for one-year-old 103
  slow-eating babies 75
  mixed feeding 100
  spoonfeeding 100
  see also Bottle feeding, Breast feeding,
    Mealtimes
Feet: exercises for (during pregnancy) 29
  flat (of children) 154
Fertilization (of egg) 10, *11*
Fever 109
  constipation after 110
  convulsions due to 111
  to reduce 131
Fevers, infectious 132-5
Fibbing (children) 175
'Finger foods' 102, *103*, 120
Fingers, swelling of the (during
  pregnancy) 24
Fire, to put out 155
First aid 154-5
Fits 111
Flea bites, allergy to 152

Fluid retention *see* Pre-eclampsia
Fluoride: tablets 102, 129
  toothpaste 129
Flying: when pregnant 15
  with a baby 122
Foetus: definition of 10
  development of (0-36 weeks) 16-18
  distress to 56
Folic acid 22
Folliculitis 153, 171
Fontanelle 67
Food: cravings for (during pregnancy) 11
  distaste for (during pregnancy) 11
  faddiness about 147-8, 167
  'finger' 102, *103*, 120
  nutritious 126-7
  for pre-school children 166-7
  snack 126
  solid 100-1
  tins or home-cooked? 120-1
  for toddlers 147-8
  see also Diet
Forceps delivery 54, 55, *57*, 57-8
Foreskin, tight (in newborn) 87
Forewaters 45
Formula 70
  vitamins in 102

Games: with young babies 93, 118
  with pre-school children 168
Gas-and-air machine *48*, 52
General Practitioner Maternity Unit 34
Genital organs: awareness of
  formation of 17
  touching 178
  of the newborn 85
German measles 133
  effects on foetus 23
  inoculation against 23
  symptoms 135
  vaccination 113
Germs, protection against 109
Grant, maternity 34, 35
Grasp reflex (in the newborn) 69
Gripe water 135
Growing pains 171
Growth 104
  see also Weight
Gums: changes in during pregnancy 29

Haemorrhoids (during pregnancy) 29
Hair: effects of pregnancy on 71
  lanugo 17, 68
Hair washing 104
  of the newborn *80*, *82*
  making it pleasant 183
Hands: swollen during pregnancy 29
  use of in young baby 106
  use of in one-year-old 128, *128*
  see also Manual dexterity, increasing
Harnesses, safety 123
  in car 122, *123*
Head: banging (of a baby) 119
  cleaning a baby's 86
  control of 105
  'engagement' of *21*
  flexion of 55
  misshapen in newborn 85
  washing *80*, *82*
Headache, recurrent 171
Health visitors 34, 92
Hearing: of the newborn 67
  see also Deafness
Hearing aids 112
Heart: effects of pregnancy on 21
  pregnant women with heart disease 30
Heartburn (during pregnancy) 28
Heat: baby's temperature 36, 68, 84, 85
Heat rash 85
Hernia 87
Herpes simplex (cold sores) 152
Hiccups 68

High chairs 120, *121*
Hip-strengthening exercises *14*
Hives 152
Home confinement 60-1
Home helps 34
Hormones: avoidance of during pregnancy 22
    placental 10
Horse riding during pregnancy 15
Hospitals: reasons for hospital confinement 61
    feeding routine 62
    going to 50-1
    nursing your child in 151-2
    routines 59, 61-2
    stay in 34
    useful items to take to 63
    types of 34
    visiting hours 62
    on the ward 61-2
House, safety procedures in the 36, 141
Hunger, crying from 97
Husbands: antenatal classes for 25
    involvement in pregnancy 32-3, 88
    and labour 59
    see also Fathers
Hypnotic drugs (used in labour) 51

Illnesses: of babies 109
    of young children 152-4
    emotional 170-1
    in the newborn 84-7
Immunization: during pregnancy 23
    of babies 113
    of pre-school children 172
Impetigo 153
Implantation (of egg) 10, *11*
Independence, teaching a child 182
    to prevent jealousy of new baby 175
Induction of labour 42-3
    medical reasons for 42
    social reasons for 42
Infantile eczema 113
Infections: baby 109
    minor skin 153
Infectious diseases 132-5
Injections *see* Immunization
    Triple injection (Diphtheria, whooping cough, tetanus) 113
Inoculation *see* Immunization
Insomnia (during pregnancy) 13
Insulin 172
Internal examinations 12, 24, 51
Intra-uterine device (contraceptive) 71, 115-16
Intussusception, acute 110
Iron: requirements of a one-year-old 126-7
    supplements 21, 22
Irritability: during pregnancy 33
    post-natal 89-90
Isolation of sick child 130
IUD *see* Intra-uterine device

'Jargoning' 117
Jaundice: at birth 86
    due to rhesus incompatibility 31, 86
Jealousy of new baby, and how to prevent it 175-6

Knock knees 154
'Koplik's' spots 133

Labour: abnormal contractions during 55
    contractions during 45
    drugs used during 51-2
    your husband and 59
    hypnotic drugs used in 51
    induction of 42-3
    length of 45
    pain relief during 51-3
    preparation for 33
    prolonged 55-6

sedatives used in 51
signs of 45
three stages of 46-8
    1st stage 46
    delay in 1st stage 55
    2nd stage 46-8
    delay in 2nd stage 55
    3rd stage 48
    delay in 3rd stage 56
start of 44-5, 51
tranquillizers used in 51
Language development *see* Speech, Talk, learning to
Lanugo hair 17, 68
Laughing (of babies) 117
Lavatory, use of: by one-and-a-half to two-year-olds 148
    by pre-school children 177
    making it easy for a child 182
Laxatives 110
Layette, basic essentials of the *36*, 36-8
'Lazy eye' 113
Learning and understanding:
    birth to six months old 117-118
    eight to twelve months old 118
    eighteen months to two-and-a-half years old 156-7
    critical phases 136
Leboyer's methods of childbirth 43
Legs: aches and pains in 171
    bow 154
    control of 106
    inability to straighten 87
    see Walk, learning to
'Let-down' reflex (in breast feeding) 73-4
Lie, the 43
    longitudinal 43, *43*
    oblique 43, *43*
    transverse 43, *43*
Lifting when pregnant 15
Limbs, aches and pains in 171
Lochia 72
'Loop', the (contraceptive) 115-16
Low birth weight babies 54, 84
Lying (children) 175

Manual dexterity, increasing 118, 128, 136, 146, *147*, 158
    see also under Hands
Masturbation 178
Maternal distress 56
Maternity allowance 34-5
Maternity grant 34, 35
Mealtimes: 1-1½ year olds 148
    pre-school children 166-7
Measles 133
    bronchitis from 133
    immunization against 113, 172
    symptoms 135
Measles, German *see* German measles
Meconium 56, 70
Medicine: giving a baby 87
    giving children 131
    safe for babies 39
    safe for children 135
    use of old medicines 135
    warnings 135
Meningitis 134
Menstruation: causes of delay in 11
    after delivery 72
    inhibited by breast feeding 115
Middle ear, infection of *see* Otitis media
Midwives 34, 61, 81
Milia 68, 85
Milk: making it palatable 130
    vitamins in 73, 102
    qualifications for free 34
    see also next entry
Milk, breast: manual expression of 74, 75
    production of 73-4, 75
    to stimulate production 89

to stop production 84
    vitamins in 73, 102
Milk teeth 129
Mineral needs during pregnancy 12
Miscarriages 12
    in rhesus negative mothers 31
    sexual intercourse after 12
Mobiles 35, *121*
    making 118
Molars, cutting 150
Monitoring equipment in labour ward 52, *52*
Moods during pregnancy 33
Morning sickness 11, 28
Moro reflex 69
Movements: co-ordination of 118
    of the newborn baby 66
Mumps 134
    symptoms 135
Muscle strengthening exercises 14, *14*
Muscular cramps 22
Musical toys 160

Naevus 85
Nails: care of baby's 87
    nail-biting 174
Nappies 37
    changing 37, 39, *82-3*, 139
    cleaning *83*
    discarding 148-9
Nappy liners 37
Nappy rash 70, 85-6
Naps 139-40
National Childbirth Trust 59
National Health Service benefits 34-5
Natural childbirth 42
Nausea during pregnancy 11, 28
Neck muscles, use of 105, *105*
Nettle rash 152
Night feeds 75-6
Nightmares 169
'Night terrors' 169
Nipples: care of during pregnancy 22
    changes in during pregnancy 11, 21
    cracked 76
    inverted 22
    sore 76
Nosebleeds 111
    during pregnancy 29
Nose drops 111
Nurseries, day 122
Nursery, planning the 35-6, *37*
Nursery school: choosing a 180
    starting at 180

Oedema *see* Swelling
Operations, children's 152
Oral contraceptives 115, 116
Otitis media 112, 172
    from measles 133
    from mumps 134
    from tonsillitis 112
'Overlying' 99
Overweight babies 100, 148
Overweight children 166, 167
Ovulation 10
    after birth of baby 115
    temperature chart to confirm pattern of 115
Ovum 10
    fertilization of 10, *11*
    implantation of 10, *11*
Oxytocic drugs 42, 43, 56
Oxytocin 73, 74

Pain: abdominal 110-11, 171
    emotionally induced 170-1
    relief of during labour 51-3
Papula urticaria 152
Paracervical block 52-3
Paracetamol 135
Pelvic bones, abnormal 56

Pelvic muscles, exercises for 71-2
Periods see Menstruation
Pethidine 51-2
Pets and babies 118, 119
Physical activities, pre-school 168
Pigmentation: increase in (during pregnancy) 21
  fading of 71
Piles (during pregnancy) 29
'Pill', the (contraceptive):
  'combined' 116
  'mini' 116
  breast feeding and 116
Pills: giving children 131
  use of sleeping pills during pregnancy 13
Pillows, baby 99, 99
Pitocin tablets 43
Placenta 10
  delivery of the 48
Placental hormones 10
Placental insufficiency, induction due to 42
Play: for development of intellectual skills 158-9
  for development of physical skills 158
  for development of social skills 159
  see also Games
Playgroups 180
Playing with other children 158
Play pens 140
Poliomyelitis vaccination 113
Possetting 86-7, 109
Postnatal discomforts 84
Postnatal examination 115
Postnatal exercises 70, 71, 71-2
Post-partum clinic 115
'Potty', use of 148, 149, 149
Prams 39, 123
Pre-eclampsia 24, 42
  with twins 25
Pregnancy: allowable activities 14, 15
  air travel and 15
  anaesthetics and 22
  anxiety during 32
  appetite during 13
  body changes due to 11, 12, 18, 21, 70-2
  car journeys and 15
  special clothing for 14-15
  common minor complaints of 28-30
  confirmation of 12
  cravings during 11
  dental care during 14, 30, 34
  depression during 33
  dietary requirements 12-13
  drugs to be avoided during 22
  exercises 14, 27, 29
  fears during 32
  food, distaste for 11
  German measles and 23
  hair, effects on 71
  hormones, avoidance of 22
  husbands' involvement in 32-3
  immunization and 23
  insomnia during 13
  irritability during 33
  length of 10-11
  lifting during 15
  mineral requirements during 12
  moods 33
  nausea during 11, 28
  protein requirements during 12
  resting and relaxation 13, 27
  sexual intercourse during 15
  signs of 11
  sleep requirements during 13
  smoking and 11, 22
  sport and 15, 15
  taste changes during 11
  tearfulness during 33
  tests for 12
  tooth decay during 14
  train journeys and 15
  twins 25, 25

vaccinations and 23
vitamin requirements during 12
vomiting and 11, 28
weight gain during 12-13
working during 15, 33
x-rays and 22-3
Presentation: breech 44, 44
  cephalic 44, 44
Premature babies see Pre-term babies
Pre-term babies 54
  feeding 84
Prostaglandin pessaries 43
Protein requirements: during pregnancy 12
  of a one-year-old 126-7
Psychoprophylaxis 32
Punishment (of children) 159, 176
  for telling lies 175
Push chairs 162
Pyloric stenosis 109

Questions, answering: about death 178-9
  about sex 178
Quarantine 132

Rashes: on newborn babies 85-6
  heat 85
  from infantile eczema 113
  from infectious fevers 132-5
  nappy 70, 85-6
  nettle 152
Read, learning to 179
Reading to a baby 118
'Red eye' 172
Reflexes in the newborn baby 69
Registration of birth 93
Regurgitation see Possetting
Reins, baby 146, 146
Relaxation classes 13
Relaxing postures 27
Resting during pregnancy 13
Restlessness when feeding 79
Rhesus incompatibility 31, 31
  jaundice due to 31, 86
Rhesus negative mothers:
  miscarriages 31
Rhythm method (contraception) 116
Riding (horses) during pregnancy 15
Ringworm 152
Road safety: basic rules 183
Rocking (baby's) 119
'Rooming-in' 62
Rooting reflex 69
Rubella see German measles

'Safe' period (contraception) 115
Safety procedures: in the home 36, 141
  in the road 183
Scalp, care of (baby's) 80, 86
Scarlet fever 134-5
  symptoms 135
School, nursery: choosing 180
  starting at 180
Sedatives used in labour 51, 55
Septic spots 68, 85, 153
Sex, determination of 31
Sex, telling your child about 178
Sexual intercourse: after birth of baby 115
  after miscarriage 12
  during pregnancy 15
Sheath (contraceptive) 116
Sheets, cot 38
Shingles 134
Shock: electric – treatment for 154, 154
  medical – treatment for 154
Shoes: children's 108, 162
  during pregnancy 15
'Show', the 45
Sickness: early morning 11, 28
  travel 109
  see Illnesses
Sight: defective 171

disturbances during pregnancy 30
  of the newborn baby 67
  short sightedness 171
  test at age of three 171
  see also Eyes
Sit, learning to 106-7, 107
Skiing during pregnancy 15
Skills, development of 118, 128, 136, 145-6
  toys and 118, 158-9
Skin: effects of pregnancy on 21, 71
  disorders (children) 152-3
  minor infections 153
  marks on newborn 68
  stretch marks 21, 71
  sunburn and 152-3
Sleeping and sleep requirements:
  during first few months 98-9
  between feeds 75-6
  of a one-year-old 138, 139-40
  of mothers 98
  during pregnancy 13
  where a baby should sleep 98, 99
  disturbances 149-50
  see also Nightmares, 'night terrors', Sleepwalking
Sleeping pills 13
Sleepwalking 169
Sling, baby 93
Smacking a child 159
Smallpox vaccinations (during pregnancy) 23
Smell, sense of 66
Smoking and pregnancy 11, 22
Sneezing (newborn) 68
Snuffling (newborn) 68
Social behaviour 118, 158, 159, 173
Socks, children's 108, 162
Solids: going on to 100-1
Speak, learning to see 'Talk, learning to
  see also Speech
Special care units, babies in 84, 84
Spectacles, free 34
Speech: development of 173-4
  encouragement of 117, 157, 157
  imitating (of a baby) 117
Spermicidal creams and jellies 115, 116
  'C-film' 116
Spoon feeding 100
Spoons, baby 102
Sport during pregnancy 15, 15
Spots: 'Koplik's' 133
  milia 68, 85
  on the newborn 68, 85
  on the palate 87
  septic 68, 85, 153
  see also Rashes
Squint 69, 113
Stair climbing 163, 163
Stand, learning to 108, 108
Stealing 175
Sterilizing equipment 38, 77
'Sticky eye' 86
Stings, treatment of 155
Stockings, supportive 15
Stomach ache see Abdominal pain
Stools: bloody 110
  green 70, 110
  of the newborn 70
Strangers, getting used to 118
Strawberry mark 85
Stress, children's reaction to 170
Stretch marks 21, 71
Stroking, newborn's desire for 66
Stuttering 174
Styes, treatment of 171
Sucking: reflex in newborn 69, 74-5
  of the thumb 119, 174, 174
Suction extraction 55, 57, 58
Suggestion in childbirth 51
Sunburn 152-3
Swallowing reflex 69
Sweets, giving children 126

Swelling during pregnancy: of ankles 15, 29, 71
  of face 29
  of fingers 24
  of hands 29
Swimming: during pregnancy 15
  for one-year-olds 141, *141*
Swings 160
Syntocinon 43, 55

Table manners, teaching 166, *167*
Tablets, giving a child 131
Talk, learning to: up to six months 117
  seven to eight months 117
  nine to twelve months 117
  twelve months plus 136, 138
  two to two and a half 156
  two and a half to three 157
  pre-school 173-4
  see also Speech
Tantrums 159, *159*
Taste: changes during pregnancy 11
  of a six-month-old 102
Tearfulness: during pregnancy 33
  post-natal 89-90
Tears: lack of in newborn 69
Teeth: brushing baby's 129
  cutting 129, (molars) 150
  making teeth cleaning easy 182
  making teeth cleaning pleasant 183
  tooth decay during pregnancy 14
  milk (primary) teeth 129
  order in which teeth grow *128*, 129
Teething gels 135
Teething ring 129
Television, benefits of 181-2, *182*
Temperature: when to call the doctor 114
  to bring down 131
  keeping a temperature chart 115
  taking a baby's 87, *87*
  taking a child's 131
Temper tantrums 159, *159*
Tetanus, immunization against 113
Thermometers 87, 131, *131*
Thighs, stretch marks on 71
Thrush: during pregnancy 28
  causing nappy rash 86
Thumb sucking 119, 174, *174*
Tinned baby foods 101, 120-1
Tiredness, crying from 97
Tongue tie (in the newborn) 87
Tonsillitis 112
'Topping and tailing' *82*

Towels, baby's bath 38
Toys 160
  and development of skills *129*, 158-9
  for crawling baby 140
  educational 108, 118
  from household objects 121
  making 118
  miniature 160
  musical 160
  putting away (of children) 140, 180
  soft toy as comforter 119
Train journeys: during pregnancy 15
  with a baby 122
Tranquillizers used in labour 51, 55
Travelling: when pregnant 15
  with a baby 122-3
Travel sickness 109
Turning a baby 43, 44
Twins 25, *25*
  breast-feeding 76, *77*

Ultrasonic scans *26*, 27
Umbilical cord 16
  separating the 87
Unconsciousness 155
Understanding *see* Learning and understanding
Undressing a child 139
Urine: during pregnancy 11
  lack of in newborn 69
  urine tests for pregnancy 12
Urticaria 152
Uterus, effects of pregnancy on 12, 18, 71

Vaccination *see* Immunization
Vacuum extraction *see* Suction extraction
Vagina, effects of pregnancy on 12, 21, 71-2
Vaginal discharge: during pregnancy 21, 28
  after delivery 72
  of a newborn 85
Varicose veins 15, 29
'Vernix' 18, 68
Verrucas 152
Visiting hours (in hospital) 62
Visual disturbances during pregnancy 30
Vitamins: needs during pregnancy 12
  in breast milk 102
  in cow's milk 102
  requirements of six-month-old baby 102
requirements of one-year-old 126-7
requirements of sick child 130
Vitamin A 126, 127

B vitamins 126, 127
Vitamin C 126, 127
Vitamin D 126, 127
Vomiting: during pregnancy 11, 28
  of babies 86-7, 109
  dehydration after 109
  projectile 109
  when to call the doctor 114

Wakefulness (at night) 98
Walk, learning to 144-6
  walking reflex (in newborn) 69
Walkers, baby 146
Walking during pregnancy 15
Ward, labour: monitoring equipment 52, *52*
Ward, maternity 61-2
Warm, keeping a baby 36, 68, 84
Warts 152
Washing babies *see* Bathing, 'Topping and tailing'
Washing powders 38-9
Waterproof jumpsuits *162*
Wax in ears 172
Weaning 76, 100-1, 102
  to the household diet 126
Weight: during pregnancy 12-13
  weight gain chart 13
  after delivery 70
  of newborn 89
  during first year 104
  chart 104
  during second year 147
  chart (1-1½ year old) 146
  of pre-school child 166
  chart 166, *166*
Well Baby Clinics 114
Wellington boots 162
Wetting the bed 168, 175
Wheezing 112
Whooping cough 134
  immunization against 113
  symptoms 135
Wind, crying due to 97
Winding (a bottle-fed baby) 78, 79
Words, use of *see* Talk, learning to, Speech
Working during pregnancy 15, 33
Working mothers 35, 122
Worms, thread 154

X-rays during pregnancy 22-3

Yoga during pregnancy *14*

Acknowledgements

We would like to thank all the parents for their assistance in preparing the photography and the following mothers, father and children who are featured:

Lilka and Lee Acord and James; Melanie Allan and Rachel; Mr and Mrs Jack Alvey; Cassim Arab; Mrs J. Atherton; Taehina Bailey; Mrs Beaumont and Emily; Laura and Emma Birch; Helen Broughton; Jasar and Cheryl Brown; Kelly Ann Butler; Simon Carnel; Barbara Dale; Arabella Dancy; Pamela Fettes; Mr V. Freiherger; Mrs Finbow; Vanessa and Rod Gamba Barata and Jonathon; Peter Gardner and Sam; Isabel George, Henry and Eleanor; Moira Glyn and Laura; Joanna Gowan and Alice; Alistair and Ian Gray; Lavinia Grimshaw and Isabelle; Alicia Howard and John; Sally and Barry Hutchinson, Katie and Victoria; Judith Jenne; Penny and Steen Lagoni and Sarah; Mrs Legge, Louisa and Octavia; Thomas Leslie; Wendy Marler and Oliver (and Polly, still expected); Rupert and Katie Mitchell; Sophie Patterson and Edward; Marcus and Jenny Pearce and Camilla; Patsy and Tony Pearce and Thomas; Charlotte Pimm; Suzie Powling and Daisy; Mandy Prout; Carol Ray and Danny; Eliza and Polly Redfern; Angela Rice; Debbie Routh, Roan and Tom; Tony Schavarien and Carly; Nicola Tham; Andrea Thomas, Marina and Wayne; Marcus Levi Thompson; Tom Wakeford; Kit Wilkins; Josephine Winstanley and Richard.

The photographs of the inside of a hospital in sections 2 and 3 were taken with the kind permission and co-operation of King's College Hospital and the Royal Free Hospital, to illustrate as clearly as possible typical situations. Details of policy, particularly in the management of labour, vary from hospital to hospital taking into account facilities available, therefore not all of the procedures described in the text will necessarily be available in these or other hospitals.

We would like to thank the following for their assistance:
Bedford Northwing Hospital: Glennys Culverwell
Belgrave Hospital: Miss M.L. Taylor, SRN, RSCN, NDN(Cert)
King's College Hospital: Sister D. Baker, SRN, SCM; Dr H.R. Gamsu, MB, BSCh, FRCP, DCH; Miss M.J. Lilley, SRN, SCM, MTD, HV; Sister J. Piper, SRN, SCM, MTD; Sister J. Ratnarajah, SRN, SCM
Royal Free Hospital: Miss J.M. McKenna, MSCP, ACPOG, SR
The Berkeley Play Group: Judith Holder

Thanks also to those who kindly lent their products for the photographs:
Boots Co. Ltd. (equipment); Hennes (children's clothes); Laura Ashley (clothes); Lunn Antiques (lacy bedspread, pillows and nightdress); Marks and Spencer p.l.c.: (children's clothes and kitchenware); Monsoon (clothes); Mothercare (children's clothes, toys and equipment); Mothers Ruin, 126 Holland Pk Av, London W11 (clothes); Tigermoth, 166 Portobello Rd, London NW11 (children's and mothers' clothes).

Photography of children and parents by Sandra Lousada.
Still life photography by Theo Bergström.
Full colour artwork by Dee Maclean.
Line drawings by Clive Spong.
Styling by Sarajane Hoare

YOUR BABY RECORD

BIRTHDAY ...... Thursday ....

First names ...... Seán Thomas ....

Date of birth ...... 6 August 1987 ....

Place of birth ...... Maternity Reg. Limerick ......

Birth weight ...... 8 lb 3 ozs ....

Length at birth ....

Colour of hair ...... Brown ....

Colour of eyes ...... Brown ....

FAMILY TREE

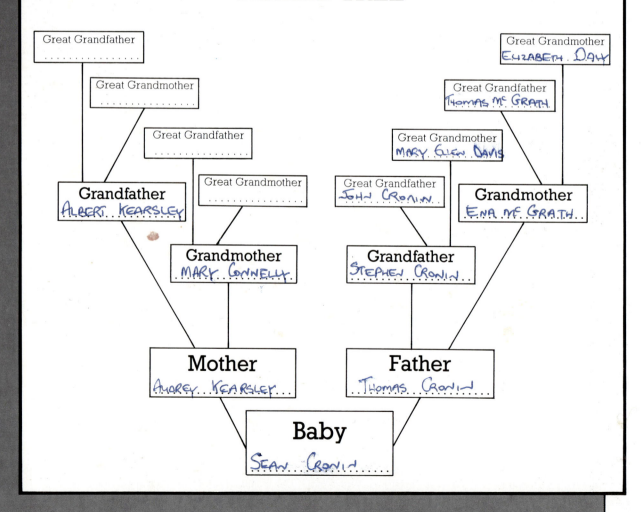

Great Grandfather
....

Great Grandmother
Elizabeth Day

Great Grandmother
....

Great Grandfather
Thomas McGrath

Great Grandfather
....

Great Grandmother
Mary Ellen Davis

Great Grandmother
....

Great Grandfather
John Cronin

Grandfather
Albert Kearsley

Grandmother
Ena McGrath

Grandmother
Mary Connelly

Grandfather
Stephen Cronin

Mother
Audrey Kearsley

Father
Thomas Cronin

Baby
Sean Cronin

YOUR BABY RECORD

FIRSTS

First day at home .... *Tuesday* ....

First smile ....

First laugh ....

First lifted head ....

First slept through the night .... *September* ....

First solid food ....

First held something ....

First picked something up ....

First sat alone ....

First crawled ....

First stood alone ....

First step ....

First word ....

First tooth ....

First outings: by pram ....

             by car ....

First visits: to hairdresser ....

               to doctor ....

               to dentist ....

YOUR BABY RECORD

FAVOURITES

Favourite toys..

Favourite fruits...

Favourite meat..

Favourite vegetables...

Favourite puddings..

Favourite sounds...

Favourite games..

Favourite stories...

GROWING UP

On first birthday   weight...............................

                       height...............................

On second birthday   weight...............................

                       height...............................

On third birthday   weight...............................

                       height...............................